MCAT COMPLETE 7-SUBJECT PREP BOOK 2025-2026

1000+ Practice Questions with Answers & Online Tests Across 7 Comprehensive Subjects

Artie Valdez

Disclaimer

Copyright © by Artie Valdez 2024. All rights reserved.

Before this document is duplicated or reproduced in any manner, the publisher's consent must be gained. Therefore, the contents within can neither be stored electronically, transferred, nor kept in a database. Neither in Part nor full can the document be copied, scanned, faxed, or retained without approval from the publisher or creator.

Please Note:

MCAT is a registered trademark of the Association of American Medical Colleges, which does not endorse this product or its methodology. Artie Valdez is not affiliated with or endorsed by any official testing organization. All organizational and test names are trademarks of their respective owners.

Visit The Last Page Of The Book To Access The Online Test Prep

Table Of Content

Introduction 10
How to Use This Book 11
What to Expect on the MCAT 14
Test-Taking Strategies for Success 15
Understanding the MCAT Question Types 17
Answer Explanations: Analyzing Your Mistakes 18
Exam Structure 19

SECTION 1

Chapter 1: Cell Structure and Function 22
    Cell Organelles and Their Functions 22
    Cell Membrane Structure and Transport Mechanisms 23

Chapter 2: Cell Genetics and Molecular Biology 25
    DNA Structure, Replication, and Repair 25
    Gene Expression and Regulation 26

Chapter 3: Cell Division: Mitosis and Meiosis 28
    Mitosis 28
    Meiosis 28
    Phases of the Cell Cycle 29
    Regulation of Cell Growth 30

Chapter 4: Metabolism and Cellular Respiration 32
    Glycolysis 32
    Krebs Cycle (Citric Acid Cycle) 32
    Oxidative Phosphorylation 33

Chapter 5: Systems Biology 35
    Nervous System 35
    Immune System 36

Chapter 6: Endocrinology and Hormonal Regulation 38

Chapter 7: Reproduction 41
Sexual vs Asexual Reproduction 41
Gametogenesis: Spermatogenesis and Oogenesis 42
Menstrual Cycle and Fertilization 43

Chapter 8: Embryogenesis and Development 44
Fertilization and Early Development 44
Germ Layers: Ectoderm, Mesoderm, Endoderm 44
Fetal Development and Birth 45

Chapter 10: The Musculoskeletal System 47
Structure and Function of Bones 47
Types of Muscles and Muscle Contraction 47
Bone Remodeling and Growth 48

Chapter 11: Homeostasis 50
Principles of Homeostasis 50
Feedback Mechanisms 50
Examples of Homeostatic Processes 51

Practical Questions For Section 1 54
Answers & Explanation 71

SECTION 2

Chapter 1: Amino Acids, Peptides, and Proteins 80
Structure and Function of Proteins 80
Enzyme Kinetics 81

Chapter 2: Carbohydrates and Lipids 83
Lipids 83
Glycolysis, Gluconeogenesis, and Glycogen Metabolism 84

Chapter 3: Bioenergetics and Regulation of Metabolism 86
ATP Production and Use 87

Chapter 4: Nucleotides and Nucleic Acids 89
DNA/RNA Structure and Function 90

Chapter 5: Biochemical Pathways 92
    Citric Acid Cycle (Krebs Cycle) 93

Chapter 6: Membrane Transport and Signal Transduction...95

Practical Question For Section 2: 98

Answers & Explanation 114

SECTION 3

Chapter 1: Atomic Structure and Periodicity...123
    Subatomic Particles..123
    Electron Configuration 124

Chapter 2: Bonding and Molecular Structure 126
    Covalent and Ionic Bonds..127

Chapter 3: States of Matter 129
    Gases, Liquids, and Solids 129

Chapter 4: Thermodynamics..133

Chapter 5: Chemical Kinetics 136
    Reaction Rates and Mechanisms 138

Chapter 6: Equilibrium...140
    Le Chatelier's Principle 141

Chapter 7: Acids and Bases 143
    pH, pKa, and Buffers 144

Chapter 8: Electrochemistry 146

Practical Question For Section 3: 149

Answers & Explanations..166

SECTION 4

Chapter 1: Structure, Nomenclature, and Properties of Organic Molecules 173
    Alkanes, Alkenes, Alkynes 174

Chapter 2: Stereochemistry 176
    Chirality and Isomers 176

Chapter 3: Reactivity and Mechanisms 179
Electrophilic Addition 179
Nucleophilic Substitution 180

Chapter 4: Functional Groups 182
Alcohols, Aldehydes, Ketones, Carboxylic Acids 182

Chapter 5: Aromatic Compounds 185
Benzene and Substitution Reactions 186

Chapter 6: Biological Molecules 188
Amino Acids and Nucleic Acids 188

Chapter 7: Spectroscopy and Analysis 191
IR, NMR, and Mass Spectrometry: Comparison and Complementarity 193

Practical Question For Section 4: 194

Answers & Explanation 222

SECTION 5

Chapter 1: Mechanics 230
Motion, Forces, and Newton's Laws 230

Chapter 2: Work and Energy 233
Kinetic and Potential Energy 234

Chapter 3: Waves and Sound 236
Frequency, Amplitude, and Resonance 236

Chapter 4: Electricity and Magnetism 238
Circuits, Voltage, and Current 239

Chapter 5: Optics 241
Reflection 241
Refraction 242

Chapter 6: Thermodynamics 244
Heat Transfer and Laws of Thermodynamics 245

Chapter 7: Fluid Dynamics 247
Bernoulli's Equation and Applications 248

Practical Question For Section 5: 250

Answers and Explanation 268

SECTION 6

Chapter 1: Cognitive Processes 277
Perception...277
Attention 278
Memory...278

Chapter 2: Learning and Behavior 280
Classical and Operant Conditioning 280

Chapter 3: Sociological Theories 283
Social Structures and Institutions 284

Chapter 4: Identity and Self-Concept 286
Gender and Cultural Identity 287

Chapter 5: Social Relationships 289
Group Dynamics, Socialization, and Communication 289

Chapter 6: Mental Health Disorders 292
Depression 292
Anxiety 293
Personality Disorders 294

Chapter 7: Demographics and Social Inequality 295

Practical Question For Section 6: 298

Answers and Explanation 317

SECTION 7

Chapter 1: Approaching CARS Passages 327
Types of Passages and Questions 328

Chapter 2; Analyzing Arguments 330
Main Idea, Tone, and Author's Purpose 331

Chapter 3: Strategies for Answering Questions...333
Inference, Deduction, and Application 334

Chapter 4: Practice Passages 336
    Timed CARS Questions and Explanations 337
Conclusion 339

Introduction

The MCAT Complete 7-Book Subject Review 2025-2026 is designed to be a focused tool to help you prepare for the MCAT exam with a straightforward approach. The MCAT is a comprehensive exam that assesses your knowledge across several subjects, including biology, chemistry, physics, biochemistry, psychology, sociology, and critical thinking. To succeed, you need not only a strong foundation in each of these areas but also practice with the kinds of questions you'll face on test day. This book provides just that—hundreds of practice questions, each paired with detailed explanations to help you solidify your understanding and improve your test-taking skills.

Unlike content-heavy textbooks, this book emphasizes direct practice. It focuses solely on questions and answers, ensuring that you spend your time on what will make the most impact—answering questions similar to those on the actual exam. This allows you to apply what you have learned, reinforce key concepts, and develop the reasoning skills necessary for success on the MCAT.

Each chapter is structured to cover specific topics within the broader subjects tested on the MCAT. After each topic, you'll find a section of questions that test your comprehension and problem-solving ability. These questions are written in a format similar to those found on the MCAT, ensuring that you get realistic practice. Following each question set, you will find detailed explanations that go beyond merely stating the correct answer. These explanations break down why the correct answer is right and why the other options are incorrect. This method helps to deepen your understanding, allowing you to see the thought process behind each question and identify patterns in MCAT question construction.

The MCAT doesn't just test your ability to recall facts; it tests your ability to apply those facts in complex scenarios. This book is designed to help you build that skill. By working through the practice questions in this book, you'll learn how to approach difficult questions, eliminate wrong answers, and select the best answer based on logic and evidence.

It's important to use this book regularly throughout your MCAT preparation. The more questions you practice, the more familiar you will become with the types of challenges the MCAT presents. Consistent practice will not only help you retain the necessary information but will also improve your confidence and pacing for the exam. This book provides the opportunity to engage in targeted, effective practice in each subject area, allowing you to focus your efforts on mastering the material most critical to your success.

Additionally, the structure of the book allows you to customize your study plan. You can work through each subject sequentially, or you can focus on areas where you feel you need the most improvement. Either way, this book is a flexible tool that can fit into your broader study schedule.

The goal of this book is simple: to help you become fully prepared to face the MCAT. By focusing on high-quality questions and detailed explanations, it offers you the practice and insight needed to excel on the exam.

How to Use This Book

The MCAT Complete 7-Book Subject Review 2025-2026 is designed to give you a clear and structured approach to your MCAT preparation, ensuring that every topic you study is backed by relevant practice questions and detailed answers. Here's how to make the most out of this book:

1. Subject Breakdown for Targeted Study

This book covers the seven key subjects you'll encounter on the MCAT:

- Biology
- Biochemistry
- General Chemistry
- Organic Chemistry
- Physics
- Psychology and Sociology
- Critical Analysis and Reasoning Skills (CARS)

Each subject is divided into logical sections that focus on specific topics. The book is designed to be used as either a comprehensive review or a targeted practice tool. If you're just starting your MCAT preparation, work through each subject chapter-by-chapter. For those further along in their study process, use this book to focus on your weaker areas. Each section has practice questions at the end, designed to simulate actual MCAT questions in both content and difficulty.

2. Master the Fundamentals Before Tackling Complex Topics

Each subject starts with fundamental concepts and gradually moves to more advanced material. If you're unsure where to begin, start from the basics and build up your knowledge. It's important to have a strong grasp of foundational topics before moving to more complex ones, as the MCAT tests your ability to apply basic principles to challenging problems. Use the questions that follow each section to reinforce what you've learned. This will give you a better understanding of how the material might appear in different forms on the exam.

3. Answer Questions Without Looking at the Explanations First

Once you've reviewed a section, attempt the practice questions without referring to the explanations. This will mimic test conditions and allow you to identify which areas need further review. After completing the questions, review the answers and explanations. Whether you answered correctly or not, reading the explanation for each question will solidify your understanding of the concept being tested.

The explanations go beyond simply identifying the correct answer. They provide a breakdown of why the right choice is correct and why the other options are wrong. This method of reviewing will not only help you grasp the material better but also teach you to think critically about each question.

4. Simulate Real Test Conditions

The MCAT is a timed test, and one of the biggest challenges is managing your time effectively during the exam. As you work through this book, set time limits for yourself. Try to complete a set number of questions in the time you'd have during the actual MCAT. This practice will help you develop a rhythm for answering questions and improve your pacing. Remember, it's not just about knowing the material—it's also about being able to apply that knowledge efficiently under pressure.

In addition, complete your practice in an environment that is free from distractions. The more closely you can replicate test conditions, the better prepared you will be for the real exam.

5. Review Every Question You Miss

It's crucial to spend extra time reviewing the questions you missed or found challenging. Understanding why you got a question wrong is often more valuable than getting it right on the first try. As you work through the explanations, look for patterns in the types of mistakes you're making. Are they content-related, where you didn't know the answer, or strategy-related, where you misinterpreted the question? Use this reflection to guide your future study sessions, focusing on the areas where you struggle the most.

Even for questions you answered correctly, take the time to review the explanations. You may have guessed correctly or arrived at the right answer without fully understanding why. Reading through the reasoning behind the correct answer will deepen your understanding and prepare you for similar questions on test day.

6. Track Your Progress

As you work through this book, it's important to keep track of your performance. After completing each section, take note of your scores and the areas where you made mistakes. By tracking your progress, you'll be able to identify which subjects you need to spend more time on and which ones you've mastered. This will allow you to focus your study efforts more effectively and make the most of your preparation time.

7. Use This Book Alongside Other Study Materials

While this book provides an extensive collection of practice questions and explanations, it's not meant to be your only resource. Use it alongside other study materials, such as content review books and full-length practice tests. This book is designed to give you practical, test-like experience with MCAT questions, but you should also ensure that you have a deep understanding of the material by reviewing textbooks, study guides, and other resources.

8. Take Full Advantage of Online Prep Resources

After studying through the questions and answers in this book, be sure to visit the last page to access the online prep resources provided. These resources offer additional practice exams, interactive question sets, and further study tools that will help you refine your skills and boost your confidence before test day. The combination of this book and the online tools will give you a comprehensive preparation strategy that covers both content review and practical application.

By using this book effectively and consistently, you'll develop the skills, confidence, and knowledge needed to perform well on the MCAT. Each section is designed to build your understanding progressively, ensuring you're fully prepared for the range of topics and question styles you'll encounter on test day.

What to Expect on the MCAT

The Medical College Admission Test (MCAT) is a rigorous, standardized examination that assesses your understanding of key science concepts, critical thinking skills, and reasoning abilities necessary for success in medical school. The MCAT is broken down into four sections:

1. **Biological and Biochemical Foundations of Living Systems:**

This section tests your knowledge of biology and biochemistry, along with some general and organic chemistry. It focuses on the processes that allow living organisms to grow, reproduce, and maintain homeostasis. You'll be expected to apply your knowledge to understand how these systems function and respond to environmental changes.

2. **Chemical and Physical Foundations of Biological Systems:**

This section covers general chemistry, organic chemistry, physics, and biochemistry. It evaluates your understanding of how physical principles, like energy and molecular interactions, apply to biological systems. Topics range from atomic structure and chemical reactions to thermodynamics and the properties of solutions.

3. **Psychological, Social, and Biological Foundations of Behavior:**

This part of the exam assesses how psychological and social factors influence health and well-being. You'll encounter questions about human behavior, mental processes, social structures, and how these factors affect the overall health of individuals and communities.

4. **Critical Analysis and Reasoning Skills (CARS):**

This section tests your ability to comprehend complex passages and assess arguments. Unlike the other sections, CARS doesn't require scientific knowledge but instead focuses on reading comprehension, reasoning, and argument evaluation. You'll be tested on your ability to critically evaluate the author's tone, main ideas, and logical connections in the text.

The MCAT is a 7.5-hour exam, including breaks, so endurance is key. The test comprises multiple-choice questions, with 59 questions in the first three sections and 53 in the CARS section. Each section is timed for 90 to 95 minutes.

You should expect questions that assess both foundational knowledge and your ability to apply that knowledge to problem-solving scenarios. The exam is structured to challenge not only what you know but how well you can use that knowledge in novel situations, similar to real-world medical practice.

Finally, your MCAT score is vital for medical school applications. Scores range from 472 to 528, with a median score of around 500. Many top medical schools expect scores above 510. Knowing what to expect on test day helps minimize surprises and enables better preparation, leading to a more focused study approach.

Test-Taking Strategies for Success

The MCAT is a challenging exam that requires not only knowledge but also strategy to perform well. Proper test-taking strategies can significantly boost your score. Here are essential strategies that will help you approach the exam confidently and efficiently:

1. Time Management

One of the biggest challenges on the MCAT is time pressure. With 230 questions to answer in a limited time, effective time management is crucial. Develop a habit of tracking time during practice exams to ensure that you can complete each section within the allotted time frame. Aim to spend no more than 1 minute and 30 seconds per question in the science sections and around 2 minutes per question in the CARS section.

A good strategy is to flag difficult questions and return to them if time permits. Spending too much time on any single question may hurt your overall performance, as unanswered questions will negatively affect your score. Use a balanced approach: answer the easy questions first, build momentum, and save the more time-consuming or challenging questions for later.

2. Understanding the Question Types

The MCAT presents several types of questions, including stand-alone questions and passage-based questions. In passage-based questions, you are expected to interpret and analyze scientific texts and apply your knowledge. These questions are often more complex than stand-alone ones, so practice carefully reading and interpreting scientific passages under time constraints.

To improve in CARS, focus on understanding the author's main argument and identifying how supporting details relate to it. For science passages, ensure that you fully understand the experiment, results, or theoretical argument presented before answering the questions.

3. Elimination Method

Even when you are unsure about a particular question, you can still increase your chances of answering it correctly by eliminating obviously incorrect options. On the MCAT, there is no penalty for guessing, so it's important to always select an answer, even if you're uncertain. By narrowing down the answer choices, you can make a more informed guess and improve your odds.

When practicing, focus on honing your ability to recognize distractors—choices that may seem plausible but are incorrect. These distractors often rely on common misconceptions or slight misinterpretations of the material. By refining your ability to spot them, you'll increase the accuracy of your answers.

4. Practice with Full-Length Exams

Taking full-length practice tests under simulated exam conditions is one of the best ways to prepare for the MCAT. These tests help you build stamina for the actual test day and provide an opportunity to refine your pacing and question-answering strategies. After each practice test, review your wrong answers thoroughly to understand why you missed the question. This will highlight areas where you need further study and help you avoid making the same mistakes on test day.

In addition to content review, practicing with full-length exams helps reduce anxiety and improve your mental endurance, as the MCAT is a long exam that requires sustained focus.

5. Active Reading Strategies for CARS

The CARS section is notorious for being difficult, especially for science students who are more comfortable with concrete facts than abstract arguments. To succeed in CARS, adopt active reading strategies, such as summarizing paragraphs as you read, identifying the main idea, and predicting where the author's argument is heading.

Focus on the author's tone, attitude, and point of view. If you can discern the author's perspective, you'll have a better sense of how to approach questions that ask you to infer their intent or analyze their reasoning. Be mindful of extreme language in answer choices, as the MCAT often uses subtler conclusions.

6. Maintaining Composure and Confidence

Test anxiety can significantly impair performance on test day. To combat this, build confidence through thorough preparation. Engage in mindfulness or relaxation exercises, such as deep breathing, before and during the test to calm your nerves.

Additionally, adopt a growth mindset. Understand that every practice exam or question you miss is an opportunity to learn and improve, rather than a sign of failure. A positive attitude helps maintain composure, especially if you encounter difficult questions during the exam.

7. Focus on High-Yield Topics

While the MCAT covers a broad range of subjects, some topics are more heavily represented than others. Focus your studies on high-yield topics like amino acids, metabolism, acid-base chemistry, and genetics. These are frequently tested on the MCAT, so mastering them will give you a solid foundation.

Utilize official AAMC resources and question banks to target these high-yield areas. By concentrating on the most frequently tested topics, you can optimize your study time and maximize your score potential.

Understanding the MCAT Question Types

The MCAT exam consists of multiple-choice questions (MCQs) designed to test a wide range of skills and knowledge. Each question type evaluates a specific competency, and understanding these can improve performance and strategy during the test.

1. **Factual Recall Questions:**

These questions assess your knowledge of basic scientific facts and principles. They require direct recall of memorized information, such as definitions, formulas, and biological processes. Although these questions are straightforward, they require thorough preparation to ensure recall under time pressure.

2. **Conceptual Questions:**

Conceptual questions test your understanding of broader scientific ideas and their application to new scenarios. They often involve interpreting data, recognizing patterns, or understanding how multiple processes interact. These questions require more than just memorization; they demand a deep understanding of how different concepts are related.

3. **Passage-Based Questions:**

Passage-based questions are a major component of the MCAT. These are tied to a scientific passage that provides context, data, or a scenario, and the questions require you to analyze this information to answer correctly. This type of question tests your ability to apply knowledge to unfamiliar situations. Key skills include identifying the main idea, understanding experiments, and analyzing results or hypotheses presented in the passage.

4. **Experimental Design and Data Interpretation:**

These questions assess your ability to interpret data from tables, graphs, or research studies. You may be asked to make conclusions based on the data, predict outcomes, or critique experimental designs. Success in these questions depends on your ability to interpret trends, recognize patterns, and apply statistical reasoning.

5. **Reasoning Beyond the Text:**

These questions focus on how well you can apply your knowledge to scenarios not directly presented in the MCAT. They challenge your ability to connect scientific principles with hypothetical or real-world situations, evaluating your problem-solving skills and ability to think critically in unfamiliar contexts.

6. **Critical Analysis and Reasoning Skills (CARS) Questions:**

The CARS section assesses your comprehension and reasoning abilities. The passages in this section cover topics from the humanities and social sciences. The questions test your ability to draw conclusions, evaluate arguments, and make inferences based on the passage's content without relying on outside knowledge.

Answer Explanations: Analyzing Your Mistakes

Understanding your mistakes is a crucial part of improving your performance on the MCAT. Here's how to analyze your errors effectively:

1. **Identify the Type of Mistake:**

When reviewing practice exams or question banks, categorize each incorrect answer. Did you make a factual error, misinterpret the question, or fail to apply a concept correctly? By recognizing the pattern in your mistakes, you can focus your study efforts more effectively.

- Factual Errors: These occur when you simply do not know the correct answer. This might signal the need for more review of specific content areas. Focus on strengthening your understanding of weak topics by revisiting your notes, reviewing textbooks, or watching relevant educational videos.
- Misreading the Question: Misinterpretations often stem from hasty reading or misunderstanding what is being asked. This error is common under time pressure, so practice slowing down during your practice exams to ensure you understand the question fully before answering.
- Application Errors: These mistakes occur when you fail to apply a known concept properly. This indicates a need to work on bridging the gap between knowledge and application, which is a critical skill for the MCAT.

2. **Evaluate the Reasoning Process:**

For each incorrect answer, examine your thought process. Did you fall into a common trap, or were you led astray by the complexity of the question? Understanding why you chose the wrong answer helps prevent similar mistakes in the future. Break down your reasoning step by step to see where your logic faltered.

3. **Review Correct Answer Explanations:**

For each incorrect question, thoroughly review the explanation for the correct answer. Pay special attention to why the right answer is correct and the rationale for eliminating the other options. By focusing on the reasoning behind the answer, you will improve your ability to approach similar questions correctly in the future.

4. **Refine Your Test-Taking Strategy:**

If time pressure or exam anxiety contributed to your mistakes, adjust your strategy accordingly. This may include pacing yourself better during the test, flagging questions to return to later, or practicing stress management techniques. Building your endurance through timed practice exams will help you get used to the pacing and reduce the likelihood of errors caused by rushing.

Exam Structure

The MCAT is a computer-based exam, comprising 230 questions that are divided into four main sections. Each section evaluates specific skills and knowledge across various subjects:

1. **Biological and Biochemical Foundations of Living Systems:**

This section consists of 59 questions and is designed to test your understanding of biology and biochemistry in the context of living organisms. It focuses on foundational concepts such as cell function, energy production, and the interaction between systems in living organisms. Key topics include:

- Cellular structure and function
- Genetic transmission of information
- Bioenergetics and metabolism
- Molecular biology of the cell

2. **Chemical and Physical Foundations of Biological Systems:**

This section also contains 59 questions and evaluates your knowledge of general chemistry, organic chemistry, physics, and biochemistry as they relate to biological systems. It covers the physical principles underlying the mechanics of living organisms, the chemical processes of life, and the properties of biological molecules. Key concepts include:

- Molecular interactions and reactions
- Laws of physics in biological contexts
- The role of electrochemical gradients in cellular processes

3. **Psychological, Social, and Biological Foundations of Behavior:**

This section evaluates your understanding of the behavioral sciences with 59 questions. It focuses on how psychological, social, and biological factors influence behavior and decision-making. The section includes topics such as:

- Theories of learning and cognition
- Social influences on behavior
- Identity and personality development
- Mental health disorders and their biological bases

4. Critical Analysis and Reasoning Skills (CARS):

The CARS section consists of 53 questions and focuses on your ability to comprehend, analyze, and apply information from passages in the humanities and social sciences. This section evaluates your ability to assess complex texts and reason through arguments and conclusions without relying on outside knowledge.

Section 1: Biology

Chapter 1: Cell Structure and Function

Cells are the fundamental units of life, and they can be classified into two main categories: eukaryotic and prokaryotic cells. Understanding the structural differences and functional roles of these cell types is crucial to grasp the basics of biology.

Eukaryotic Cells: Eukaryotic cells are complex and highly organized, typically larger than prokaryotic cells. They contain membrane-bound organelles, including a true nucleus, which houses the cell's genetic material. This compartmentalization allows for specialized functions within different regions of the cell. Eukaryotic cells are found in multicellular organisms such as animals, plants, fungi, and protists.

The most distinguishing feature of eukaryotic cells is the presence of the nucleus, which is enclosed by a nuclear envelope. Inside the nucleus, DNA is organized into chromosomes. Eukaryotic cells also contain other organelles such as mitochondria, responsible for energy production, and the endoplasmic reticulum (ER), which is involved in protein and lipid synthesis.

Prokaryotic Cells: Prokaryotic cells are simpler and generally smaller than eukaryotic cells. They do not have a true nucleus; instead, their DNA is located in a region called the nucleoid. Prokaryotic cells lack membrane-bound organelles, which means their cellular functions are less compartmentalized. These cells are typically found in single-celled organisms such as bacteria and archaea.

Despite their simplicity, prokaryotic cells are highly efficient. Many possess a cell wall that provides structural support and protection. Some also have structures like flagella or pili for movement and interaction with their environment. The lack of membrane-bound organelles allows prokaryotes to grow and divide rapidly, making them highly adaptable to various environments.

Cell Organelles and Their Functions

Eukaryotic cells contain a variety of organelles, each performing specific functions essential for the cell's survival and operation.

Nucleus: The nucleus is the control center of the cell, containing the genetic material (DNA). It is surrounded by the nuclear envelope, a double membrane that protects the DNA and controls the passage of molecules in and out of the nucleus. Inside, the nucleolus is responsible for ribosome production. The DNA within the nucleus dictates cellular activity through the production of RNA, which then directs protein synthesis.

Mitochondria: Known as the powerhouse of the cell, mitochondria are responsible for producing energy in the form of adenosine triphosphate (ATP). Mitochondria have their own DNA, which supports the endosymbiotic theory that they originated from ancient bacteria. Through a process called oxidative phosphorylation, mitochondria generate the energy needed for various cellular activities.

Endoplasmic Reticulum (ER): The ER is a network of membranes involved in the synthesis and transport of proteins and lipids. There are two types of ER: rough ER (RER) and smooth ER (SER). The RER is studded with ribosomes, giving it a "rough" appearance, and is primarily involved in protein synthesis. The SER lacks ribosomes and is responsible for lipid synthesis and detoxification processes.

Golgi Apparatus: The Golgi apparatus modifies, sorts, and packages proteins and lipids for transport. It acts as a shipping center, ensuring that molecules are correctly modified and sent to their appropriate destinations, whether inside or outside the cell. Proteins from the ER are processed in the Golgi before being delivered to their final locations.

Lysosomes: Lysosomes are membrane-bound organelles containing enzymes that break down cellular waste, foreign material, and damaged organelles. They act as the cell's recycling system, digesting unwanted materials so that their components can be reused.

Ribosomes: Ribosomes are responsible for protein synthesis. They read the messenger RNA (mRNA) produced in the nucleus and translate it into polypeptides, which then fold into functional proteins. Ribosomes can be found floating freely in the cytoplasm or attached to the RER.

Cytoskeleton: The cytoskeleton provides structural support to the cell, maintains its shape, and aids in cellular movement. It is composed of microfilaments, intermediate filaments, and microtubules. These structures also play a role in intracellular transport and cell division.

Chloroplasts (in plant cells): Chloroplasts are responsible for photosynthesis in plant cells. Like mitochondria, they have their own DNA and are thought to have originated from ancient symbiotic bacteria. Chloroplasts convert light energy into chemical energy (glucose), which can be used by the plant for growth and development.

Cell Membrane Structure and Transport Mechanisms

The cell membrane, also known as the plasma membrane, is a vital structure that surrounds the cell, protecting its internal components while regulating what enters and leaves the cell. The cell membrane is primarily composed of a lipid bilayer, proteins, and carbohydrates, each contributing to its function.

Phospholipid Bilayer: The core structure of the cell membrane is the phospholipid bilayer. Phospholipids have a hydrophilic (water-attracting) head and two hydrophobic (water-repelling) tails. This dual nature causes the phospholipids to arrange themselves in a bilayer, with the heads facing the external and internal environments of the cell and the tails facing each other. This arrangement creates a semi-permeable barrier that allows only certain molecules to pass through.

Membrane Proteins: Proteins embedded within the cell membrane perform a variety of functions, including transport, communication, and structural support. Integral proteins span the entire membrane and often function as channels or transporters, helping to move substances in and out of the cell. Peripheral proteins are attached to the surface of the membrane and play roles in signaling or structural integrity.

Carbohydrates: Carbohydrates attached to proteins or lipids on the extracellular side of the membrane form structures known as glycoproteins and glycolipids. These structures are crucial for cell recognition, communication, and adhesion. They also play a role in immune responses by helping the body distinguish between its own cells and foreign cells.

- Transport Mechanisms: The cell membrane's semi-permeability allows it to control the movement of substances, which can occur through passive or active transport mechanisms.
- Passive Transport: This occurs without the need for cellular energy (ATP). Substances move from areas of high concentration to low concentration (down their concentration gradient). Examples of passive transport include diffusion, osmosis, and facilitated diffusion (which involves the use of membrane proteins).
- Active Transport: In contrast to passive transport, active transport requires ATP to move substances against their concentration gradient (from low to high concentration). Protein pumps, such as the sodium-potassium pump, are a common example. Another type of active transport is endocytosis, where the cell engulfs large particles, and exocytosis, where materials are expelled from the cell.

The structure and function of cells are intricately designed to maintain life processes. Whether it's through the organelles that manage cellular functions or the membrane that controls the exchange of materials, each component plays a vital role in the overall operation and survival of the cell.

Chapter 2: Cell Genetics and Molecular Biology

Cell genetics and molecular biology are crucial fields in understanding how living organisms function at the most fundamental level. Genetics refers to the study of genes, heredity, and how certain traits are passed down from one generation to the next, while molecular biology focuses on the molecular mechanisms that govern cellular functions. Both areas overlap in their exploration of DNA, RNA, proteins, and the intricate processes that regulate cellular behavior.

The study of cell genetics begins with understanding the organization of genetic material within cells. In eukaryotic cells, DNA is located in the nucleus, while in prokaryotic cells, it exists in a simpler form, often referred to as a nucleoid region. DNA stores all the necessary information required for the growth, development, reproduction, and functioning of organisms.

Molecular biology focuses on how cells replicate their genetic material, express genes, and respond to their environment. A critical aspect of this field is the central dogma of molecular biology: DNA is transcribed into RNA, which is then translated into proteins. These proteins serve as the workhorses of the cell, responsible for carrying out all cellular processes, from maintaining structure to catalyzing biochemical reactions.

DNA Structure, Replication, and Repair

DNA Structure: Deoxyribonucleic acid (DNA) is a molecule that encodes genetic information in living organisms. The structure of DNA was first described by James Watson and Francis Crick in 1953 as a double helix, consisting of two strands of nucleotides. Each nucleotide is composed of a phosphate group, a deoxyribose sugar, and one of four nitrogenous bases: adenine (A), thymine (T), cytosine (C), and guanine (G). The two strands of DNA are held together by hydrogen bonds between complementary bases: A pairs with T, and C pairs with G.

The double-helix structure of DNA allows it to store genetic information efficiently. The sequence of bases along the DNA strand encodes instructions for building proteins, which are crucial for all cellular activities. This information is transmitted from one generation to the next through the process of replication.

DNA Replication: DNA replication is the process by which a cell duplicates its DNA before cell division. This ensures that each new cell receives an exact copy of the genetic material. The process begins at specific regions called origins of replication. Helicase, an enzyme, unwinds the DNA strands, creating a replication fork where the two strands are separated.

One of the separated strands, known as the leading strand, is synthesized continuously by the enzyme DNA polymerase, which adds complementary nucleotides in the 5' to 3' direction. The other strand, the lagging strand, is synthesized discontinuously in short fragments known as Okazaki fragments, also in the 5' to 3' direction. These fragments are later joined by DNA ligase to form a continuous strand. Replication is highly accurate, but mistakes can occur. These errors are corrected by proofreading mechanisms within the polymerase enzymes, ensuring the fidelity of the replication process.

DNA Repair: While DNA replication is highly accurate, it is not immune to errors or damage. DNA can be altered by environmental factors such as UV radiation, chemicals, and biological agents, which can lead to mutations. Fortunately, cells have evolved several repair mechanisms to correct these errors.

- Base Excision Repair (BER): This mechanism fixes small, non-helix-distorting base lesions such as those caused by oxidation or deamination. It involves removing the damaged base, followed by DNA polymerase filling the gap and DNA ligase sealing the strand.
- Nucleotide Excision Repair (NER): This pathway repairs bulky lesions like thymine dimers caused by UV radiation. NER removes a short single-stranded segment of the DNA that contains the lesion, after which the DNA is filled in and sealed.
- Mismatch Repair (MMR): This mechanism corrects errors that escape the proofreading activity of DNA polymerase, such as base mismatches or small insertions/deletions that occur during DNA replication.

Without effective DNA repair mechanisms, organisms would accumulate mutations that could lead to diseases like cancer.

Gene Expression and Regulation

Gene expression refers to the process by which information from a gene is used to synthesize functional gene products, typically proteins. This process involves two main steps: transcription and translation.

Transcription: During transcription, the DNA sequence of a gene is transcribed into messenger RNA (mRNA) by the enzyme RNA polymerase. Transcription begins at the promoter region of a gene, where RNA polymerase binds and initiates the synthesis of a complementary RNA strand from one of the DNA strands (the template strand). The RNA strand grows in the 5' to 3' direction, adding complementary RNA nucleotides (A, U, C, G) to the template strand. Once the RNA polymerase reaches a termination signal in the DNA, it stops transcription, and the newly formed mRNA molecule is released.

In eukaryotes, the mRNA undergoes further processing, including splicing, capping, and polyadenylation, before it is transported out of the nucleus to the ribosome for translation. During splicing, non-coding regions (introns) are removed, and the coding regions (exons) are joined together to form the mature mRNA.

Translation: Once the mature mRNA reaches the ribosome, it serves as a template for protein synthesis. During translation, transfer RNA (tRNA) molecules, each carrying a specific amino acid, recognize the codons on the mRNA through complementary base-pairing with their anticodons. The ribosome catalyzes the formation of peptide bonds between the amino acids, creating a polypeptide chain that will fold into a functional protein.

Regulation of Gene Expression: Not all genes are expressed at all times; gene expression is tightly regulated depending on the cell's needs. This regulation can occur at multiple levels, including:

- Transcriptional Regulation: The most common form of gene regulation, where proteins called transcription factors bind to specific DNA sequences to either promote or inhibit the binding of RNA polymerase to the promoter region of a gene. Enhancers and silencers are regulatory elements that influence transcription rates by interacting with transcription factors.
- Post-Transcriptional Regulation: After transcription, gene expression can be regulated through RNA splicing, stability, and transport. Alternative splicing, for instance, allows a single gene to produce multiple protein variants by rearranging exons.
- Translational Regulation: Gene expression can also be controlled during translation. Certain sequences in the mRNA or regulatory proteins can influence the rate at which translation occurs.
- Post-Translational Regulation: After a protein is synthesized, its activity can be regulated by chemical modifications, such as phosphorylation or ubiquitination, which can activate or deactivate the protein, or signal it for degradation.

Understanding the regulation of gene expression is crucial for comprehending how cells differentiate, adapt, and respond to their environment.

Chapter 3: Cell Division: Mitosis and Meiosis

Cell division is a fundamental biological process that allows organisms to grow, develop, repair damaged tissues, and reproduce. There are two main types of cell division: mitosis and meiosis. Both processes involve the replication of genetic material, but they differ in their outcomes and roles within an organism.

Mitosis

Mitosis is the process by which somatic (non-reproductive) cells divide, resulting in two identical daughter cells. Each daughter cell contains the same number of chromosomes as the parent cell, which ensures genetic consistency across all cells in an organism. Mitosis occurs during growth, tissue repair, and cellular replacement.

Mitosis can be divided into five stages:

- Prophase: The chromatin condenses into visible chromosomes, each consisting of two sister chromatids held together by a centromere. The nuclear envelope begins to disintegrate, and spindle fibers emerge from the centrosomes.
- Prometaphase: The nuclear envelope breaks down completely, allowing spindle fibers to attach to the kinetochores, which are protein structures on the centromeres of the chromosomes.
- Metaphase: Chromosomes align along the metaphase plate, an imaginary plane in the center of the cell. This ensures that each daughter cell will receive one copy of each chromosome.
- Anaphase: The sister chromatids are pulled apart by the spindle fibers and move toward opposite poles of the cell. Each chromatid is now considered an individual chromosome.
- Telophase: Chromosomes reach the poles and begin to decondense back into chromatin. The nuclear envelope reforms around each set of chromosomes, creating two distinct nuclei.

After telophase, cytokinesis occurs, which physically separates the cytoplasm into two daughter cells. In animal cells, a contractile ring forms and pinches the cell membrane, while in plant cells, a cell plate forms to divide the two cells.

Meiosis

Meiosis, in contrast, occurs only in germ cells (sperm and egg cells) and results in the production of four genetically distinct daughter cells, each with half the number of chromosomes as the parent cell. This reduction in chromosome number is crucial for maintaining genetic stability in sexually reproducing organisms.

Meiosis consists of two rounds of division: meiosis I and meiosis II. Each round has its own stages, similar to mitosis.

1. Meiosis I: This is the reductional division, where homologous chromosomes (pairs of chromosomes, one from each parent) are separated.
   - Prophase I: Homologous chromosomes pair up in a process called synapsis, and crossing over occurs, where segments of genetic material are exchanged between chromatids. This increases genetic diversity.
   - Metaphase I: Homologous pairs align along the metaphase plate.
   - Anaphase I: Homologous chromosomes are pulled to opposite poles.
   - Telophase I: The cell divides into two cells, each with half the original number of chromosomes (haploid).
2. Meiosis II: This resembles mitosis and involves the separation of sister chromatids.
   - Prophase II: Chromosomes condense again, and the spindle apparatus forms.
   - Metaphase II: Chromosomes align at the metaphase plate.
   - Anaphase II: Sister chromatids are separated and pulled toward opposite poles.
   - Telophase II: Each of the two cells divides, resulting in a total of four haploid daughter cells.

These four daughter cells have a unique combination of genetic material due to the processes of crossing over and independent assortment of chromosomes, both of which occur during meiosis I.

Phases of the Cell Cycle

The cell cycle is the series of events that cells go through as they grow and divide. It consists of four main phases: G1, S, G2, and M, with an additional resting phase called G0. Each phase plays a critical role in preparing the cell for division.

G1 Phase (Gap 1)

G1 is the first phase after a cell has divided. During this phase, the cell grows in size and synthesizes various proteins and organelles that are needed for DNA replication. The cell also checks for DNA damage and other errors. If conditions are unfavorable or the cell is not needed for division, it may enter the G0 phase, where it remains inactive but functional.

G1 is a critical checkpoint because the cell commits to the process of division. If there is extensive DNA damage or other issues, the cell may enter a state of repair or undergo apoptosis (programmed cell death) to prevent the propagation of damaged DNA.

S Phase (Synthesis)

During the S phase, the cell replicates its DNA, resulting in two identical sets of chromosomes. This process ensures that each daughter cell will have a complete set of genetic material after division. DNA replication is tightly regulated to prevent errors, and various proteins, such as DNA polymerases, play a key role in ensuring the accuracy of replication.

G2 Phase (Gap 2)

After the S phase, the cell enters G2, during which it continues to grow and prepares for mitosis. The cell synthesizes proteins necessary for chromosome manipulation and cell division. G2 serves as another checkpoint, where the cell checks the integrity of the replicated DNA and ensures all organelles and cellular structures are in place for division.

M Phase (Mitosis)

The M phase is where the actual division occurs, encompassing mitosis (or meiosis in reproductive cells) and cytokinesis. This phase leads to the formation of two daughter cells in mitosis or four genetically diverse cells in meiosis.

G0 Phase (Resting Phase)

Cells that are not actively dividing can enter the G0 phase. In this phase, the cell remains metabolically active but does not replicate or divide. Some cells, such as neurons and muscle cells, remain in G0 for their entire lifespan, while others, like liver cells, may re-enter the cell cycle when needed for repair or growth.

Regulation of Cell Growth

Cell growth and division are tightly regulated processes, controlled by various signals and checkpoints to ensure proper function. Unregulated cell growth can lead to cancer and other disorders. There are several key mechanisms involved in the regulation of cell growth.

Growth Factors and Signals: Cells rely on external signals, such as growth factors, to stimulate division. Growth factors bind to specific receptors on the cell surface, triggering a cascade of intracellular signals that promote cell cycle progression. For example, epidermal growth factor (EGF) promotes the proliferation of skin cells.

Cell Cycle Checkpoints

Throughout the cell cycle, checkpoints ensure that the cell is ready to progress to the next phase. There are three main checkpoints:

- G1 Checkpoint: Checks for DNA damage before the cell commits to division.
- G2 Checkpoint: Ensures DNA replication was successful and checks for any damage before mitosis.
- M Checkpoint: Ensures that chromosomes are properly aligned on the metaphase plate before they are separated.

If any abnormalities are detected at these checkpoints, the cell may either repair the damage or undergo apoptosis.

Cyclins and Cyclin-Dependent Kinases (CDKs): Cyclins are proteins that regulate the cell cycle by activating CDKs, which are enzymes that drive the cell through the different phases. Cyclins bind to CDKs, forming a complex that phosphorylates target proteins involved in cell cycle progression. The levels of cyclins fluctuate throughout the cell cycle, ensuring that CDKs are activated at the appropriate times.

Tumor Suppressors and Oncogenes: Genes that regulate cell growth can be categorized as either tumor suppressors or oncogenes. Tumor suppressors, such as p53 and Rb, prevent uncontrolled cell growth by halting the cell cycle in response to DNA damage or other issues. Oncogenes, when mutated, promote unchecked cell division, leading to the formation of tumors.

Proper regulation of cell growth is essential for maintaining tissue homeostasis and preventing diseases like cancer. Misregulation can result in excessive or insufficient cell division, with severe consequences for the organism.

Chapter 4: Metabolism and Cellular Respiration

Metabolism is the sum of all chemical reactions in a living organism that allow for the conversion of energy and the synthesis of necessary molecules. In humans, metabolism includes catabolic pathways that break down molecules to release energy and anabolic pathways that build complex molecules from simpler ones. One of the key metabolic processes is cellular respiration, which is how cells generate energy, primarily in the form of adenosine triphosphate (ATP).

Cellular respiration involves breaking down glucose and other organic molecules in the presence of oxygen to produce ATP, water, and carbon dioxide. The process can be divided into three main stages: glycolysis, the Krebs cycle, and oxidative phosphorylation. These pathways allow cells to harvest the chemical energy stored in nutrients.

Glycolysis

Glycolysis is the first step of cellular respiration and occurs in the cytoplasm of the cell. It is an anaerobic process, meaning it does not require oxygen. Glycolysis begins with a glucose molecule (a six-carbon sugar) and ends with two molecules of pyruvate (a three-carbon compound), generating a small amount of ATP and NADH in the process.

- The glycolysis pathway can be divided into two phases: the energy investment phase and the energy payoff phase.
- Energy Investment Phase: In this phase, two ATP molecules are used to phosphorylate glucose, making it more chemically reactive. The six-carbon glucose is ultimately split into two three-carbon molecules of glyceraldehyde-3-phosphate (G3P).
- Energy Payoff Phase: In this phase, each G3P molecule is oxidized, and in the process, two NAD^+ molecules are reduced to NADH. Additionally, four ATP molecules are produced through substrate-level phosphorylation, resulting in a net gain of two ATP molecules for the cell. At the end of this phase, two pyruvate molecules are produced.

The overall reaction for glycolysis is:

$$\text{Glucose} + 2NAD^+ + 2ADP + 2P_i \rightarrow 2\text{Pyruvate} + 2NADH + 2ATP + 2H_2O$$

Although glycolysis produces ATP, it is not very efficient compared to the later stages of cellular respiration. However, glycolysis is essential because it can occur without oxygen, allowing cells to generate some ATP even in anaerobic conditions.

Krebs Cycle (Citric Acid Cycle)

The pyruvate molecules produced in glycolysis are transported into the mitochondria, where they undergo further processing in the Krebs cycle (also known as the citric acid cycle or tricarboxylic acid cycle). Before entering the cycle, pyruvate is converted into acetyl coenzyme A (acetyl-CoA), which serves as the substrate for the Krebs cycle.

The Krebs cycle occurs in the mitochondrial matrix and is responsible for the complete oxidation of acetyl-CoA into carbon dioxide. For each acetyl-CoA molecule, the cycle generates three NADH molecules, one FADH2 molecule, one GTP (or ATP), and two carbon dioxide molecules as waste products. The NADH and FADH2 molecules produced are rich in electrons and will play a critical role in oxidative phosphorylation.

The Krebs cycle can be broken down into several steps:

- Formation of Citrate: Acetyl-CoA (a two-carbon molecule) combines with oxaloacetate (a four-carbon molecule) to form citrate (a six-carbon molecule).
- Isomerization of Citrate to Isocitrate: Citrate is rearranged to form isocitrate, an isomer of citrate.
- Oxidative Decarboxylation of Isocitrate: Isocitrate is oxidized to alpha-ketoglutarate, a five-carbon molecule, in a reaction that produces NADH and releases carbon dioxide.
- Oxidation of Alpha-Ketoglutarate: Alpha-ketoglutarate is further oxidized, reducing NAD+ to NADH and releasing another molecule of carbon dioxide. The remaining four-carbon compound binds to coenzyme A, forming succinyl-CoA.
- Substrate-Level Phosphorylation: Succinyl-CoA is converted to succinate, and this reaction generates one GTP (which can be converted into ATP).
- Oxidation of Succinate to Fumarate: Succinate is oxidized to fumarate, and FAD is reduced to FADH2.
- Hydration of Fumarate to Malate: Fumarate undergoes hydration to form malate.
- Oxidation of Malate: Malate is oxidized to regenerate oxaloacetate, and NAD+ is reduced to NADH.

The Krebs cycle is a cyclic process, meaning oxaloacetate is regenerated at the end of each cycle to combine with another acetyl-CoA molecule. The energy captured in NADH and FADH2 will be used in the final stage of cellular respiration—oxidative phosphorylation.

Oxidative Phosphorylation

Oxidative phosphorylation is the final stage of cellular respiration and occurs in the inner mitochondrial membrane. This stage is where the majority of ATP is produced, as the energy stored in NADH and FADH2 is used to power ATP synthesis. The process involves two key components: the electron transport chain (ETC) and chemiosmosis.

1. Electron Transport Chain (ETC): The ETC consists of a series of protein complexes (Complexes I-IV) embedded in the inner mitochondrial membrane. Electrons from NADH and FADH2 are transferred through these complexes, with each transfer releasing energy. This energy is used to pump protons (H+) from the mitochondrial matrix into the intermembrane space, creating a proton gradient.

2. **Chemiosmosis and ATP Synthesis:** The proton gradient generated by the ETC creates potential energy across the inner mitochondrial membrane. Protons flow back into the matrix through ATP synthase, a protein that uses the energy of the proton flow to convert ADP and inorganic phosphate (Pi) into ATP. This process of ATP generation is called chemiosmosis.
3. The total yield of ATP from one molecule of glucose through oxidative phosphorylation is approximately 32-34 ATP molecules, depending on the efficiency of the system.

The overall equation for cellular respiration, combining glycolysis, the Krebs cycle, and oxidative phosphorylation, is:

$$Glucose + 6O_2 \rightarrow 6CO_2 + 6H_2O + ATP$$

Metabolism and cellular respiration provide the energy necessary for all cellular functions. Glycolysis breaks down glucose into pyruvate, the Krebs cycle oxidizes acetyl-CoA to generate electron carriers, and oxidative phosphorylation uses these electrons to produce large amounts of ATP. Together, these pathways ensure that cells have a constant supply of energy to maintain homeostasis and carry out essential biological processes.

Chapter 5: Systems Biology

Systems biology is an interdisciplinary field that seeks to understand complex biological systems as integrated wholes. It focuses on the interactions and relationships between different parts of a system, such as genes, proteins, cells, and tissues, to grasp how they contribute to the overall function of an organism. This approach moves beyond reductionist views, which look at individual parts in isolation, and instead examines the dynamic interactions that lead to emergent properties—characteristics of a system that cannot be understood just by analyzing the components separately.

A central aspect of systems biology is its reliance on mathematical models and computational simulations to represent biological processes. By applying these tools, researchers can predict how changes in one part of a system, such as a genetic mutation, might influence the entire organism. Data from various sources, such as genomics, proteomics, and metabolomics, are integrated to give a more comprehensive understanding of how biological systems function and respond to changes in their environment.

For example, in human health, systems biology is used to study how disruptions in molecular networks contribute to diseases. Researchers can map the interactions between genes and proteins in diseases like cancer or diabetes, identifying critical pathways that could be targeted for treatment. Moreover, systems biology plays an essential role in personalized medicine by predicting how individuals with unique genetic makeups will respond to specific treatments.

The development of new technologies such as high-throughput sequencing, mass spectrometry, and advanced imaging techniques has significantly contributed to the progress of systems biology. These tools generate large amounts of data, which can be analyzed using computational algorithms to uncover hidden patterns and relationships that are not easily observed through traditional biological methods.

Nervous System

The nervous system is a highly specialized network responsible for transmitting signals throughout the body to coordinate actions and sensory information. It is divided into two major parts: the central nervous system (CNS), comprising the brain and spinal cord, and the peripheral nervous system (PNS), which includes all other neural elements such as nerves and sensory receptors.

The central nervous system (CNS) is the control center for the entire body. The brain processes sensory input, initiates responses, stores memories, and generates thoughts and emotions. The spinal cord, on the other hand, acts as a conduit for signals between the brain and the rest of the body, and it also controls reflex actions that do not require brain input, like pulling your hand away from a hot surface.

Neurons are the functional units of the nervous system. These cells are specialized for rapid communication through electrical impulses known as action potentials. A neuron consists of three main parts: the cell body, dendrites, and axon. The cell body contains the nucleus and organelles, while dendrites receive signals from other neurons, and the axon transmits those signals to target cells. When a neuron is activated by a stimulus, it generates an electrical signal that travels down the axon to the synapse, where neurotransmitters are released to carry the signal to the next neuron or target cell.

The peripheral nervous system (PNS) is further divided into the somatic and autonomic nervous systems. The somatic nervous system controls voluntary movements by transmitting signals from the CNS to skeletal muscles. In contrast, the autonomic nervous system regulates involuntary functions such as heart rate, digestion, and respiratory rate. The autonomic nervous system is further divided into the sympathetic and parasympathetic divisions, which work together to maintain homeostasis. The sympathetic division is responsible for the "fight or flight" response, increasing heart rate and blood flow to muscles during times of stress. The parasympathetic division promotes "rest and digest" functions, slowing the heart rate and enhancing digestion when the body is at rest.

The nervous system is crucial for maintaining homeostasis, allowing the body to respond to internal and external changes. Damage to the nervous system, such as from traumatic injury or degenerative diseases like multiple sclerosis, can have profound effects on an individual's ability to control movement, process sensory information, or perform basic bodily functions. Understanding the structure and function of the nervous system is essential for diagnosing and treating neurological conditions.

Immune System

The immune system is the body's defense mechanism against pathogens, including bacteria, viruses, fungi, and parasites. It consists of a complex network of cells, tissues, and organs that work together to protect the body from infections and diseases. The immune system can be divided into two main components: the innate immune system and the adaptive immune system.

The innate immune system is the body's first line of defense. It provides a rapid, non-specific response to pathogens. Key components of the innate immune system include physical barriers, such as the skin and mucous membranes, which prevent pathogens from entering the body. Additionally, innate immune cells, like macrophages, neutrophils, and dendritic cells, patrol the body and attack any foreign invaders they encounter.

Macrophages and neutrophils are types of phagocytes, meaning they engulf and destroy pathogens. Dendritic cells act as messengers between the innate and adaptive immune systems. They capture antigens from pathogens and present them to T cells, which are part of the adaptive immune system, thereby initiating a more specific immune response.

The adaptive immune system is slower to respond but provides a highly specific defense against pathogens. It is capable of "remembering" previous infections, allowing the body to mount a faster and stronger response upon subsequent exposure to the same pathogen. This process is the basis for immunological memory, which is why vaccines are effective in preventing diseases.

The key players in the adaptive immune system are T cells and B cells, both types of lymphocytes. T cells have various roles, including killing infected cells (cytotoxic T cells) and coordinating the immune response (helper T cells). B cells produce antibodies, proteins that bind to specific antigens on pathogens, marking them for destruction by other immune cells.

In addition to its role in defending against infections, the immune system is also involved in detecting and destroying cancerous cells. Immune surveillance is a process by which the immune system identifies and eliminates cells that have become abnormal, such as cancer cells. However, some cancers can evade the immune system, which is why immunotherapy—a treatment that enhances the body's immune response to cancer—has become a promising area of research.

Immune system dysfunction can lead to a range of health problems. Autoimmune diseases, such as rheumatoid arthritis and lupus, occur when the immune system mistakenly attacks the body's own tissues. Immunodeficiency disorders, like HIV/AIDS, weaken the immune system, making individuals more susceptible to infections. In contrast, allergies result from an overactive immune response to harmless substances, such as pollen or pet dander.

Maintaining a balanced immune response is crucial for overall health. Researchers are continually exploring ways to boost the immune system through nutrition, lifestyle changes, and medical interventions. For instance, adequate sleep, regular exercise, and a diet rich in vitamins and minerals support immune function, while stress, poor diet, and lack of sleep can weaken the immune system.

Chapter 6: Endocrinology and Hormonal Regulation

Endocrinology is the branch of biology and medicine focused on the endocrine system, which comprises glands that release hormones. Hormones are chemical messengers that regulate various physiological processes such as growth, metabolism, reproduction, and mood. Proper hormonal regulation is crucial for maintaining homeostasis— the stable internal environment that keeps the body functioning efficiently.

The Endocrine System and Its Glands

The endocrine system consists of several glands, each responsible for secreting specific hormones. These hormones travel through the bloodstream to target organs or tissues, where they trigger specific responses. Here is an overview of the primary glands and the hormones they secrete:

1. Pituitary Gland: Often referred to as the "master gland," the pituitary controls other endocrine glands and regulates processes such as growth, metabolism, and reproduction. The anterior pituitary secretes hormones such as growth hormone (GH), thyroid-stimulating hormone (TSH), adrenocorticotropic hormone (ACTH), and prolactin, while the posterior pituitary stores and releases oxytocin and antidiuretic hormone (ADH).
2. Hypothalamus: This gland serves as a link between the nervous and endocrine systems. It produces releasing and inhibiting hormones that control the pituitary gland's secretion of hormones. Key hormones include thyrotropin-releasing hormone (TRH) and corticotropin-releasing hormone (CRH).
3. Thyroid Gland: Located in the neck, the thyroid secretes thyroxine (T4) and triiodothyronine (T3), which regulate the body's metabolic rate, heart function, and digestive processes. It also releases calcitonin, a hormone that helps regulate calcium levels in the blood.
4. Parathyroid Glands: These small glands behind the thyroid produce parathyroid hormone (PTH), which plays a critical role in maintaining calcium balance in the blood and bones.
5. Adrenal Glands: Located on top of the kidneys, the adrenal glands consist of two regions: the cortex and the medulla. The adrenal cortex produces steroid hormones such as cortisol (which regulates metabolism and the immune response), aldosterone (which controls blood pressure), and androgens (sex hormones). The adrenal medulla produces catecholamines like adrenaline and noradrenaline, which are involved in the body's fight-or-flight response.
6. Pancreas: As both an exocrine and endocrine organ, the pancreas regulates blood sugar levels through the secretion of insulin and glucagon. Insulin decreases blood glucose levels, while glucagon increases them.
7. Gonads (Ovaries and Testes): The gonads produce sex hormones. In females, the ovaries secrete estrogen and progesterone, which regulate reproductive cycles, pregnancy, and secondary sexual characteristics. In males, the testes produce testosterone, which governs sperm production and secondary sexual traits.
8. Pineal Gland: This small gland in the brain produces melatonin, which helps regulate sleep-wake cycles and circadian rhythms.

Hormonal Regulation Mechanisms

The endocrine system operates largely through feedback mechanisms, most notably negative feedback loops, to regulate hormone levels. This ensures that the concentration of hormones within the bloodstream remains within a narrow range, preventing imbalances that could disrupt bodily functions.

- Negative Feedback: In this system, the release of a hormone leads to conditions that suppress further hormone release. For example, the hypothalamus releases TRH, which stimulates the pituitary to release TSH. In turn, TSH stimulates the thyroid gland to release T3 and T4. Once levels of T3 and T4 are sufficient, these hormones inhibit the release of TRH and TSH, thereby maintaining balance.
- Positive Feedback: Less common than negative feedback, positive feedback amplifies hormone production in response to a stimulus. For example, during childbirth, oxytocin is released to intensify uterine contractions, and as contractions increase, more oxytocin is released.

Hormonal Regulation of Major Body Functions

1. Growth and Development: Growth hormone (GH) from the pituitary gland plays a vital role in promoting body growth, particularly during childhood and adolescence. GH stimulates the growth of bones, muscles, and tissues by triggering protein synthesis and cell division. A deficiency in GH can lead to growth disorders like dwarfism, while excessive production can result in gigantism or acromegaly.
2. Metabolism: Thyroid hormones (T3 and T4) are essential regulators of metabolic rate. They increase the rate at which cells convert nutrients into energy, impacting heart rate, body temperature, and digestion. Hypothyroidism (low thyroid hormone production) can lead to weight gain, fatigue, and cold intolerance, while hyperthyroidism (excessive thyroid hormone production) can cause weight loss, rapid heartbeat, and irritability.
3. Reproductive Functions: In females, estrogen and progesterone regulate menstrual cycles, pregnancy, and breast development. In males, testosterone stimulates sperm production and the development of secondary sexual characteristics such as body hair and muscle mass. Hormonal imbalances in the gonads can lead to fertility issues, irregular menstrual cycles, and developmental disorders.
4. Stress Response: The adrenal glands play a critical role in managing stress. In response to stress, the hypothalamus secretes CRH, prompting the pituitary to release ACTH, which stimulates the adrenal cortex to release cortisol. Cortisol increases blood glucose levels, suppresses the immune system, and promotes the use of fats and proteins for energy, preparing the body for a prolonged stress response. Chronic stress can lead to excessive cortisol production, resulting in conditions like Cushing's syndrome.
5. Blood Sugar Regulation: Insulin and glucagon from the pancreas work in opposition to maintain stable blood glucose levels. After eating, insulin promotes the uptake of glucose by

cells for energy or storage as glycogen in the liver and muscles. When blood sugar drops between meals, glucagon signals the liver to break down glycogen into glucose, releasing it into the bloodstream.

6. Calcium Homeostasis: The balance of calcium in the blood is regulated by calcitonin from the thyroid and PTH from the parathyroid glands. PTH increases calcium levels by stimulating bone resorption (breaking down bone tissue to release calcium into the bloodstream), increasing calcium absorption in the intestines, and promoting calcium reabsorption in the kidneys. Calcitonin works to lower calcium levels by inhibiting bone resorption.

Hormonal Disorders

Disruptions in hormonal regulation can lead to various disorders, including:

- Diabetes Mellitus: A condition characterized by the body's inability to produce sufficient insulin (Type 1 diabetes) or to use insulin effectively (Type 2 diabetes), resulting in elevated blood glucose levels. Long-term complications include damage to the eyes, kidneys, and nerves.
- Hyperthyroidism and Hypothyroidism: Hyperthyroidism occurs when the thyroid gland produces too much T3 and T4, leading to symptoms such as rapid weight loss, increased heart rate, and anxiety. Hypothyroidism is marked by insufficient thyroid hormone production, resulting in fatigue, weight gain, and depression.
- Cushing's Syndrome: This disorder results from prolonged exposure to high levels of cortisol. Symptoms include weight gain, high blood pressure, and a characteristic "moon face."

Addison's Disease: Caused by insufficient production of cortisol and aldosterone, Addison's disease can lead to fatigue, low blood pressure, and weight loss.

Chapter 7: Reproduction

Reproduction is a fundamental biological process through which organisms produce offspring, ensuring the continuity of their species. In humans and most animals, reproduction occurs through two primary modes: sexual reproduction and asexual reproduction. These mechanisms differ significantly in terms of genetic variation and the biological processes involved.

Sexual vs Asexual Reproduction

Sexual reproduction involves the combination of genetic material from two distinct parent organisms, resulting in offspring that are genetically different from both parents. This genetic diversity is achieved through the fusion of two gametes—one from each parent—in a process known as fertilization. Sexual reproduction ensures variation within a population, which is crucial for evolution and adaptation. In humans, sexual reproduction occurs between male and female individuals, where sperm (from the male) and eggs (from the female) fuse to form a zygote.

Key advantages of sexual reproduction include:

- Genetic diversity: It provides variation in the offspring, helping species adapt to environmental changes.
- Evolutionary advantage: It facilitates natural selection, allowing populations to develop resistance to diseases or changing habitats.

However, sexual reproduction has disadvantages, such as requiring two parents and generally consuming more time and energy compared to asexual reproduction.

Asexual reproduction, on the other hand, involves a single parent and does not require the fusion of gametes. The offspring are genetically identical to the parent, resulting in clones. This method is common in many plants, bacteria, and some invertebrates. While asexual reproduction is efficient and allows for rapid population growth, it lacks the genetic diversity found in sexual reproduction.

Forms of asexual reproduction include:

- Binary fission: Common in bacteria, where a single cell divides into two identical cells.
- Budding: Seen in organisms like hydra, where new individuals grow from a bud on the parent's body.
- Fragmentation: In some animals like starfish, where parts of an organism break off and regenerate into new individuals.

In humans and most multicellular animals, asexual reproduction is not a primary form of reproduction but may occur in certain cases, such as cloning or cellular repair.

Gametogenesis: Spermatogenesis and Oogenesis

Gametogenesis is the process by which gametes—sperm in males and eggs in females—are produced. It is a crucial aspect of sexual reproduction, as it ensures that each gamete contains half the number of chromosomes found in normal body cells, allowing the restoration of the full chromosome number upon fertilization.

Spermatogenesis

Spermatogenesis is the process of sperm production in males, occurring in the seminiferous tubules of the testes. This process begins at puberty and continues throughout life, producing millions of sperm each day. Spermatogenesis involves several stages:

- Mitosis of Spermatogonia: Diploid cells called spermatogonia undergo mitosis to produce primary spermatocytes, which are also diploid.
- Meiosis I: Primary spermatocytes undergo the first meiotic division to produce two haploid secondary spermatocytes.
- Meiosis II: Each secondary spermatocyte undergoes the second meiotic division to produce two spermatids, resulting in four haploid cells in total.
- Spermiogenesis: Spermatids undergo a maturation process to become motile sperm cells, or spermatozoa. During this phase, spermatids develop tails (flagella) for movement and shed excess cytoplasm.

A mature sperm consists of three parts: the head (containing the nucleus and DNA), the midpiece (packed with mitochondria for energy), and the tail (responsible for motility). This entire process takes approximately 64 days in humans, and it is highly efficient, ensuring continuous sperm production.

Oogenesis

Oogenesis is the process by which eggs, or ova, are produced in females. Unlike spermatogenesis, which results in four viable sperm cells from each precursor, oogenesis produces only one viable egg and three polar bodies, which are non-functional. Oogenesis begins before birth, pauses during childhood, and resumes at puberty, continuing until menopause. It takes place in the ovaries and involves the following stages:

- Oogonia Formation: During fetal development, diploid oogonia undergo mitosis to produce primary oocytes. These primary oocytes begin meiosis but are arrested in prophase I until puberty.
- Meiosis I: At puberty, hormonal changes trigger the completion of meiosis I in a few primary oocytes during each menstrual cycle, resulting in one secondary oocyte (haploid) and a smaller polar body.

- Meiosis II: The secondary oocyte begins meiosis II but is arrested in metaphase II until fertilization. If fertilization occurs, meiosis II is completed, resulting in a mature ovum and another polar body. The mature ovum then combines with the sperm to form a zygote.

The process of oogenesis is cyclical and tied to the menstrual cycle, with only one oocyte typically reaching full maturation during each cycle.

Menstrual Cycle and Fertilization

The menstrual cycle is a monthly sequence of events that prepares the female body for pregnancy. It involves the coordination of hormonal changes in the hypothalamus, pituitary gland, and ovaries, and can be divided into four key phases:

1. Menstrual Phase: This phase begins with menstruation, the shedding of the uterine lining (endometrium), and typically lasts 3 to 7 days. During this time, hormone levels, including estrogen and progesterone, are low.
2. Follicular Phase: After menstruation, the pituitary gland secretes follicle-stimulating hormone (FSH), which stimulates the growth of ovarian follicles. Each follicle contains an immature egg, and as one dominant follicle matures, it secretes increasing amounts of estrogen. Estrogen promotes the thickening of the endometrium in preparation for potential implantation.
3. Ovulation: Around day 14 of the cycle, a surge in luteinizing hormone (LH) triggers the release of the mature egg from the dominant follicle, a process known as ovulation. The egg is then swept into the fallopian tube, where it can encounter sperm.
4. Luteal Phase: After ovulation, the ruptured follicle transforms into the corpus luteum, which secretes progesterone. Progesterone maintains the endometrium, making it receptive to implantation. If fertilization does not occur, the corpus luteum degenerates, causing progesterone levels to drop and triggering menstruation, restarting the cycle.

Fertilization occurs when a sperm cell successfully penetrates the secondary oocyte, usually within the fallopian tube. The fusion of the sperm and egg nuclei restores the diploid number of chromosomes, forming a zygote. The zygote undergoes several rounds of cell division as it travels toward the uterus, where it implants into the thickened endometrium, marking the beginning of pregnancy.

If fertilization does not occur, the egg disintegrates, and the menstrual cycle repeats. Fertilization typically happens within 24 hours after ovulation, and the window of fertility is generally considered to be a few days before and after ovulation.

Chapter 8: Embryogenesis and Development

Embryogenesis is the process by which a fertilized egg (zygote) develops into a fully formed fetus. It encompasses a series of well-orchestrated cellular divisions, migrations, and differentiation events that give rise to the various tissues and organs of the body. This process is essential for understanding the complex development of an organism, including the formation of germ layers, organ systems, and body structures.

Fertilization and Early Development

Fertilization is the initial step in embryogenesis, occurring when a sperm cell successfully penetrates an egg (ovum), leading to the formation of a zygote. This process typically takes place in the fallopian tube in humans. Upon sperm entry, cortical reactions in the egg prevent additional sperm from entering, ensuring monospermy. The zygote now contains a full set of chromosomes—23 from the mother and 23 from the father, making up 46 chromosomes in total.

Cleavage follows fertilization, consisting of rapid mitotic divisions without an increase in the overall size of the zygote. These divisions produce smaller cells called blastomeres. Cleavage divisions are important for increasing the number of cells, which allows for future differentiation without the zygote increasing in size initially. The end result of cleavage is a solid ball of cells known as the morula.

The morula undergoes further development into a fluid-filled structure called the blastocyst. The blastocyst contains an inner cell mass (ICM), which will give rise to the embryo, and an outer layer of cells called the trophoblast, which will contribute to the formation of the placenta. Around five to seven days after fertilization, the blastocyst implants itself into the endometrium of the uterus, initiating the next phase of development.

Germ Layers: Ectoderm, Mesoderm, Endoderm

Once implantation is complete, the process of gastrulation begins, which is pivotal for forming the three primary germ layers of the developing embryo. These layers—ectoderm, mesoderm, and endoderm—are the foundation from which all tissues and organs arise.

1. Ectoderm: This outermost germ layer gives rise to structures associated with the outer body and the nervous system. Key derivatives of the ectoderm include:
   - The nervous system, including the brain and spinal cord, through a process called neurulation. The neural tube, which forms from the ectoderm, will eventually develop into the central nervous system.
   - The epidermis, or outer layer of the skin, as well as hair, nails, and sweat glands.
   - Sensory organs, including parts of the eyes and ears.

2. Mesoderm: The middle germ layer differentiates into tissues involved in support, movement, and transport. Key derivatives include:
   - Musculoskeletal system: Bones, muscles, and cartilage are derived from the mesoderm.
   - Circulatory system: The heart, blood vessels, and blood cells arise from this layer, playing a critical role in forming the body's transportation system for oxygen and nutrients.
   - Excretory system: The kidneys and other components of the urinary system also develop from the mesoderm.
   - Reproductive system: Structures such as the gonads (ovaries and testes) arise from mesodermal cells.
3. Endoderm: The innermost germ layer forms the linings of the body's internal systems. The main derivatives include:
   - The gastrointestinal (GI) tract, including the stomach, intestines, and liver.
   - The respiratory system, including the lungs and trachea.
   - Endocrine glands such as the pancreas and the thyroid, which play roles in regulating metabolism and other critical body functions.

As the germ layers differentiate, they give rise to all the tissues and organs of the body, leading to increasingly specialized structures that function in an integrated manner.

Fetal Development and Birth

Following the formation of the germ layers, the embryo undergoes a process called organogenesis, where the primary tissues begin to form functional organs. This process extends throughout embryonic and fetal development.

1. First Trimester:
   - During the first trimester (weeks 1-12), the basic structures of the body are established. By the end of the first trimester, all major organs have begun to form. For instance, neurulation, the process by which the neural tube forms, occurs early in this period. The neural tube will later develop into the central nervous system.
   - Around week 8, the embryo is now referred to as a fetus. While the organs are formed, they are not yet fully functional, and significant development still needs to occur.
   - The fetus undergoes rapid growth in size during this trimester.
2. Second Trimester:
   - From weeks 13 to 26, the fetus grows in size and weight, with many organ systems maturing significantly.
   - Structures such as bones begin to harden, and the nervous system continues to develop, allowing for some reflex movements to begin by the end of the trimester.
   - The cardiovascular system also continues to mature, as blood vessels and the heart become more functional.
   - The fetus develops fine hair (lanugo) on its skin, and some sensory functions, such as hearing, begin to develop.

3. Third Trimester:
   - The final trimester (weeks 27 to 40) focuses on the continued growth and maturation of the fetus, preparing it for birth. The lungs mature significantly during this time, with surfactant production enabling the lungs to function outside the womb. Surfactant prevents the collapse of alveoli, essential for breathing post-birth.
   - Fat deposition increases, which helps regulate the baby's body temperature after birth. The baby also gains considerable weight, and its movements become more pronounced.
   - The placenta continues to support the fetus by providing oxygen and nutrients and removing waste products.

Birth, also known as parturition, involves several coordinated processes to bring the baby from the uterus into the external environment. Labor typically progresses in three stages:

- Stage 1: The cervix dilates and effaces, preparing for the passage of the baby.
- Stage 2: The baby is delivered through the birth canal.
- Stage 3: The placenta is expelled from the uterus.

Hormones, particularly oxytocin and prostaglandins, play critical roles in stimulating uterine contractions necessary for labor. Once the baby is born, its circulatory system undergoes significant changes, such as the closure of the ductus arteriosus, allowing the lungs to take over oxygen exchange.

Overall, embryogenesis and fetal development are intricate processes that involve a series of highly regulated events. From fertilization through birth, the transformation of a single-celled zygote into a complex, multicellular organism is one of the most fascinating aspects of human biology.

Chapter 10: The Musculoskeletal System

The musculoskeletal system is responsible for providing structural support, enabling movement, and protecting vital organs. This system is made up of bones, muscles, joints, and associated connective tissues like tendons and ligaments. It plays a crucial role in maintaining the body's posture, facilitating locomotion, and allowing for a wide range of movements. Additionally, the musculoskeletal system stores minerals like calcium and phosphorus in bones, and it is essential for hematopoiesis, the production of blood cells within the bone marrow.

Structure and Function of Bones

Bones are rigid structures that make up the skeletal framework of the body. They are primarily composed of a matrix of collagen fibers and calcium phosphate, which gives them strength and rigidity. Bones serve several key functions:

4. Support and Protection: Bones provide a solid framework that supports the body's soft tissues and organs. The skull protects the brain, the rib cage shields the heart and lungs, and the vertebrae protect the spinal cord.
5. Movement: Bones, in conjunction with muscles, facilitate movement. Muscles attach to bones via tendons, and the contraction of muscles results in the pulling of bones at joints, creating motion.
6. Mineral Storage: Bones act as a reservoir for essential minerals, especially calcium and phosphorus, which can be released into the bloodstream as needed to maintain homeostasis.
7. Blood Cell Production: Bone marrow, found in the hollow cavities of certain bones, is responsible for producing red and white blood cells, as well as platelets.
8. Energy Storage: Yellow bone marrow, composed of adipose tissue, serves as a store for fats, which can be used for energy when needed.

Bone is classified into two types based on structure: compact bone, which is dense and forms the outer layer of bones, and spongy bone, which is lighter and found in the interior of bones, particularly in areas that experience stress from multiple directions.

Types of Muscles and Muscle Contraction

There are three main types of muscles in the human body:

1. Skeletal Muscle: Skeletal muscles are attached to bones and are under voluntary control. They are responsible for body movements such as walking, lifting, and posture maintenance. Skeletal muscles are striated, meaning they have a banded appearance due to the arrangement of actin and myosin filaments in their cells.
2. Smooth Muscle: Smooth muscles are found in the walls of internal organs like the intestines, blood vessels, and the bladder. These muscles are not under voluntary control and function automatically to perform tasks such as peristalsis (the movement of food through the digestive system) and regulation of blood vessel diameter. Smooth muscles lack the striated appearance of skeletal muscles.

3. Cardiac Muscle: Cardiac muscles are found only in the heart. They are involuntary and have a striated appearance similar to skeletal muscles. Cardiac muscle cells are interconnected by intercalated discs, which allow for coordinated contractions essential for pumping blood.

Muscle Contraction is governed by the sliding filament theory, which describes how actin (thin) and myosin (thick) filaments slide past one another to produce contraction. The process begins with the release of calcium ions, which bind to troponin, causing a conformational change that moves tropomyosin away from actin's binding sites. Myosin heads then bind to actin, forming cross-bridges, and through a series of steps involving ATP, the myosin heads pull the actin filaments toward the center of the sarcomere, shortening the muscle fiber.

Muscle contractions can be classified into two main types:

- Isotonic Contraction: In isotonic contractions, the muscle changes length as it contracts, causing movement of a body part. For example, lifting a weight involves shortening the muscle (concentric contraction), while lowering it involves lengthening the muscle (eccentric contraction).
- Isometric Contraction: In isometric contractions, the muscle generates force without changing length. This type of contraction occurs when a muscle is activated but not allowed to shorten or lengthen, such as holding a weight in a fixed position.

Bone Remodeling and Growth

Bone Remodeling is a continuous process where old or damaged bone tissue is replaced with new bone tissue. This process is essential for maintaining bone strength and integrity throughout life. It involves two key cell types:

1. Osteoclasts: These cells break down bone tissue by secreting enzymes and acids that dissolve the bone matrix, a process known as bone resorption. This process releases minerals, such as calcium, back into the bloodstream.
2. Osteoblasts: These cells are responsible for forming new bone. They secrete collagen and other components that form the bone matrix, which is then mineralized to create strong bone tissue.

Bone remodeling is regulated by several factors, including mechanical stress, hormones (such as parathyroid hormone and calcitonin), and dietary intake of calcium and vitamin D. The balance between osteoclast and osteoblast activity is crucial for maintaining healthy bones. Disruptions in this balance can lead to conditions like osteoporosis, where bones become weak and brittle.

Bone Growth occurs through two primary processes:

1. Endochondral Ossification: This process is responsible for the formation of long bones, such as the femur and humerus. It begins with a cartilage model, which is gradually replaced by bone tissue. Growth in length occurs at the epiphyseal plate (growth plate), where new cartilage is produced and then ossified to become bone.

2. Intramembranous Ossification: This process forms flat bones like the skull and clavicles. In this method, bone develops directly from mesenchymal tissue without a cartilage precursor.

During childhood and adolescence, bones grow in length due to the activity at the growth plates. Once these plates close, usually after puberty, bones no longer increase in length, though they can continue to grow in thickness through the addition of new bone tissue by osteoblasts.

Joint Structure and Movement

Joints, or articulations, are the points where two or more bones meet. They allow for various types of movement and are classified based on their structure and the type of movement they permit:

1. Fibrous Joints: These joints are immovable and are held together by dense connective tissue. Examples include the sutures between the bones of the skull.
2. Cartilaginous Joints: These joints allow limited movement and are connected by cartilage. An example is the intervertebral discs between the vertebrae.
3. Synovial Joints: These are the most common and movable type of joints in the body. Synovial joints have a fluid-filled joint cavity that allows for smooth movement between bones. They include:
   - Hinge Joints: Allow movement in one direction, like the elbow or knee.
   - Ball-and-Socket Joints: Permit a wide range of motion, such as in the shoulder and hip.
   - Pivot Joints: Allow rotational movement, such as the joint between the first and second cervical vertebrae (the atlas and axis).

Each joint is stabilized by ligaments, which are strong bands of connective tissue that connect bone to bone. Additionally, tendons, which connect muscle to bone, help facilitate movement at the joints. Synovial fluid within the joint cavity lubricates the joint, reducing friction and allowing for smooth, pain-free movement.

Chapter 11: Homeostasis

Homeostasis refers to the maintenance of a stable internal environment within an organism, crucial for the proper functioning of cells and systems. The human body, like other organisms, relies on a series of regulatory mechanisms to keep variables such as temperature, pH, glucose levels, and electrolyte balance within narrow limits. Any deviation from these limits can lead to dysfunction and disease. Homeostasis is achieved through dynamic processes that constantly adjust to changes in the external and internal environment.

Principles of Homeostasis

The core principle of homeostasis is maintaining equilibrium in the body's internal conditions despite fluctuations in the external environment. Homeostasis is regulated through three primary components:

1. Receptors (Sensors): These detect any changes or deviations from the set point (normal range) in the body's internal environment. For example, thermoreceptors detect changes in body temperature, while chemoreceptors monitor pH or CO_2 levels in the blood.
2. Control Centers: The control center, typically part of the central nervous system (e.g., the brain or spinal cord), receives information from receptors. It compares the data to the set point and initiates appropriate responses. The hypothalamus, for example, is a key control center for regulating body temperature, hunger, and thirst.
3. Effectors: Effectors are muscles, glands, or organs that bring about the necessary changes to restore balance. They carry out the response dictated by the control center. For example, when body temperature drops, muscles (effectors) contract to generate heat via shivering.

Together, these components form a regulatory loop that is critical for homeostatic control, ensuring that the body's internal environment remains within a functional range.

Feedback Mechanisms

Feedback mechanisms are integral to the homeostatic process. They ensure that the body responds appropriately to changes by either amplifying or reducing the initial stimulus. Feedback mechanisms can be classified into two types: negative feedback and positive feedback.

Negative Feedback

Negative feedback mechanisms are the most common in maintaining homeostasis. They work by reversing a change to return the system to its normal range. When a physiological variable deviates from its set point, negative feedback mechanisms reduce or shut down the stimulus that caused the deviation. This process effectively restores the variable to the normal state.

Example of Negative Feedback: Temperature Regulation

- Receptor: Thermoreceptors in the skin and hypothalamus detect a drop in body temperature.

- Control Center: The hypothalamus compares the actual body temperature to the normal set point (~37°C).
- Effector: The hypothalamus triggers shivering (muscle contractions) to generate heat and vasoconstriction to reduce heat loss. As the body warms, the stimulus (cold) decreases, and the effectors slow or stop their activity.

Other examples include blood glucose regulation via insulin and glucagon, blood pressure regulation through baroreceptors, and fluid balance via antidiuretic hormone (ADH).

Positive Feedback

Positive feedback mechanisms amplify the initial stimulus, driving the body further away from the set point. While less common in maintaining daily homeostasis, positive feedback plays a critical role in processes that require a self-perpetuating cycle, often until a specific endpoint is reached.

Example of Positive Feedback: Childbirth

- Receptor: Stretch receptors in the cervix detect the baby's head pushing against it.
- Control Center: The brain (hypothalamus) sends signals to the pituitary gland to release oxytocin.
- Effector: Oxytocin stimulates stronger uterine contractions, which push the baby further down, increasing the stimulus on the stretch receptors. This process continues until childbirth occurs, after which the cycle is interrupted.

Another example of positive feedback is the blood clotting cascade, where each step in the clotting process triggers the next, resulting in rapid formation of a blood clot.

Examples of Homeostatic Processes

Various physiological systems rely on homeostatic mechanisms to maintain balance and proper function. Key examples include temperature regulation, glucose homeostasis, and fluid and electrolyte balance.

1. Temperature Regulation

The human body must maintain a core temperature of around 37°C to function properly. Thermoregulation involves multiple systems working together to prevent overheating (hyperthermia) or overcooling (hypothermia).

When body temperature rises, the hypothalamus triggers:

- Sweating: Sweat glands release water onto the skin's surface, and as it evaporates, it cools the body.
- Vasodilation: Blood vessels in the skin dilate to increase blood flow, promoting heat loss.

When body temperature drops, the body initiates:

- Shivering: Muscles contract rapidly, generating heat.
- Vasoconstriction: Blood vessels constrict, reducing blood flow to the skin and minimizing heat loss.

2. Glucose Homeostasis

Maintaining stable blood glucose levels is crucial for cellular function, especially for organs like the brain that rely on glucose as their primary energy source. The pancreas plays a central role in glucose homeostasis by releasing insulin and glucagon.

- Insulin: When blood glucose levels rise after eating, insulin is released from the pancreas, promoting glucose uptake by cells and storage as glycogen in the liver. This lowers blood glucose levels.
- Glucagon: When blood glucose levels drop, the pancreas releases glucagon, which signals the liver to break down glycogen into glucose and release it into the bloodstream, raising blood glucose levels.

Diabetes is a condition where this feedback mechanism is impaired, leading to chronically high blood glucose levels.

3. Fluid and Electrolyte Balance

The body must carefully regulate its fluid and electrolyte levels to ensure normal cellular function, blood pressure, and volume. The kidneys are the primary organs responsible for maintaining this balance through the following processes:

- Antidiuretic Hormone (ADH): When the body is dehydrated, the hypothalamus signals the release of ADH, which prompts the kidneys to reabsorb more water and produce less urine. This helps maintain blood volume and pressure.
- Aldosterone: This hormone, secreted by the adrenal glands, regulates sodium and potassium levels in the blood. Aldosterone increases sodium reabsorption by the kidneys, which helps retain water and maintain blood pressure.

Proper electrolyte balance is vital for nerve impulse transmission, muscle contraction, and other cellular processes.

4. pH Regulation

The body's internal pH must be kept within a narrow range (7.35-7.45) for enzymes and other biochemical processes to function optimally. Several systems work together to regulate pH, including:

- Buffer Systems: Chemicals like bicarbonate in the blood neutralize excess acids or bases to prevent drastic pH changes.

- Respiratory System: By altering the rate of carbon dioxide exhalation, the respiratory system helps control pH. Increased CO_2 removal reduces acidity (increases pH), while retention of CO_2 increases acidity.
- Renal System: The kidneys excrete hydrogen ions and reabsorb bicarbonate to regulate blood pH over a longer period.

Practical Questions For Section 1

1. Hyperbaric oxygen therapy is used for certain bacterial infections by placing the patient in a chamber where oxygen pressure is raised, increasing oxygen levels in the tissues. This treatment is most likely effective against:
   a) obligate aerobic bacteria.
   b) facultative anaerobic bacteria.
   c) aerotolerant anaerobic bacteria.
   d) obligate anaerobic bacteria.

2. Which of the following statements is NOT true regarding connective tissue cells?
   a) They form the majority of cells in muscles, bones, and tendons.
   b) They release substances to create the extracellular matrix.
   c) They often contribute to forming the stroma in organs.
   d) They offer structural support to epithelial cells in organs.

3. Which of these types of nucleic acid could make up a virus's genome?
   I. Single-stranded RNA
   II. Double-stranded DNA
   III. Single-stranded DNA
   a) I only
   b) II only
   c) I and II only
   d) I, II, and III

4. The theory of spontaneous generation, which suggested that life can arise from non-living matter, was challenged by Pasteur in 1859 when he demonstrated that no organisms grew in sterilized media. This supports which concept of cell theory?
   a) All living things consist of cells.
   b) The cell is the fundamental unit of life.
   c) Cells can only come from pre-existing cells.
   d) Cells store genetic material in the form of DNA.

5. Mitochondrial DNA has the following characteristics:
   I. Circular structure
   II. Ability to replicate independently
   III. Single-stranded nature
   a) I only
   b) II only
   c) I and II only
   d) I, II, and III

6. Which of the following is NOT a task performed by the smooth endoplasmic reticulum?
   a) Lipid production
   b) Detoxification of harmful substances
   c) Protein synthesis

d) Protein transportation
7. What is the primary role of the nucleolus?
   a) Synthesis of ribosomal RNA
   b) DNA duplication
   c) Cell division
   d) Assembly of chromosomes
8. Which of the following organelles is enclosed by a single membrane?
   a) Lysosomes
   b) Mitochondria
   c) Nuclei
   d) Ribosomes
9. Which of these differences would NOT help differentiate a prokaryotic cell from a eukaryotic cell?
   a) Ribosomal size and weight
   b) Presence of a nucleus
   c) Having an outer cell membrane
   d) Having membrane-bound organelles
10. Which structure does NOT contain tubulin?
    a) Cilia
    b) Flagella
    c) Microfilaments
    d) Centrioles
11. Herpes simplex virus (HSV) remains dormant in the nervous system and can cause outbreaks triggered by factors like heat or radiation. Which statement best describes HSV?
    a) During dormancy, the virus is in its lytic phase.
    b) The virus is in the lysogenic phase during outbreaks.
    c) HSV integrates its genetic material into the host's genome.
    d) HSV possesses a tail sheath and tail fibers.
12. Antibiotic resistance in bacteria is a critical issue. Which processes contribute to a bacterium's ability to increase genetic diversity and resist antibiotics?
   I. Binary fission
   II. Conjugation
   III. Transduction
    a) I and II only
    b) I and III only
    c) II and III only
    d) I, II, and III

13. A penicillin-resistant bacterium is transferred to a colony lacking the fertility factor, yet the resistance does not spread. Additionally, the bacterium exhibits new traits like secreting a novel protein. Which form of bacterial recombination is least likely to explain this change?
    a) Conjugation
    b) Transformation
    c) Transduction
    d) Infection by a bacteriophage
14. Alzheimer's disease involves the production of β-amyloid, which forms plaques in the brain through a β-pleated sheet structure. This disease mechanism is most similar to which pathogen?
    a) Bacteria
    b) Viruses
    c) Prions
    d) Viroids
15. After infecting a cell, a virus must travel to the nucleus to produce viral proteins. What is the most likely type of genome this virus contains?
    a) Double-stranded DNA
    b) Double-stranded RNA
    c) Positive-sense RNA
    d) Negative-sense RNA
16. During bacterial reproduction, which process involves direct transfer of genetic material through a pilus?
    a) Binary fission
    b) Conjugation
    c) Transformation
    d) Transduction
17. Which of the following structures is responsible for synthesizing proteins in a eukaryotic cell?
    a) Smooth ER
    b) Ribosomes
    c) Golgi apparatus
    d) Lysosomes
18. The primary function of the rough endoplasmic reticulum is:
    a) Lipid metabolism
    b) Protein synthesis
    c) DNA replication
    d) Glucose storage
19. What cellular structure is responsible for energy production in eukaryotic cells?
    a) Mitochondria
    b) Chloroplasts
    c) Ribosomes
    d) Nucleus

20. Which of the following types of cells does NOT have membrane-bound organelles?
    a) Eukaryotic cells
    b) Prokaryotic cells
    c) Fungal cells
    d) Animal cells
21. Which process involves the uptake of foreign DNA from the surrounding environment by a bacterium?
    a) Conjugation
    b) Transformation
    c) Transduction
    d) Binary fission
22. Which of the following is NOT a function of the Golgi apparatus?
    a) Modification of proteins
    b) Packaging of proteins for secretion
    c) Breakdown of fatty acids
    d) Sorting of proteins
23. In the cell membrane, which type of molecule forms the bilayer that separates the internal environment from the external environment?
    a) Proteins
    b) Phospholipids
    c) Carbohydrates
    d) Nucleotides
24. Which of the following organelles contains enzymes that break down waste material in a cell?
    a) Ribosomes
    b) Lysosomes
    c) Mitochondria
    d) Nucleus
25. What is the function of centrioles in animal cells?
    a) Protein synthesis
    b) Cell division
    c) Energy production
    d) Waste disposal
26. Which organelle is primarily involved in the detoxification of drugs and poisons?
    a) Lysosomes
    b) Smooth ER
    c) Golgi apparatus
    d) Ribosomes
27. The structure responsible for organizing microtubules during cell division is:
    a) Lysosome
    b) Ribosome

c) Centriole
   d) Mitochondrion
28. The genetic material in eukaryotic cells is contained within the:
   a) Ribosome
   b) Nucleus
   c) Lysosome
   d) Plasma membrane
29. In which organelle does the process of photosynthesis occur?
   a) Mitochondria
   b) Golgi apparatus
   c) Chloroplast
   d) Nucleus
30. What is the role of the plasma membrane in cells?
   a) Providing energy
   b) Storing genetic material
   c) Regulating entry and exit of substances
   d) Synthesizing proteins
31. What is the correct progression in the formation of a mature sperm cell?
   a) Spermatid → primary spermatocyte → spermatogonium → secondary spermatocyte → spermatozoan
   b) Spermatogonium → primary spermatocyte → secondary spermatocyte → spermatid → spermatozoan
   c) Spermatozoan → primary spermatocyte → secondary spermatocyte → spermatogonium → spermatid
   d) Spermatogonium → primary spermatocyte → secondary spermatocyte → spermatozoan → spermatid
32. Which developmental stage of an egg cell corresponds to the appropriate phase in a woman's life?
   a) From birth to puberty—prophase II
   b) At ovulation—metaphase I
   c) At ovulation—metaphase II
   d) At fertilization—prophase II
33. In Alzheimer's patients, spindle apparatus issues in attaching to kinetochore fibers are found. At what mitotic stage would this defect first appear?
   a) Prophase
   b) Metaphase
   c) Anaphase
   d) Telophase

34. If a scientist wants to introduce a radiolabeled deoxyadenine into one of two daughter cells produced during mitosis, what is the latest stage at which this could occur?
    a) G1 phase
    b) G2 phase
    c) M phase
    d) S phase
35. Excessive estrogen production is common in granulosa cell tumors. Which reproductive organ should be examined for a secondary tumor?
    a) Fallopian tubes
    b) Cervix
    c) Endometrium
    d) Vagina
36. After ovulation, where does the oocyte go?
    a) Fallopian tube
    b) Follicle
    c) Abdominal cavity
    d) Uterus
37. Cancer cells undergo uncontrolled mitosis. Which stage(s) of the cell cycle could chemotherapy potentially disrupt to stop cell division?
    a) S phase only
    b) S phase and prophase only
    c) Prophase and metaphase only
    d) S phase, prophase, and metaphase
38. Which pair of male reproductive structures and their features is incorrect?
    a) Seminal vesicles—produce alkaline fructose-containing secretions
    b) Prostate gland—has muscles that raise and lower the testes
    c) Vas deferens—connects the epididymis to the ejaculatory duct
    d) Cowper's glands—clear urine residue from the urethra
39. At what point in meiosis is the diploid chromosome number maintained?
    a) Interphase
    b) Telophase I
    c) Interkinesis
    d) Telophase II
40. Which of the following does NOT contribute significantly to genetic diversity?
    a) Random sperm fertilization of an egg
    b) Random homologous chromosome segregation
    c) Crossing over between homologous chromosomes
    d) DNA replication in S phase

41. Which key distinction between mitosis and meiosis is accurately stated?
    a) During metaphase of mitosis, chromosomes align single file; in metaphase II of meiosis, chromosomes align on opposite sides of the metaphase plate.
    b) In anaphase of mitosis, homologous chromosomes separate; in anaphase of meiosis I, sister chromatids separate.
    c) At the end of mitosis, daughter cells are identical; at the end of meiosis I, daughter cells are identical to the parent cell.
    d) In metaphase of mitosis, centromeres lie on the metaphase plate; in metaphase I of meiosis, centromeres do not.
42. Which statement about prophase is accurate?
    a) Chromosomes migrate to opposite poles.
    b) Spindle apparatus disintegrates.
    c) Chromosomes unravel.
    d) Nucleoli disappear.
43. A phenotypically female individual with a recessive X-linked allele and disease symptoms likely has which genotype due to parental nondisjunction?
    a) 46,XX
    b) 46,XY
    c) 45,X
    d) 47,XXY
44. During which part of the menstrual cycle does progesterone reach its highest concentration?
    a) Follicular phase
    b) Ovulation
    c) Luteal phase
    d) Menses
45. Which of the following would NOT be expected during pregnancy?
    a) High hCG levels in the first trimester
    b) Elevated progesterone throughout the pregnancy
    c) Low FSH levels in the first trimester
    d) Increased GnRH levels during pregnancy
46. What sequence of events describes the correct development of a mature sperm?
    a) Spermatid → primary spermatocyte → spermatogonium → secondary spermatocyte → spermatozoan
    b) Spermatogonium → primary spermatocyte → secondary spermatocyte → spermatid → spermatozoan
    c) Spermatozoan → primary spermatocyte → secondary spermatocyte → spermatogonium → spermatid
    d) Spermatogonium → primary spermatocyte → secondary spermatocyte → spermatozoan → spermatid

47. At ovulation, the egg is arrested in which stage?
    a) Prophase II
    b) Metaphase I
    c) Metaphase II
    d) Telophase I
48. Which structure in the male reproductive system produces a secretion high in fructose?
    a) Prostate gland
    b) Seminal vesicles
    c) Cowper's glands
    d) Epididymis
49. At which stage of the cell cycle does genetic recombination primarily occur?
    a) Prophase I
    b) Telophase I
    c) Anaphase II
    d) Metaphase I
50. Which cellular stage is linked to the highest probability of cancer cell suppression by chemotherapy?
    a) S phase
    b) M phase
    c) G1 phase
    d) G2 phase
51. During mitosis, when do centromeres align along the metaphase plate?
    a) Metaphase I
    b) Metaphase II
    c) Anaphase
    d) Prophase
52. Which of the following best defines homeostasis?
    a) The process of breaking down food for energy
    b) The maintenance of a constant internal environment
    c) The ability of an organism to move toward a stimulus
    d) The production of heat through muscle contractions
53. Which component in a homeostatic control system detects changes in the environment?
    a) Effector
    b) Control center
    c) Receptor
    d) Hormone
54. Negative feedback in homeostasis is characterized by which of the following?
    a) Amplifying the initial stimulus
    b) Reversing the change in the variable
    c) Triggering a new change in the opposite direction

d) Maintaining the initial stimulus
55. Which of the following is an example of a negative feedback mechanism?
    a) Blood clotting during injury
    b) Uterine contractions during childbirth
    c) Regulation of blood glucose levels
    d) Oxytocin release during labor
56. Which hormone is primarily responsible for reducing blood glucose levels after a meal?
    a) Glucagon
    b) Insulin
    c) ADH
    d) Aldosterone
57. In response to an increase in body temperature, which process helps restore homeostasis?
    a) Vasoconstriction
    b) Shivering
    c) Sweating
    d) Increased heart rate
58. Which of the following systems is involved in regulating blood pH?
    a) Digestive system
    b) Respiratory system
    c) Lymphatic system
    d) Muscular system
59. Which of the following is NOT typically involved in homeostasis?
    a) Nerves
    b) Hormones
    c) Skin
    d) Bone marrow
60. The hormone aldosterone helps regulate homeostasis by affecting which of the following?
    a) Blood glucose levels
    b) Sodium and potassium balance
    c) Body temperature
    d) Oxygen transport
61. Which of the following describes a positive feedback mechanism?
    a) It stabilizes body temperature when it fluctuates
    b) It enhances the effect of a stimulus until a specific event concludes
    c) It minimizes deviations from the body's normal state
    d) It decreases heart rate to lower blood pressure
62. Which of the following nitrogenous bases pairs with cytosine in the DNA double helix?
    a) Adenine
    b) Guanine
    c) Thymine

d) Uracil
63. Which enzyme is responsible for unwinding the DNA double helix during replication?
    a) DNA ligase
    b) DNA polymerase
    c) Helicase
    d) RNA polymerase
64. In which direction does DNA polymerase synthesize the new DNA strand?
    a) 5' to 3'
    b) 3' to 5'
    c) Both directions simultaneously
    d) Random direction depending on the strand
65. Which repair mechanism is used to correct bulky lesions, such as thymine dimers, caused by UV radiation?
    a) Mismatch Repair
    b) Nucleotide Excision Repair
    c) Base Excision Repair
    d) Homologous Recombination
66. What is the role of RNA polymerase during transcription?
    a) Binding to the promoter and synthesizing mRNA
    b) Unwinding the DNA and binding Okazaki fragments
    c) Joining nucleotides together during replication
    d) Proofreading and correcting DNA replication errors
67. In eukaryotic cells, the removal of non-coding sequences (introns) from pre-mRNA occurs during which process?
    a) Translation
    b) Transcription
    c) Splicing
    d) DNA Replication
68. Which of the following is a feature of the leading strand during DNA replication?
    a) Synthesized in short Okazaki fragments
    b) Synthesized continuously in the 5' to 3' direction
    c) Synthesized by RNA polymerase
    d) Requires DNA ligase for joining fragments
69. Which of the following is NOT involved in post-transcriptional regulation of gene expression?
    a) Alternative splicing
    b) RNA capping
    c) Polyadenylation
    d) Histone modification

70. What is the first step in the process of transcription in prokaryotic cells?
    a) Binding of RNA polymerase to the terminator region
    b) Binding of RNA polymerase to the promoter region
    c) Translation of mRNA into proteins
    d) Removal of introns from mRNA
71. Which of the following best describes the relationship between a gene and a protein?
    a) A gene directly produces a protein
    b) A gene is transcribed into mRNA, which is then translated into a protein
    c) A gene is made of proteins
    d) A gene is only involved in DNA replication
72. Which phase of the cell cycle involves DNA replication?

    a) G1 phase

    b) S phase

    c) G2 phase

    d) M phase

73. During which stage of mitosis do the sister chromatids separate and move toward opposite poles of the cell?

    a) Prophase

    b) Metaphase

    c) Anaphase

    d) Telophase

74. In meiosis, crossing over occurs during which phase?

    a) Prophase I

    b) Metaphase I

    c) Anaphase I

    d) Telophase I

75. What is the role of cyclin-dependent kinases (CDKs) in the cell cycle?

    a) They initiate DNA replication

    b) They control cell cycle progression by activating specific proteins

    c) They break down cyclins after cell division

    d) They repair damaged DNA

76. Which checkpoint ensures that all chromosomes are properly aligned at the metaphase plate before proceeding to anaphase?

    a) G1 checkpoint

    b) G2 checkpoint

    c) M checkpoint

    d) G0 checkpoint

77. What process occurs during anaphase I of meiosis that contributes to genetic diversity?

    a) Separation of sister chromatids

    b) Crossing over

    c) Independent assortment of homologous chromosomes

    d) Formation of the spindle apparatus

78. Which protein acts as a tumor suppressor and is often referred to as the "guardian of the genome"?

    a) Cyclin D

    b) p53

    c) CDK4

    d) Rb

79. In which phase of mitosis does the nuclear envelope re-form around separated sets of chromosomes?

    a) Prophase

    b) Metaphase

    c) Anaphase

    d) Telophase

80. What is the main function of the G1 phase in the cell cycle?

    a) DNA replication

    b) Protein synthesis and organelle duplication

    c) Chromosome alignment

    d) Cell division

81. What process ensures the reduction of chromosome number during meiosis?

    a) DNA replication

    b) Cytokinesis

    c) Separation of homologous chromosomes in meiosis I

    d) Separation of sister chromatids in meiosis II

82. Which of the following is the primary purpose of glycolysis?

    a) To produce ATP from ADP

    b) To convert glucose into pyruvate

    c) To release oxygen

    d) To generate water as a byproduct

83. What is the net ATP gain from one molecule of glucose during glycolysis?

    a) 1 ATP

    b) 2 ATP

    c) 4 ATP

    d) 6 ATP

84. Which molecule is regenerated at the end of the Krebs cycle to allow the cycle to continue?

    a) Acetyl-CoA

    b) Citrate

    c) Oxaloacetate

    d) Pyruvate

85. During the Krebs cycle, which of the following molecules directly generates ATP (or GTP)?

    a) Succinyl-CoA

    b) Citrate

    c) Fumarate

    d) Isocitrate

86. In the electron transport chain, which molecule donates electrons to Complex I?

   a) FADH2

   b) NADH

   c) Oxygen

   d) Pyruvate

87. What role does oxygen play in oxidative phosphorylation?

   a) It pumps protons across the inner mitochondrial membrane

   b) It acts as the final electron acceptor

   c) It initiates ATP production

   d) It is required for glycolysis

88. Which of the following is a byproduct of the complete oxidation of glucose in cellular respiration?

   a) NADPH

   b) Lactic acid

   c) Carbon dioxide

   d) Ethanol

89. Which process produces the majority of ATP in cellular respiration?

   a) Glycolysis

   b) The Krebs cycle

   c) Oxidative phosphorylation

   d) Fermentation

90. Which enzyme is responsible for synthesizing ATP during chemiosmosis?

   a) Pyruvate dehydrogenase

   b) Hexokinase

   c) ATP synthase

   d) Citrate synthase

91. How many molecules of carbon dioxide are released during one turn of the Krebs cycle?

    a) 1

    b) 2

    c) 3

    d) 4

92. In systems biology, which of the following is essential for understanding the interactions within biological systems?
    a) DNA replication
    b) Reductionist analysis
    c) Computational modeling
    d) Mitochondrial function

93. Which component of the central nervous system is primarily responsible for processing sensory input and generating responses?
    a) Brain
    b) Spinal cord
    c) Peripheral nerves
    d) Autonomic nervous system

94. What is the role of neurotransmitters in the nervous system?
    a) To transmit electrical signals within the axon
    b) To increase the speed of action potentials
    c) To carry chemical signals across synapses
    d) To regulate hormone release

95. Which division of the autonomic nervous system is responsible for the "rest and digest" functions?
    a) Sympathetic
    b) Parasympathetic
    c) Somatic
    d) Central

96. In the immune system, which cell type is primarily involved in the production of antibodies?
    a) T cells
    b) B cells
    c) Macrophages
    d) Dendritic cells

97. Which of the following is a characteristic of the innate immune system?
    a) Slow response to pathogens
    b) Highly specific to particular antigens
    c) Involves immunological memory
    d) Provides a non-specific first line of defense

98. Which process allows the adaptive immune system to recognize and respond more rapidly to pathogens it has encountered before?
    a) Phagocytosis
    b) Inflammation
    c) Immunological memory
    d) Antigen presentation
99. Which type of neuron is responsible for transmitting signals from the central nervous system to muscles, initiating movement?
    a) Sensory neurons
    b) Motor neurons
    c) Interneurons
    d) Glial cells
100. In immune surveillance, which of the following is the primary role of cytotoxic T cells?
    a) Engulf and digest pathogens
    b) Coordinate the immune response
    c) Produce antibodies
    d) Destroy infected or cancerous cells
101. The sympathetic division of the autonomic nervous system is most active during:
    a) Deep sleep
    b) Physical rest
    c) Exercise or stress
    d) Digestion and nutrient absorption
102. Which of the following glands is known as the "master gland" due to its control over other endocrine glands?
    a) Thyroid gland
    b) Pituitary gland
    c) Adrenal gland
    d) Pineal gland
103. What type of feedback mechanism is most commonly involved in regulating hormone levels in the body?
    a) Positive feedback
    b) Negative feedback
    c) Hormonal feedback
    d) Neutral feedback
104. Which hormone is primarily responsible for lowering blood glucose levels after a meal?
    a) Glucagon
    b) Insulin
    c) Cortisol
    d) Adrenaline

105. Which of the following is the primary hormone produced by the adrenal medulla in response to stress?
    a) Cortisol
    b) Aldosterone
    c) Adrenaline
    d) Testosterone

106. The secretion of which hormone is directly controlled by corticotropin-releasing hormone (CRH) from the hypothalamus?
    a) Growth hormone
    b) Adrenocorticotropic hormone (ACTH)
    c) Thyroid-stimulating hormone (TSH)
    d) Prolactin

107. Which hormone is produced by the parathyroid glands and is crucial for maintaining calcium homeostasis in the blood?
    a) Calcitonin
    b) Thyroxine
    c) Parathyroid hormone (PTH)
    d) Glucocorticoids

108. What effect does thyroid hormone (T3 and T4) have on the body's metabolic rate?
    a) It decreases the metabolic rate
    b) It increases the metabolic rate
    c) It has no effect on the metabolic rate
    d) It stabilizes the metabolic rate

109. Which of the following is a symptom of hyperthyroidism?
    a) Fatigue and weight gain
    b) Bradycardia (slow heart rate)
    c) Rapid weight loss and increased heart rate
    d) Dry skin and hair loss

110. Which of the following best describes the role of glucagon in the body?
    a) It promotes the uptake of glucose into cells
    b) It increases the storage of glycogen in the liver
    c) It increases blood glucose levels by promoting glycogen breakdown
    d) It stimulates the release of insulin from the pancreas

111. Cushing's syndrome is caused by excessive levels of which hormone?
    a) Insulin
    b) Glucagon
    c) Aldosterone
    d) Cortisol

Answers & Explanation

1. **D. obligate anaerobic bacteria.** - Hyperbaric oxygen therapy increases oxygen concentration in tissues. Since obligate anaerobic bacteria cannot survive in high oxygen environments, this treatment is most effective against them.
2. **A. They form the majority of cells in muscles, bones, and tendons.** - Connective tissue cells mainly form the extracellular matrix and provide structural support, but they do not account for most cells in muscles, bones, or tendons, which are primarily composed of muscle or bone cells.
3. **D. I, II, and III.** - Viruses can have genomes made from single-stranded RNA, double-stranded DNA, or single-stranded DNA, making all three options possible.
4. **C. Cells can only come from pre-existing cells.** - Pasteur's experiment debunked spontaneous generation, demonstrating that living organisms (cells) cannot arise from nonliving material but only from other living cells.
5. **C. I and II only.** - Mitochondrial DNA is circular and self-replicating, but it is double-stranded, not single-stranded.
6. **C. Protein synthesis.** - Protein synthesis is carried out by ribosomes and the rough endoplasmic reticulum, not the smooth endoplasmic reticulum (SER), which is responsible for lipid synthesis, detoxification, and transport.
7. **A. Synthesis of ribosomal RNA.** - The nucleolus is the site of ribosomal RNA (rRNA) synthesis and ribosome assembly within the nucleus.
8. **A. Lysosomes.** - Lysosomes are surrounded by a single membrane and contain enzymes that break down cellular waste. Mitochondria and nuclei have double membranes, and ribosomes are not membrane-bound.
9. **C. Having an outer cell membrane.** - Both prokaryotic and eukaryotic cells have an outer cell membrane. The other options describe clear differences between prokaryotes and eukaryotes.
10. **C. Microfilaments.** - Microfilaments are composed of actin, not tubulin. Cilia, flagella, and centrioles contain microtubules made of tubulin.
11. **C. HSV integrates its genetic material into the host's genome.** - HSV remains latent in the host's nervous system by integrating its DNA into the host genome. During outbreaks, the virus can enter the lytic cycle and become active.
12. **C. II and III only.** - Bacteria increase their genetic diversity through conjugation (transfer of DNA via a pilus) and transduction (transfer of DNA by a virus). Binary fission does not introduce genetic variability but simply replicates the genome.
13. **A. Conjugation.** - Conjugation requires the fertility factor (F factor), which the colony lacked, making it unlikely as the mechanism for the phenotypic changes in this case.
14. **C. Prions.** – The disease mechanism in Alzheimer's, involving misfolded β-pleated sheet proteins forming plaques, is most similar to prions, which are infectious proteins that cause misfolding in host proteins.

15. **A. Double-stranded DNA.** - Viruses that need to transport their genome to the host nucleus to produce proteins generally have double-stranded DNA, as these viruses replicate using the host's transcription machinery.
16. **B.** - Conjugation involves direct transfer of genetic material through a pilus from one bacterium to another, which can introduce genetic diversity.
17. **B. Ribosomes.** - Ribosomes are responsible for protein synthesis in eukaryotic cells, found either free in the cytoplasm or attached to the rough ER.
18. **B. Protein synthesis.** - The rough endoplasmic reticulum is associated with ribosomes and is involved in the synthesis and processing of proteins.
19. **A. Mitochondria.** - Mitochondria are the "powerhouses" of the cell and are responsible for generating ATP, the energy currency of the cell, through cellular respiration.
20. **B. Prokaryotic cells.** - Prokaryotic cells, such as bacteria, do not have membrane-bound organelles. Eukaryotic cells, including plant, animal, and fungal cells, do have membrane-bound organelles.
21. **B. Transformation.** - Transformation is the process by which a bacterium takes up foreign DNA from its environment and incorporates it into its own genome.
22. **C. Breakdown of fatty acids.** - The Golgi apparatus is primarily responsible for modifying, packaging, and distributing proteins, not for the breakdown of fatty acids (which occurs in peroxisomes).
23. **B. Phospholipids.** - The cell membrane consists of a phospholipid bilayer that separates the cell's internal environment from the external environment and regulates the passage of substances.
24. **B. Lysosomes.** - Lysosomes contain hydrolytic enzymes responsible for breaking down cellular waste and debris.
25. **B. Cell division.** - Centrioles are involved in organizing microtubules during cell division, helping to form the mitotic spindle.
26. **B. Smooth ER.** - The smooth endoplasmic reticulum (SER) plays a key role in detoxifying drugs and poisons, especially in liver cells.
27. **C. Centriole.** - Centrioles help in organizing microtubules that are crucial during cell division to separate chromosomes.
28. **B. Nucleus.** - The nucleus is the organelle that houses the cell's genetic material (DNA) in eukaryotic cells.
29. **C. Chloroplast.** - Chloroplasts are the organelles responsible for photosynthesis, where light energy is converted into chemical energy in plants and algae.
30. **C. Regulating entry and exit of substances.** - The plasma membrane controls what enters and exits the cell, maintaining the internal environment of the cell.
31. **B. Spermatogonium → primary spermatocyte → secondary spermatocyte → spermatid → spermatozoan.** - This sequence represents the correct order of sperm cell development, starting from the spermatogonium and ending with the mature spermatozoan.

32. **C. At ovulation—metaphase II.** During ovulation, the oocyte is arrested in metaphase II and will complete meiosis only if fertilization occurs.
33. **B. Metaphase.** In metaphase, the spindle fibers attach to the kinetochores, making it the first stage where defects in the spindle apparatus-kinetochore attachment can be visualized.
34. **D. S phase.** S phase is the period of the cell cycle during which DNA replication occurs, and radiolabeled nucleotides can be incorporated.
35. **C. Endometrium.** Excessive estrogen can stimulate the endometrium, potentially leading to endometrial cancer as a secondary malignancy.
36. **A. Fallopian tube.** Upon ovulation, the oocyte is released into the fallopian tube where fertilization typically occurs.
37. **D. S phase, prophase, and metaphase.** Chemotherapy can target multiple stages of the cell cycle, including S phase (DNA synthesis), prophase, and metaphase (where cell division occurs).
38. **B. Prostate gland—surrounded by muscle to raise and lower the testes.** This is incorrect because the prostate gland is not involved in raising or lowering the testes; this function is performed by the cremaster muscle.
39. **B. During telophase I.** After telophase I, the cell transitions from diploid to haploid, meaning telophase I is the last point where the cell still has a diploid number of chromosomes.
40. **D. Replication of the DNA during S stage.** DNA replication does not contribute to genetic variability, as it is a conservative process that duplicates genetic material.
41. **A. In metaphase of mitosis, replicated chromosomes line up in single file; in metaphase II of meiosis, replicated chromosomes line up on opposite sides of the metaphase plate.** Mitosis involves single-file chromosome alignment, while in meiosis II, sister chromatids are aligned for separation.
42. **D. The nucleoli disappear.** In prophase, nucleoli disappear as part of the preparatory steps for chromosome segregation.
43. **C. 45,X.** This individual likely has Turner syndrome (45,X), which can result from nondisjunction and explains the presence of symptoms despite having only one X chromosome.
44. **C. Luteal phase.** Progesterone levels peak during the luteal phase to maintain the uterine lining in preparation for potential pregnancy.
45. **D. High levels of GnRH throughout the pregnancy.** High levels of GnRH are not typically seen during pregnancy because feedback mechanisms reduce its production to prevent further ovulation.
46. **B. Spermatogonium → primary spermatocyte → secondary spermatocyte → spermatid → spermatozoan.** This describes the correct development pathway for a sperm cell from its most primitive form (spermatogonium) to the mature spermatozoan.
47. **C. Metaphase II.** At the point of ovulation, the egg is arrested in metaphase II until fertilization triggers the completion of meiosis.

48. **B. Seminal vesicles.** The seminal vesicles produce a fructose-rich secretion that nourishes sperm and helps with motility.
49. **A. Prophase I.** Genetic recombination (crossing over) occurs during prophase I of meiosis, where homologous chromosomes exchange genetic material.
50. **A. S phase.** Chemotherapy often targets rapidly dividing cells by inhibiting DNA replication during the S phase of the cell cycle.
51. **B. Metaphase II.** In metaphase II, the centromeres of the sister chromatids align along the metaphase plate before separation.
52. **B. The maintenance of a constant internal environment.** Homeostasis is the process by which organisms maintain a stable internal environment, even when external conditions change.
53. **C. Receptor.** Receptors detect changes in the environment, such as temperature or pH, and send this information to the control center for processing.
54. **B. Reversing the change in the variable.** Negative feedback works by reversing the initial change in a variable to bring it back to its normal range, thereby maintaining stability.
55. **C. Regulation of blood glucose levels.** The regulation of blood glucose levels through insulin and glucagon is a classic example of negative feedback, where insulin lowers blood glucose, and glucagon raises it.
56. **B. Insulin.** Insulin is the hormone responsible for lowering blood glucose levels by promoting the uptake of glucose into cells after a meal.
57. **C. Sweating.** Sweating helps restore homeostasis by cooling the body when the internal temperature rises above the normal set point.
58. **B. Respiratory system.** The respiratory system helps regulate blood pH by controlling the levels of carbon dioxide in the blood, which directly affects acidity.
59. **D. Bone marrow.** Bone marrow is primarily involved in the production of blood cells and is not directly involved in maintaining homeostasis.
60. **B. Sodium and potassium balance.** Aldosterone regulates sodium and potassium balance by promoting the reabsorption of sodium and the excretion of potassium by the kidneys.
61. **B. It enhances the effect of a stimulus until a specific event concludes.** Positive feedback amplifies the initial stimulus, pushing a system toward a final event, such as the release of oxytocin during childbirth, which increases contractions until delivery occurs.
62. **B. Guanine.** Cytosine pairs with guanine in the DNA double helix through three hydrogen bonds, while adenine pairs with thymine through two hydrogen bonds.
63. **C. Helicase.** Helicase is the enzyme responsible for unwinding and separating the two strands of the DNA double helix during replication, creating the replication fork.
64. **A. 5' to 3'.** DNA polymerase synthesizes the new DNA strand in the 5' to 3' direction, adding nucleotides to the 3' end of the growing strand.
65. **B. Nucleotide Excision Repair.** Nucleotide Excision Repair (NER) is a DNA repair mechanism that removes bulky lesions, such as thymine dimers caused by UV light, and replaces the damaged section with new nucleotides.

66. **A. Binding to the promoter and synthesizing mRNA.** RNA polymerase binds to the promoter region of a gene and synthesizes a complementary mRNA strand from the DNA template during transcription.
67. **C. Splicing.** In eukaryotic cells, splicing removes non-coding sequences (introns) from the pre-mRNA and joins the coding sequences (exons) to form a mature mRNA ready for translation.
68. **B. Synthesized continuously in the 5' to 3' direction.** The leading strand is synthesized continuously in the 5' to 3' direction during DNA replication, following the unwinding of the DNA by helicase.
69. **D. Histone modification.** Histone modification is involved in transcriptional regulation, not post-transcriptional regulation, which includes processes like splicing, capping, and polyadenylation.
70. **B. Binding of RNA polymerase to the promoter region.** The first step of transcription in prokaryotes is the binding of RNA polymerase to the promoter region, initiating the synthesis of mRNA from the DNA template.
71. **B. A gene is transcribed into mRNA, which is then translated into a protein.** A gene contains the instructions for building proteins. It is transcribed into mRNA, which is then translated into a protein during translation.
72. **B. S phase.** – The S phase (Synthesis phase) is when DNA replication occurs, ensuring that each daughter cell will have an identical set of chromosomes after cell division.
73. **C. Anaphase.** – During anaphase, the sister chromatids are pulled apart by the spindle fibers and move toward opposite poles of the cell, ensuring that each new cell will receive an identical set of chromosomes.
74. **A. Prophase I.** – Crossing over, the exchange of genetic material between homologous chromosomes, occurs during prophase I of meiosis, contributing to genetic diversity.
75. **B. They control cell cycle progression by activating specific proteins.** – CDKs regulate the cell cycle by partnering with cyclins, phosphorylating target proteins, and ensuring proper progression through the cell cycle stages.
76. **C. M checkpoint.** – The M checkpoint (spindle checkpoint) ensures that all chromosomes are properly aligned on the metaphase plate, preventing improper segregation of chromosomes during anaphase.
77. **C. Independent assortment of homologous chromosomes.** – During anaphase I of meiosis, homologous chromosomes are randomly separated into daughter cells, contributing to genetic diversity through independent assortment.
78. **B. p53.** – p53 is a tumor suppressor protein that regulates the cell cycle and prevents the propagation of cells with damaged DNA, often referred to as the "guardian of the genome."
79. **D. Telophase.** – During telophase, the nuclear envelope reforms around the separated sets of chromosomes, which have reached opposite poles, marking the near end of mitosis.

80. **B. Protein synthesis and organelle duplication.** – The G1 phase is characterized by the synthesis of proteins and duplication of organelles, preparing the cell for DNA replication in the S phase.
81. **C. Separation of homologous chromosomes in meiosis I.** – Meiosis I is the reductional division, where homologous chromosomes are separated, reducing the chromosome number by half in the resulting daughter cells.
82. **B. To convert glucose into pyruvate.** Glycolysis is the process that breaks down glucose into two molecules of pyruvate, which is then used in further stages of cellular respiration.
83. **B. 2 ATP.** Glycolysis produces a net gain of 2 ATP molecules per glucose molecule, as it consumes 2 ATP in the energy investment phase and generates 4 ATP in the energy payoff phase.
84. **C. Oxaloacetate.** Oxaloacetate is regenerated at the end of the Krebs cycle and combines with acetyl-CoA to start the next cycle.
85. **A. Succinyl-CoA.** Succinyl-CoA is converted to succinate, and this step produces one molecule of GTP (or ATP) via substrate-level phosphorylation.
86. **B. NADH.** NADH donates electrons to Complex I of the electron transport chain, initiating the process of electron transfer.
87. **B. It acts as the final electron acceptor.** Oxygen is the final electron acceptor in the electron transport chain, combining with electrons and protons to form water.
88. **C. Carbon dioxide.** Carbon dioxide is a byproduct of the complete oxidation of glucose during cellular respiration, specifically in the pyruvate decarboxylation and Krebs cycle stages.
89. **C. Oxidative phosphorylation.** Oxidative phosphorylation produces the majority of ATP during cellular respiration by utilizing the electron transport chain and chemiosmosis.
90. **C. ATP synthase.** ATP synthase is the enzyme responsible for synthesizing ATP as protons flow through it during chemiosmosis.
91. **B. 2.** During one turn of the Krebs cycle, two molecules of carbon dioxide are released as waste products of the oxidation of acetyl-CoA.
92. **C. Computational modeling** – Computational modeling is essential in systems biology to represent complex biological processes and predict how different parts of a system interact.
93. **A. Brain** – The brain, as part of the central nervous system, is primarily responsible for processing sensory input, generating responses, and controlling most body functions.
94. **C. To carry chemical signals across synapses** – Neurotransmitters are released from neurons to carry chemical signals across synapses to other neurons or target cells, facilitating communication within the nervous system.
95. **B. Parasympathetic** – The parasympathetic division of the autonomic nervous system is responsible for "rest and digest" functions, promoting relaxation, and recovery of the body.
96. **B. B cells** – B cells are responsible for producing antibodies, which bind to specific antigens on pathogens, marking them for destruction by other immune cells.

97. D. Provides a non-specific first line of defense – The innate immune system offers a non-specific first line of defense against pathogens through barriers like skin, phagocytic cells, and inflammatory responses.

98. C. Immunological memory – Immunological memory allows the adaptive immune system to "remember" previous pathogens and respond more rapidly upon subsequent exposures.

99. B. Motor neurons – Motor neurons transmit signals from the central nervous system to muscles, initiating movement as part of the somatic nervous system.

100. D. Destroy infected or cancerous cells – Cytotoxic T cells are responsible for identifying and destroying cells infected by viruses or cells that have become cancerous.

101. C. Exercise or stress – The sympathetic division of the autonomic nervous system is most active during times of stress or physical exertion, preparing the body for "fight or flight" responses.

102. B. Pituitary gland. The pituitary gland is often referred to as the "master gland" because it controls the function of other endocrine glands, such as the thyroid, adrenal glands, and gonads, through the hormones it secretes.

103. B. Negative feedback. Negative feedback is the most common mechanism for regulating hormone levels. It works by reducing the output or activity of any organ or system back to its normal range in response to a stimulus, ensuring that hormone levels are kept within an optimal range.

104. B. Insulin. Insulin is the hormone produced by the pancreas that lowers blood glucose levels after eating by promoting the uptake of glucose into cells and stimulating the storage of glucose as glycogen in the liver.

105. C. Adrenaline. Adrenaline (also known as epinephrine) is released by the adrenal medulla during the fight-or-flight response, preparing the body for quick physical action by increasing heart rate, blood pressure, and energy availability.

106. B. Adrenocorticotropic hormone (ACTH). CRH from the hypothalamus stimulates the release of ACTH from the anterior pituitary gland, which in turn triggers the adrenal cortex to secrete cortisol, a hormone involved in stress response and metabolism.

107. C. Parathyroid hormone (PTH). PTH is secreted by the parathyroid glands and is essential for regulating blood calcium levels. It increases calcium levels by promoting the release of calcium from bones, increasing intestinal calcium absorption, and enhancing kidney reabsorption of calcium.

108. B. It increases the metabolic rate. Thyroid hormones (T3 and T4) increase the body's metabolic rate by stimulating cells to convert nutrients into energy more rapidly, which influences various functions such as heart rate, digestion, and temperature regulation.

109. C. Rapid weight loss and increased heart rate. Hyperthyroidism, a condition of excessive thyroid hormone production, speeds up metabolism, leading to symptoms such as rapid weight loss, increased heart rate, nervousness, and sweating.

110. **C. It increases blood glucose levels by promoting glycogen breakdown.** Glucagon is secreted by the pancreas when blood glucose levels are low. It acts primarily on the liver, where it stimulates the breakdown of glycogen into glucose, raising blood sugar levels.

111. **D. Cortisol.** Cushing's syndrome is caused by excessive levels of cortisol, often due to overproduction by the adrenal glands or long-term use of corticosteroid medications. Symptoms include weight gain, high blood pressure, and a characteristic "moon face."

Section 2: Biochemistry

Chapter 1: Amino Acids, Peptides, and Proteins

Amino acids are the building blocks of proteins, which are essential macromolecules in biological systems. There are 20 standard amino acids, each characterized by an amino group ($-NH_2$), a carboxyl group (-COOH), a hydrogen atom, and a variable side chain (R group) attached to a central carbon atom (alpha-carbon). The side chains of amino acids determine their chemical properties and their roles in protein structure and function. Amino acids can be categorized based on the polarity and charge of their side chains into nonpolar, polar, acidic, and basic groups.

- Nonpolar amino acids (e.g., leucine, valine) have hydrophobic side chains that tend to be buried inside the protein structure, away from water.
- Polar amino acids (e.g., serine, threonine) have hydrophilic side chains that can form hydrogen bonds with water or other polar molecules.
- Acidic amino acids (e.g., aspartic acid, glutamic acid) have negatively charged side chains at physiological pH.
- Basic amino acids (e.g., lysine, arginine) have positively charged side chains at physiological pH.

Amino acids are linked together by peptide bonds, which are covalent bonds formed through a dehydration reaction between the amino group of one amino acid and the carboxyl group of another. This chain of amino acids is known as a polypeptide. The sequence of amino acids in a polypeptide is defined as its primary structure, and this sequence dictates how the protein will fold and function.

Peptides are short chains of amino acids, typically containing fewer than 50 residues, while proteins are longer chains that fold into complex three-dimensional structures. Proteins perform a wide variety of functions in biological systems, including catalysis, signaling, transport, and structural support. Each protein's specific function is determined by its structure, which is stabilized by interactions such as hydrogen bonds, ionic interactions, and disulfide bridges between amino acid residues.

Structure and Function of Proteins

Proteins exhibit four levels of structure: primary, secondary, tertiary, and quaternary.

1. Primary structure: The primary structure of a protein is the linear sequence of amino acids in a polypeptide chain, connected by peptide bonds. The order of amino acids is genetically determined and crucial for the protein's ultimate shape and function.
2. Secondary structure: The secondary structure refers to local folded structures that form within a polypeptide chain due to hydrogen bonding between backbone atoms. The most common secondary structures are the alpha-helix and the beta-sheet.
   - Alpha-helix: A right-handed coil in which every backbone N-H group hydrogen bonds to the backbone C=O group four residues earlier. This structure is common in fibrous proteins like keratin.

- Beta-sheet: Consists of beta strands connected laterally by hydrogen bonds, forming a sheet-like arrangement. This structure is common in silk proteins.
3. Tertiary structure: The tertiary structure is the overall three-dimensional shape of a single polypeptide chain, stabilized by various interactions between the side chains of amino acids, including hydrogen bonds, ionic bonds, hydrophobic interactions, and disulfide bridges. This level of structure determines the protein's functionality. The tertiary structure allows enzymes, for example, to form active sites where catalysis occurs.
4. Quaternary structure: Some proteins consist of more than one polypeptide chain, and the quaternary structure refers to the arrangement of these chains in a multi-subunit complex. Hemoglobin, for instance, has a quaternary structure composed of four polypeptide subunits, which allows it to efficiently carry oxygen in the bloodstream.

Proteins can function in various capacities:

- Enzymes are proteins that catalyze biochemical reactions, increasing the reaction rate without being consumed. Enzymes lower the activation energy required for reactions to occur, enabling biological processes to proceed under physiological conditions.
- Structural proteins like collagen and elastin provide support to tissues and organs, ensuring structural integrity and elasticity.
- Transport proteins such as hemoglobin carry molecules (e.g., oxygen) to different parts of the body.
- Signaling proteins like hormones and receptors play roles in cell communication, allowing cells to respond to external stimuli.

The specific function of a protein is dependent on its three-dimensional shape. A change in the protein's shape, whether due to mutation in the primary sequence or external factors such as pH or temperature changes, can lead to loss of function or gain of harmful activity, as seen in diseases like Alzheimer's and cystic fibrosis.

Enzyme Kinetics

Enzyme kinetics is the study of how enzymes bind to substrates and convert them into products. Understanding enzyme kinetics is crucial for elucidating how enzymes function in biological systems and for developing drugs that modulate enzyme activity.

The rate of an enzyme-catalyzed reaction depends on several factors, including substrate concentration, enzyme concentration, temperature, and pH. The most commonly studied model of enzyme kinetics is the Michaelis-Menten equation, which describes the rate of enzymatic reactions by relating reaction rate (v) to substrate concentration ([S]).

The equation is expressed as: $V = \dfrac{V_{max}\{S\}}{K_M + \{S\}}$

where:

- v is the reaction velocity.
- Vmax is the maximum rate of the reaction at saturating substrate concentrations.
- Km (Michaelis constant) is the substrate concentration at which the reaction rate is half of Vmax. It provides an indication of the enzyme's affinity for its substrate; a low Km suggests high affinity, while a high Km indicates lower affinity.

The initial phase of enzyme activity is characterized by a rapid increase in reaction rate as substrate concentration rises. However, as the enzyme becomes saturated with substrate, the reaction rate reaches a maximum, where all enzyme active sites are occupied (Vmax). At this point, further increases in substrate concentration do not increase the reaction rate.

Enzyme inhibition can significantly affect enzyme kinetics. There are several types of inhibitors:

- Competitive inhibitors compete with the substrate for binding to the active site of the enzyme. This increases the Km (lower affinity) without affecting Vmax, as high substrate concentrations can overcome the inhibition.
- Noncompetitive inhibitors bind to an allosteric site (not the active site), reducing the Vmax without affecting Km, as substrate binding is not prevented, but the enzyme's catalytic ability is diminished.
- Uncompetitive inhibitors bind only to the enzyme-substrate complex, lowering both Km and Vmax.

Enzyme kinetics also considers catalytic efficiency, which is the rate at which an enzyme converts substrate to product. This is influenced by both Km and Vmax, and is represented by the ratio kcat/Km, where kcat is the catalytic constant, or turnover number (the number of substrate molecules converted per enzyme molecule per second).

Understanding enzyme kinetics helps in drug development, especially when targeting enzymes in diseases. Many pharmaceutical agents function as enzyme inhibitors, designed to modulate enzyme activity by mimicking substrates or binding to allosteric sites.

Chapter 2: Carbohydrates and Lipids

Carbohydrates and lipids are fundamental biomolecules that play critical roles in energy storage, structural support, and cellular signaling. Both are essential to the functioning of living organisms, contributing to metabolic processes that sustain life. In this section, we will explore the structure, function, and metabolism of carbohydrates and lipids.

Carbohydrates: Carbohydrates are organic molecules consisting of carbon, hydrogen, and oxygen, typically with a hydrogen ratio of 2:1, as found in water. The basic units of carbohydrates are monosaccharides, which can polymerize to form disaccharides, oligosaccharides, and polysaccharides.

Monosaccharides: Monosaccharides are the simplest form of carbohydrates, consisting of single sugar molecules such as glucose, fructose, and galactose. These sugars are classified based on the number of carbon atoms present and the location of the carbonyl group. Glucose, a hexose sugar with six carbon atoms, is the primary energy source for most organisms. Its structure allows it to undergo various metabolic processes, including glycolysis, gluconeogenesis, and the citric acid cycle.

Disaccharides and Polysaccharides: When two monosaccharides join through a glycosidic bond, they form disaccharides. For instance, glucose and fructose combine to form sucrose, while two glucose molecules create maltose. Polysaccharides, such as starch, glycogen, and cellulose, are long chains of monosaccharides. Glycogen is the storage form of glucose in animals and is primarily found in liver and muscle tissues.

Functions of Carbohydrates: Carbohydrates serve several essential functions:

- Energy Source: Glucose, derived from carbohydrates, is a critical source of ATP through cellular respiration.
- Energy Storage: In the form of glycogen or starch, carbohydrates act as reservoirs of energy that can be mobilized when needed.
- Structural Role: Some carbohydrates, like cellulose, provide structural support to plant cell walls.
- Cell Signaling and Recognition: Oligosaccharides attached to proteins and lipids on cell membranes play roles in cell-cell recognition and signaling.

Lipids

Lipids are hydrophobic or amphipathic molecules that include fats, oils, waxes, phospholipids, and steroids. They are primarily composed of long chains of hydrocarbons and play a crucial role in energy storage, membrane structure, and signaling pathways.

Fatty Acids and Triglycerides: Fatty acids are long hydrocarbon chains with a carboxyl group at one end. They can be saturated (no double bonds) or unsaturated (one or more double bonds). Saturated fatty acids, such as those found in animal fats, are typically solid at room temperature, while unsaturated fatty acids, found in plants and fish, are liquid. Fatty acids are esterified with glycerol to form triglycerides, the primary storage form of lipids in adipose tissue.

Phospholipids: Phospholipids consist of two fatty acids, a glycerol molecule, and a phosphate group. They are essential components of cell membranes, forming a bilayer that serves as a barrier and provides structural integrity. Their amphipathic nature—having both hydrophobic and hydrophilic regions—allows them to form the dynamic and selective membrane that regulates the entry and exit of molecules in and out of cells.

Steroids: Steroids, such as cholesterol, are a distinct class of lipids with a characteristic four-ring structure. Cholesterol is a precursor to steroid hormones, vitamin D, and bile salts. It also modulates membrane fluidity, ensuring that cellular membranes remain flexible across a range of temperatures.

Functions of Lipids:

- Energy Storage: Triglycerides store more energy per gram than carbohydrates, making them the body's primary long-term energy reserve.
- Membrane Structure: Phospholipids and cholesterol are integral to maintaining cellular integrity by forming the lipid bilayer of cell membranes.
- Insulation and Protection: Lipids provide thermal insulation and protect vital organs by cushioning them.
- Signaling Molecules: Steroid hormones and other lipid-derived molecules regulate various physiological processes.

Glycolysis, Gluconeogenesis, and Glycogen Metabolism

The metabolism of carbohydrates is a complex and tightly regulated process that ensures the body has a continuous supply of energy. Three key metabolic pathways—glycolysis, gluconeogenesis, and glycogen metabolism—are central to this system.

Glycolysis: Glycolysis is the process by which glucose is broken down into two molecules of pyruvate, generating energy in the form of ATP and NADH. It occurs in the cytoplasm of cells and does not require oxygen, making it an anaerobic pathway.

Key Steps in Glycolysis:

1. Glucose Activation: The first step involves the phosphorylation of glucose to glucose-6-phosphate by the enzyme hexokinase. This step consumes one molecule of ATP.
2. Fructose-1,6-bisphosphate Formation: Glucose-6-phosphate is converted to fructose-1,6-bisphosphate, a key intermediate, through a series of reactions catalyzed by phosphofructokinase-1 (PFK-1). This is the rate-limiting step of glycolysis.
3. Energy Generation: The latter stages of glycolysis involve the conversion of fructose-1,6-bisphosphate into pyruvate, producing four ATP molecules and two NADH molecules.

Since two ATP molecules were consumed earlier, the net gain is two ATP per glucose molecule.

Glycolysis is a vital process because it provides energy quickly, especially in anaerobic conditions, such as during intense exercise.

Gluconeogenesis: Gluconeogenesis is essentially the reverse of glycolysis. It is the process by which the liver and kidneys synthesize glucose from non-carbohydrate precursors, such as lactate, glycerol, and amino acids. This pathway is crucial during periods of fasting or intense exercise when blood glucose levels are low, and the body must produce glucose to maintain homeostasis.

Key Differences from Glycolysis:

1. Enzyme Substitution: Several steps of glycolysis are irreversible; hence, gluconeogenesis uses different enzymes to bypass these steps. For example, pyruvate carboxylase and phosphoenolpyruvate carboxykinase (PEPCK) bypass the pyruvate kinase step of glycolysis.
2. Energy Consumption: Gluconeogenesis is an energy-consuming process, requiring six ATP molecules to produce one molecule of glucose, in contrast to the net gain of two ATP molecules during glycolysis.

Gluconeogenesis helps maintain blood glucose levels during starvation, prolonged exercise, or carbohydrate-deficient diets.

Glycogen Metabolism

Glycogen metabolism involves two opposing processes: glycogenesis (the synthesis of glycogen) and glycogenolysis (the breakdown of glycogen).

Glycogenesis: Glycogenesis is the process of synthesizing glycogen from glucose for storage in the liver and muscle tissues. The enzyme glycogen synthase catalyzes the addition of glucose molecules to a growing glycogen chain, using UDP-glucose as the glucose donor. Glycogenesis occurs when there is an excess of glucose in the blood, such as after a meal.

Glycogenolysis: Glycogenolysis is the breakdown of glycogen into glucose-1-phosphate, which is converted into glucose-6-phosphate. In the liver, glucose-6-phosphate is further converted into free glucose and released into the bloodstream to maintain blood glucose levels during fasting or between meals.

Regulation of Glycogen Metabolism: The regulation of glycogen metabolism is tightly controlled by hormones such as insulin and glucagon. Insulin promotes glycogenesis, whereas glucagon and adrenaline stimulate glycogenolysis.

Chapter 3: Bioenergetics and Regulation of Metabolism

Bioenergetics is the study of how energy flows through living organisms, which is a crucial aspect of understanding metabolism. In biological systems, energy is required for maintaining cellular processes, growth, and overall function. The key focus of bioenergetics is how cells convert energy from nutrients like carbohydrates, fats, and proteins into a usable form. This energy is primarily harnessed through metabolic pathways, which are tightly regulated to meet the energy demands of the organism.

The Role of Bioenergetics in Cellular Function

At the core of bioenergetics is the concept of energy transformation. In cells, energy is stored in chemical bonds of molecules such as glucose, fatty acids, and amino acids. These molecules are broken down through catabolic pathways to release energy. This process occurs through a series of enzymatic reactions that transfer energy from these molecules to adenosine triphosphate (ATP), the energy currency of the cell.

There are two major types of metabolism:

- Catabolism: The breakdown of larger molecules into smaller units, releasing energy in the process.
- Anabolism: The building of complex molecules from simpler ones, which requires energy input.

Bioenergetic pathways are highly regulated to ensure that energy production matches cellular demand. Cells have several mechanisms to sense energy status, primarily through the levels of ATP, adenosine diphosphate (ADP), and adenosine monophosphate (AMP). These molecules act as signals to either increase or decrease metabolic activity depending on the energy needs of the cell.

Key Bioenergetic Pathways

Several metabolic pathways play critical roles in bioenergetics, and they are all interconnected:

1. Glycolysis: This pathway occurs in the cytoplasm and involves the breakdown of glucose into pyruvate. Glycolysis produces a net gain of 2 ATP molecules per glucose molecule and is a fast method of generating energy under both aerobic and anaerobic conditions.
2. Citric Acid Cycle (Krebs Cycle): After glycolysis, pyruvate is transported into the mitochondria where it is further oxidized in the citric acid cycle. This cycle produces high-energy electron carriers NADH and FADH2, which are crucial for the next stage of energy production.
3. Electron Transport Chain (ETC): Located in the inner mitochondrial membrane, the ETC utilizes electrons from NADH and FADH2 to drive the production of ATP. This process requires oxygen and generates the majority of ATP in cells through oxidative phosphorylation.

4. Fatty Acid Oxidation: This pathway breaks down fatty acids into acetyl-CoA, which then enters the citric acid cycle. Fatty acid oxidation is a significant source of energy, especially during periods of fasting or prolonged physical activity when glucose levels are low.

Regulation of Metabolism

The regulation of metabolism is essential for maintaining homeostasis. Cells regulate metabolic pathways at various levels, including gene expression, enzyme activity, and availability of substrates. Some key regulatory mechanisms include:

- Allosteric Regulation: Enzymes involved in metabolic pathways often have allosteric sites where molecules such as ATP, ADP, or AMP can bind. This binding can either activate or inhibit enzyme activity, depending on the energy status of the cell.
- Hormonal Control: Hormones such as insulin, glucagon, and epinephrine play significant roles in regulating metabolism. For example, insulin promotes glucose uptake and storage, while glucagon stimulates the release of glucose from stores during fasting.
- Feedback Inhibition: In some metabolic pathways, the end product can inhibit an enzyme early in the pathway, preventing the overproduction of that product. This helps maintain balance and prevents wasteful energy expenditure.

ATP Production and Use

ATP, or adenosine triphosphate, is the primary energy carrier in all living organisms. Its role in the cell is critical because it provides the energy necessary for various biological processes. ATP is often referred to as the "molecular currency" of energy transfer because of its central role in metabolism.

Structure and Function of ATP

- ATP consists of three components:
- Adenine: A nitrogenous base.
- Ribose: A five-carbon sugar molecule.
- Three Phosphate Groups: These are linked together by high-energy bonds, and the energy stored in these bonds is released when ATP is hydrolyzed to ADP (adenosine diphosphate) and inorganic phosphate (Pi).

The hydrolysis of ATP releases a significant amount of free energy, which can then be used to drive various cellular processes such as muscle contraction, active transport of molecules across membranes, and biosynthetic reactions.

ATP Production Pathways

Cells produce ATP through several interconnected processes. The primary pathways of ATP production include:

1. Substrate-Level Phosphorylation: This occurs during glycolysis and the citric acid cycle. It involves the direct transfer of a phosphate group from a substrate molecule to ADP, forming ATP. While substrate-level phosphorylation is important, it accounts for a small fraction of the total ATP generated in cells.
2. Oxidative Phosphorylation: The majority of ATP in cells is produced through oxidative phosphorylation, which occurs in the mitochondria. This process uses the electron transport chain to generate a proton gradient across the inner mitochondrial membrane. The energy from this gradient is used by ATP synthase to produce ATP from ADP and Pi.
3. Photophosphorylation: In plants, ATP is produced through photophosphorylation during photosynthesis. This process captures energy from sunlight to generate ATP, which is used in the Calvin cycle to synthesize sugars.

Cellular Uses of ATP

ATP is used to power a variety of essential cellular functions, including:

1. Muscle Contraction: ATP binds to myosin, a motor protein involved in muscle contraction. The energy released from ATP hydrolysis allows myosin to change shape and interact with actin filaments, leading to muscle contraction.
2. Active Transport: ATP provides the energy for active transport mechanisms, such as the sodium-potassium pump, which maintains proper ion balance across cell membranes.
3. Biosynthesis: The synthesis of macromolecules such as proteins, nucleic acids, and lipids requires energy in the form of ATP. For example, ATP is used during transcription and translation to form peptide bonds between amino acids.
4. Cell Signaling: ATP is also involved in cell signaling pathways, particularly in phosphorylation cascades where protein kinases transfer phosphate groups from ATP to target proteins, modulating their activity.
5. Thermogenesis: ATP hydrolysis also contributes to heat production, which is important in maintaining body temperature, especially in endothermic organisms.

ATP Regulation and Energy Efficiency

The production and use of ATP are tightly regulated to ensure efficient energy use. Cells constantly monitor their energy status through the levels of ATP, ADP, and AMP. When ATP levels are high, energy production pathways are downregulated to prevent excess energy generation, while low ATP levels trigger an increase in metabolic activity to restore energy balance.

The regulation of ATP production ensures that energy is produced on an as-needed basis, preventing wastage and maintaining efficient cellular function. Energy conservation is crucial for long-term survival, particularly in cells with high energy demands such as neurons, muscle cells, and hepatocytes.

Chapter 4: Nucleotides and Nucleic Acids

Nucleotides are the fundamental building blocks of nucleic acids, which include DNA (deoxyribonucleic acid) and RNA (ribonucleic acid). These macromolecules are essential for storing and transmitting genetic information, as well as for various cellular processes that involve protein synthesis and regulation. A nucleotide consists of three components: a nitrogenous base, a five-carbon sugar, and one or more phosphate groups.

1. Nitrogenous Bases: Nucleotides contain nitrogenous bases, which are divided into two categories: purines and pyrimidines. Purines, which include adenine (A) and guanine (G), have a double-ring structure. Pyrimidines, which include cytosine (C), thymine (T), and uracil (U), have a single-ring structure. In DNA, the nitrogenous bases are adenine, guanine, cytosine, and thymine. In RNA, uracil replaces thymine.

The specific pairing of these nitrogenous bases, called complementary base pairing, is crucial for the structure and function of DNA and RNA. In DNA, adenine pairs with thymine via two hydrogen bonds, and guanine pairs with cytosine via three hydrogen bonds. In RNA, adenine pairs with uracil.

2. Five-Carbon Sugar: The five-carbon sugar, also known as a pentose, differs between DNA and RNA. In DNA, the sugar is deoxyribose, which lacks an oxygen atom at the 2' position of the sugar ring. This small difference makes DNA more stable and less reactive than RNA. In RNA, the sugar is ribose, which contains a hydroxyl group (-OH) at the 2' position. This hydroxyl group makes RNA more reactive and less stable in cellular environments.

3. Phosphate Group: The phosphate group in nucleotides is attached to the 5' carbon of the pentose sugar. Nucleotides can have one, two, or three phosphate groups, forming nucleoside monophosphates, diphosphates, or triphosphates, respectively. The most common example is adenosine triphosphate (ATP), which is a nucleotide with three phosphate groups. Phosphate groups are negatively charged, contributing to the overall negative charge of nucleic acids.

The phosphate group plays a critical role in forming the backbone of nucleic acids. In both DNA and RNA, nucleotides are linked together through phosphodiester bonds, which occur between the 5' phosphate of one nucleotide and the 3' hydroxyl group of the next nucleotide. This linkage creates a sugar-phosphate backbone, which gives nucleic acids their structural stability and integrity.

4. Nucleic Acids Nucleic acids, DNA and RNA, are long polymers made up of repeating nucleotide units. They differ in structure, function, and chemical properties but share the common role of storing and transmitting genetic information.

DNA (Deoxyribonucleic Acid): DNA is a double-stranded molecule that forms a helical structure, known as the double helix. The two strands run in opposite directions (antiparallel) and are held together by hydrogen bonds between the complementary nitrogenous bases. The sequence of nucleotides in DNA encodes genetic information, which is used by cells to synthesize proteins and regulate cellular functions.

RNA (Ribonucleic Acid): RNA is typically single-stranded and plays several roles in the cell, including acting as a messenger (mRNA), transferring amino acids (tRNA), and forming part of the ribosome (rRNA). RNA molecules can fold into complex structures due to intramolecular base pairing, allowing them to perform a wide range of functions.

DNA/RNA Structure and Function

1. DNA Structure DNA is a double-stranded helix with a backbone made of alternating sugar (deoxyribose) and phosphate groups. The nitrogenous bases, which extend inward from the backbone, form the "rungs" of the ladder-like structure. These bases pair specifically: adenine with thymine (A-T) and guanine with cytosine (G-C), forming complementary base pairs.

Each strand of DNA has directionality, meaning it has a 5' end (phosphate group attached to the 5' carbon of the sugar) and a 3' end (hydroxyl group attached to the 3' carbon of the sugar). The two strands of DNA are antiparallel, meaning one strand runs from 5' to 3', and the other runs from 3' to 5'.

The stability of the DNA structure is largely due to the hydrogen bonding between the complementary base pairs and the hydrophobic interactions between the stacked base pairs. The double helix structure allows DNA to be highly compact and capable of storing vast amounts of genetic information in a relatively small space within the cell.

2. DNA Function The primary function of DNA is to store genetic information that dictates the development, function, and reproduction of all living organisms. DNA serves as a template for transcription, where specific genes are transcribed into messenger RNA (mRNA). This mRNA is then translated into proteins, which perform a variety of cellular functions.

DNA replication is another critical function. During cell division, the two strands of the DNA helix separate, and each serves as a template for the formation of a new complementary strand. This ensures that each new cell receives an identical copy of the genetic material.

3. RNA Structure Unlike DNA, RNA is typically single-stranded and consists of a ribose sugar instead of deoxyribose. Uracil (U) replaces thymine (T) in RNA, so adenine pairs with uracil. RNA molecules can fold into complex three-dimensional structures due to intramolecular base pairing, where complementary bases within the same RNA strand pair with each other.

The different types of RNA have distinct structures and functions. Messenger RNA (mRNA) is a linear strand that carries genetic information from DNA to the ribosome for protein synthesis. Transfer RNA (tRNA) has a cloverleaf structure that helps translate the genetic code into amino acids. Ribosomal RNA (rRNA) forms the core of the ribosome and catalyzes protein synthesis.

4. RNA Function RNA plays a key role in gene expression and protein synthesis. The central dogma of molecular biology describes the flow of genetic information from DNA to RNA to protein. In transcription, a gene's DNA sequence is copied into mRNA, which then travels from the nucleus to the ribosome. At the ribosome, mRNA is translated into a specific sequence of amino acids, forming a protein.

RNA is also involved in various regulatory and catalytic functions. For example, small interfering RNAs (siRNAs) and microRNAs (miRNAs) regulate gene expression by binding to complementary mRNA sequences, leading to their degradation or inhibition of translation.

Nucleotides are the essential components of nucleic acids, and both DNA and RNA play vital roles in cellular function. DNA stores the genetic information necessary for the development and function of organisms, while RNA is involved in translating that information into proteins. The specific structures of these molecules enable them to carry out their critical roles in biology, ensuring the continuity of life and the regulation of cellular processes.

Chapter 5: Biochemical Pathways

Biochemical pathways represent the series of chemical reactions that occur within living cells to sustain life. These pathways are intricately regulated to control the flow of molecules through various metabolic processes, ensuring the efficient production of energy, synthesis of biomolecules, and removal of waste products. Each pathway is linked to others, forming a network that supports cellular function and homeostasis. One of the most critical biochemical pathways involves the breakdown of glucose and other nutrients to generate energy in the form of ATP, a process known as cellular respiration.

Glycolysis: The process of glycolysis is the first step in the breakdown of glucose to extract energy for cellular metabolism. It occurs in the cytoplasm of the cell and does not require oxygen, making it an anaerobic process. Glycolysis begins with one molecule of glucose (a six-carbon sugar) and ends with two molecules of pyruvate (a three-carbon compound), along with a net gain of two molecules of ATP and two molecules of NADH.

The steps of glycolysis can be divided into two phases: the energy investment phase and the energy payoff phase. In the energy investment phase, two ATP molecules are consumed to phosphorylate glucose and its derivatives, making them more reactive. In the energy payoff phase, four ATP molecules are produced via substrate-level phosphorylation, resulting in a net gain of two ATP. Additionally, two NAD+ molecules are reduced to NADH, which will be used later in the electron transport chain.

The pyruvate produced at the end of glycolysis can proceed into the citric acid cycle if oxygen is present, or it can undergo fermentation if oxygen is unavailable. In aerobic conditions, the pyruvate enters the mitochondria, where it is converted into acetyl-CoA, the starting molecule for the citric acid cycle.

Pentose Phosphate Pathway: The pentose phosphate pathway (PPP) is another crucial biochemical pathway that branches off from glycolysis. The PPP serves two main functions: the production of ribose-5-phosphate, a precursor for nucleotide synthesis, and the generation of NADPH, which is essential for anabolic reactions such as fatty acid synthesis and maintaining the reducing environment of the cell.

The PPP has two phases: the oxidative phase and the non-oxidative phase. In the oxidative phase, glucose-6-phosphate is oxidized, producing NADPH and ribulose-5-phosphate. In the non-oxidative phase, the pathway generates intermediates that can feed back into glycolysis or be used for biosynthetic processes.

Fatty Acid Oxidation: Fatty acid oxidation, also known as beta-oxidation, is the process by which fatty acids are broken down in the mitochondria to produce acetyl-CoA, NADH, and FADH2. These products feed into the citric acid cycle and electron transport chain to generate ATP. Beta-oxidation occurs in cycles, with each cycle shortening the fatty acid chain by two carbons and producing one acetyl-CoA, one NADH, and one FADH2.

The breakdown of fatty acids provides a highly efficient source of energy, especially during times of fasting or prolonged exercise when glucose stores are depleted. The acetyl-CoA produced by fatty acid oxidation can be used for energy production via the citric acid cycle, or it can be diverted into the synthesis of ketone bodies in the liver, which serve as an alternative energy source for tissues like the brain during periods of low glucose availability.

Protein Catabolism: Proteins can also be broken down to provide energy, though this is typically a less favored pathway compared to carbohydrate and fat metabolism. Protein catabolism involves the breakdown of amino acids into intermediates that can enter the citric acid cycle or be converted into glucose via gluconeogenesis.

Each amino acid undergoes deamination, a process that removes the amino group, leaving behind a carbon skeleton. The carbon skeletons of different amino acids are converted into various metabolites, such as pyruvate, acetyl-CoA, or intermediates of the citric acid cycle. The nitrogen from the amino group is converted into ammonia, which is subsequently detoxified into urea in the liver and excreted via the kidneys.

Citric Acid Cycle (Krebs Cycle)

The citric acid cycle, also known as the Krebs cycle or tricarboxylic acid (TCA) cycle, is a key component of cellular respiration. This cycle takes place in the mitochondrial matrix and serves as the final pathway for the oxidation of carbohydrates, fats, and proteins. The primary function of the citric acid cycle is to produce high-energy molecules (NADH and $FADH_2$) that are used in the electron transport chain to generate ATP. Additionally, the citric acid cycle provides intermediates for various biosynthetic pathways.

Entry into the Citric Acid Cycle

The citric acid cycle begins with the entry of acetyl-CoA, which is produced from the breakdown of carbohydrates, fatty acids, and amino acids. Acetyl-CoA combines with oxaloacetate, a four-carbon molecule, to form citrate, a six-carbon molecule. This reaction is catalyzed by the enzyme citrate synthase.

Step-by-Step Breakdown of the Citric Acid Cycle

1. Formation of Citrate: Acetyl-CoA and oxaloacetate combine to form citrate, catalyzed by citrate synthase. This is a highly exergonic reaction that drives the cycle forward.
2. Isomerization of Citrate: Citrate is then isomerized into isocitrate by the enzyme aconitase. This step involves the removal and readdition of water to rearrange the molecular structure of citrate.
3. Oxidative Decarboxylation of Isocitrate: Isocitrate is oxidized by isocitrate dehydrogenase to form alpha-ketoglutarate, a five-carbon molecule. In this reaction, NAD+ is reduced to NADH, and one molecule of carbon dioxide is released.
4. Formation of Succinyl-CoA: Alpha-ketoglutarate undergoes another oxidative decarboxylation, catalyzed by alpha-ketoglutarate dehydrogenase, to produce succinyl-CoA.

This reaction generates another molecule of NADH and releases a second molecule of carbon dioxide.

5. Conversion of Succinyl-CoA to Succinate: Succinyl-CoA is converted into succinate by the enzyme succinyl-CoA synthetase. This step generates one molecule of GTP (which can be converted to ATP), making it the only substrate-level phosphorylation in the citric acid cycle.
6. Oxidation of Succinate: Succinate is oxidized to fumarate by the enzyme succinate dehydrogenase, which is embedded in the inner mitochondrial membrane. This reaction reduces FAD to FADH2, which enters the electron transport chain.
7. Hydration of Fumarate: Fumarate is converted into malate by the addition of a water molecule, catalyzed by fumarase.
8. Oxidation of Malate: In the final step, malate is oxidized to regenerate oxaloacetate, catalyzed by malate dehydrogenase. This reaction produces another molecule of NADH.

Energy Yield from the Citric Acid Cycle

Each turn of the citric acid cycle produces:

- 3 NADH molecules
- 1 FADH2 molecule
- 1 GTP (equivalent to ATP)
- 2 CO2 molecules

Since each glucose molecule produces two acetyl-CoA molecules, the citric acid cycle must turn twice for each glucose molecule, effectively doubling these yields. The NADH and FADH2 generated during the cycle carry high-energy electrons to the electron transport chain, where they play a crucial role in oxidative phosphorylation and ATP production.

Chapter 6: Membrane Transport and Signal Transduction

Membrane transport and signal transduction are essential processes that maintain the cellular environment and mediate communication within cells and between cells and their environment. Membrane transport ensures that molecules move in and out of cells appropriately, while signal transduction pathways interpret external signals to elicit specific cellular responses.

Membrane Transport: Membrane transport refers to the movement of substances across the cellular membrane. This membrane, composed primarily of a lipid bilayer, selectively allows molecules to enter or exit the cell. There are two main types of membrane transport: passive and active.

Passive Transport: Passive transport does not require energy and occurs down the concentration gradient, from an area of higher concentration to an area of lower concentration. Types of passive transport include:

1. Simple Diffusion In simple diffusion, small nonpolar molecules, such as oxygen (O_2) and carbon dioxide (CO_2), move directly across the lipid bilayer. These molecules move down their concentration gradient without the need for any transport proteins. Since the lipid bilayer is hydrophobic, only lipid-soluble and small uncharged molecules can easily diffuse across the membrane.
2. Facilitated Diffusion Facilitated diffusion is the transport of larger or polar molecules, such as glucose or ions, across the cell membrane with the help of specific transport proteins. Two main classes of transport proteins are involved:
   - Channel Proteins: These proteins form pores in the membrane that allow specific molecules or ions, such as sodium (Na^+), potassium (K^+), or water, to pass through by diffusion. The movement is still down the concentration gradient, and channel proteins can be gated, meaning they open or close in response to certain stimuli.
   - Carrier Proteins: These proteins bind to the molecule they transport and undergo a conformational change to move the molecule across the membrane. For example, the glucose transporter facilitates the movement of glucose into cells.

Active Transport

Active transport requires energy, typically in the form of ATP, because it moves substances against their concentration gradient—from an area of lower concentration to an area of higher concentration. There are two main types of active transport:

1. Primary Active Transport In primary active transport, ATP is directly used to move molecules against their gradient. A classic example is the Na^+/K^+ pump (sodium-potassium pump), which is vital for maintaining the electrochemical gradient in cells. The pump moves three sodium ions out of the cell and two potassium ions into the cell, using one molecule of ATP for each cycle. This process is critical in maintaining cellular ion balance and electrical potential across the membrane.

2. Secondary Active Transport Secondary active transport, also known as cotransport, does not directly use ATP. Instead, it relies on the energy stored in the form of a concentration gradient, which was established by primary active transport. Secondary transport is subdivided into two types:
   - Symport: Both molecules move in the same direction across the membrane. An example is the sodium-glucose symporter, which uses the sodium ion gradient established by the Na+/K+ pump to bring glucose into the cell alongside sodium.
   - Antiport: The molecules move in opposite directions. For example, the sodium-calcium exchanger removes calcium from the cell by utilizing the sodium gradient.

Signal Transduction

Signal transduction refers to the process by which cells respond to external signals, typically through receptor proteins located on the cell surface or inside the cell. These receptors recognize specific signaling molecules (ligands), such as hormones, growth factors, or neurotransmitters, and initiate a series of intracellular events that lead to a cellular response.

Types of Signaling Molecules

There are several types of signaling molecules that bind to receptors to initiate signal transduction:

1. Hormones: Hormones are long-distance signaling molecules, often released by glands in the body, that travel through the bloodstream to reach target cells. Examples include insulin, which regulates glucose uptake, and cortisol, which modulates stress responses.
2. Neurotransmitters: These are short-range signaling molecules that transmit signals across synapses between neurons or between neurons and other cell types. Examples include acetylcholine and dopamine.
3. Cytokines: Cytokines are small proteins involved in immune responses. They help in cell signaling, particularly in regulating the immune system's response to infection or injury.

Signal Transduction Pathways

Once a signaling molecule binds to its receptor, the signal is transduced (converted) into a specific cellular response. Several key pathways mediate signal transduction:

1. G-Protein-Coupled Receptors (GPCRs) GPCRs are one of the most common types of receptors. When a ligand binds to a GPCR, it activates a G-protein inside the cell. The activated G-protein can then interact with other enzymes or ion channels to produce secondary messengers, such as cyclic AMP (cAMP), that amplify the signal and trigger a response. GPCRs play roles in numerous physiological processes, including vision, taste, and immune responses.
2. Receptor Tyrosine Kinases (RTKs) RTKs are receptors that, upon ligand binding, undergo dimerization and autophosphorylation on tyrosine residues. These phosphorylated tyrosines then serve as docking sites for various intracellular signaling proteins, initiating multiple

signaling cascades. RTKs are crucial in processes like cell growth, differentiation, and metabolism. A well-known example is the epidermal growth factor receptor (EGFR), which is involved in cell proliferation.
3. Ion Channel-Linked Receptors These receptors are involved in rapid signaling events. When a ligand binds to the receptor, it causes the opening or closing of ion channels in the membrane, altering the flow of ions such as Na+, K+, or Ca2+. This change in ion concentration can lead to rapid cellular responses, such as the propagation of electrical signals in neurons.

Intracellular Signaling Molecules

Once a signal is received by the receptor, a cascade of intracellular signaling molecules relays the message to the appropriate cellular machinery:

1. Secondary Messengers Secondary messengers, such as cAMP, inositol triphosphate (IP3), and diacylglycerol (DAG), are small molecules that amplify the signal within the cell. For instance, cAMP activates protein kinase A (PKA), which then phosphorylates target proteins to elicit specific responses, such as changes in metabolism or gene expression.
2. Kinase Cascades Many signal transduction pathways involve kinase cascades, where one kinase activates another, leading to a phosphorylation chain that ultimately modifies cellular function. For example, the mitogen-activated protein kinase (MAPK) pathway is a kinase cascade that regulates cell division, differentiation, and survival.

Termination of Signal Transduction

- Signal transduction must be tightly regulated to ensure that signals are terminated once the appropriate response has been achieved. Mechanisms for signal termination include:
- Dephosphorylation: Phosphatases remove phosphate groups from proteins, effectively reversing the signal.
- Receptor Desensitization: Receptors can be inactivated through internalization or by conformational changes that prevent further signaling.
- Degradation of Signaling Molecules: Secondary messengers and other signaling proteins can be degraded or inactivated to stop the signaling process.

Practical Question For Section 2:

1. Which of the following is NOT a property of amino acids?
   a) They contain a carboxyl group.
   b) They contain an R group.
   c) They form disulfide bonds through peptide linkages.
   d) They contain an amino group.
2. The peptide bond is formed between which two groups of adjacent amino acids?
   a) Amino and carboxyl groups
   b) Carboxyl and R groups
   c) Amino and hydroxyl groups
   d) R groups and hydroxyl groups
3. Which of the following is an example of a basic amino acid?
   a) Lysine
   b) Glutamate
   c) Serine
   d) Valine
4. The quaternary structure of a protein refers to:
   a) The sequence of amino acids in a polypeptide chain
   b) The three-dimensional shape of a single polypeptide
   c) The interaction between multiple polypeptide chains
   d) The formation of alpha-helices and beta-sheets
5. Which type of bond is primarily responsible for the secondary structure of proteins?
   a) Hydrogen bonds
   b) Disulfide bonds
   c) Ionic bonds
   d) Peptide bonds
6. What is the main structural feature of an alpha-helix?
   a) It is a coiled structure stabilized by hydrogen bonds.
   b) It is a flat sheet-like structure with hydrogen bonds between strands.
   c) It is formed by hydrophobic interactions.
   d) It contains disulfide bridges between cysteine residues.
7. Which of the following is true regarding beta-sheets in proteins?
   a) Beta-sheets are formed by covalent bonds between side chains.
   b) Beta-sheets result from hydrogen bonds between backbone atoms of different strands.
   c) Beta-sheets are more flexible than alpha-helices.
   d) Beta-sheets are only found in extracellular proteins.
8. The primary structure of a protein is determined by:
   a) Hydrogen bonding patterns between the backbone atoms
   b) The sequence of amino acids
   c) The interaction of hydrophobic side chains

d) The formation of beta-sheets and alpha-helices
9. Which of the following amino acids is likely to be found in the interior of a protein's tertiary structure?
   a) Glutamine
   b) Serine
   c) Valine
   d) Lysine
10. Enzymes catalyze reactions by:
    a) Increasing the activation energy
    b) Decreasing the activation energy
    c) Increasing the reaction temperature
    d) Altering the equilibrium constant of the reaction
11. In enzyme kinetics, what does Km represent?
    a) The maximum velocity of the enzyme
    b) The substrate concentration at which the reaction rate is half of Vmax
    c) The enzyme's turnover number
    d) The rate of product formation
12. A competitive inhibitor of an enzyme:
    a) Binds to an allosteric site
    b) Increases the Vmax of the reaction
    c) Can be overcome by increasing substrate concentration
    d) Binds to the enzyme-substrate complex
13. Which of the following is true about a noncompetitive inhibitor?
    a) It decreases Km.
    b) It binds only to the active site.
    c) It decreases the enzyme's Vmax.
    d) It increases the affinity of the enzyme for the substrate.
14. Which kinetic parameter provides an indication of an enzyme's catalytic efficiency?
    a) Km
    b) Vmax
    c) kcat
    d) kcat/Km
15. A Lineweaver-Burk plot is used to:
    a) Determine the Km and Vmax of an enzyme-catalyzed reaction
    b) Identify the specific amino acids in the enzyme active site
    c) Measure the rate of enzyme degradation
    d) Study the effects of pH on enzyme structure
16. Which type of bond stabilizes the tertiary structure of a protein?
    a) Peptide bonds
    b) Hydrogen bonds

c) Covalent bonds like disulfide bridges
d) Van der Waals forces

17. The rate of an enzyme-catalyzed reaction increases with increasing substrate concentration until:
    a) The enzyme becomes denatured.
    b) The active sites of the enzyme are saturated with substrate.
    c) The substrate is consumed.
    d) The reaction reaches equilibrium.

18. Which of the following statements about enzyme specificity is correct?
    a) Enzymes can bind to any substrate.
    b) Enzyme specificity is due to the fit between the enzyme's active site and the substrate.
    c) Enzymes alter their structure to fit any substrate.
    d) Enzyme specificity is due to random interactions between substrates and enzymes.

19. The catalytic constant (kcat) refers to:
    a) The maximum rate achieved by the enzyme
    b) The number of substrate molecules converted into product per enzyme molecule per second
    c) The substrate concentration at which the reaction rate is half-maximal
    d) The inhibition constant for a competitive inhibitor

20. Which of the following amino acids can form disulfide bonds, contributing to protein stability?
    a) Serine
    b) Cysteine
    c) Methionine
    d) Tyrosine

21. Which of the following is a polysaccharide commonly used for energy storage in animals?
    a) Starch
    b) Cellulose
    c) Glycogen
    d) Chitin

22. Which monosaccharide is the most important energy source for the human body?
    a) Fructose
    b) Glucose
    c) Galactose
    d) Ribose

23. Fatty acids that have no double bonds between carbon atoms are classified as:
    a) Saturated fatty acids
    b) Unsaturated fatty acids
    c) Polyunsaturated fatty acids
    d) Trans fatty acids

24. Phospholipids play a crucial role in which of the following cellular structures?
    a) Mitochondria

- b) Ribosome
- c) Cell membrane
- d) Nucleus

25. Which of the following molecules is a precursor for steroid hormones?
    a) Glycerol
    b) Triglyceride
    c) Cholesterol
    d) Phospholipid

26. Which of the following is a structural component of plant cell walls?
    a) Glycogen
    b) Starch
    c) Cellulose
    d) Glucose

27. Triglycerides are composed of:
    a) Three fatty acids and one glycerol
    b) Two fatty acids and one glycerol
    c) Three fatty acids and one phosphate group
    d) Two fatty acids and one phosphate group

28. Which type of lipid is involved in cell signaling and acts as a precursor to prostaglandins?
    a) Phospholipids
    b) Triglycerides
    c) Eicosanoids
    d) Cholesterol

29. Which of the following statements is true about unsaturated fats?
    a) They have no double bonds between carbon atoms
    b) They are typically solid at room temperature
    c) They contain one or more double bonds between carbon atoms
    d) They are found primarily in animal fats

30. Glycogen is stored in which of the following organs?
    a) Liver and muscles
    b) Pancreas and kidneys
    c) Brain and spinal cord
    d) Heart and lungs

31. The first step of glycolysis involves the conversion of glucose into:
    a) Fructose-6-phosphate
    b) Pyruvate
    c) Glucose-6-phosphate
    d) Fructose-1,6-bisphosphate

32. What is the net gain of ATP molecules per molecule of glucose in glycolysis?
    a) 1
    b) 2
    c) 4
    d) 6
33. Which enzyme is responsible for the rate-limiting step of glycolysis?
    a) Hexokinase
    b) Pyruvate kinase
    c) Phosphofructokinase-1 (PFK-1)
    d) Aldolase
34. Gluconeogenesis primarily occurs in which organ?
    a) Brain
    b) Muscle
    c) Liver
    d) Heart
35. Which of the following molecules can serve as a substrate for gluconeogenesis?
    a) Fatty acids
    b) Lactate
    c) Acetyl-CoA
    d) Urea
36. Which of the following enzymes is NOT involved in gluconeogenesis?
    a) Pyruvate carboxylase
    b) Phosphoenolpyruvate carboxykinase (PEPCK)
    c) Pyruvate kinase
    d) Fructose-1,6-bisphosphatase
37. Glycogen synthesis is primarily regulated by which hormone?
    a) Glucagon
    b) Insulin
    c) Epinephrine
    d) Cortisol
38. The breakdown of glycogen into glucose is known as:
    a) Glycolysis
    b) Glycogenesis
    c) Gluconeogenesis
    d) Glycogenolysis
39. Which enzyme is responsible for breaking down glycogen into glucose-1-phosphate?
    a) Glycogen phosphorylase
    b) Glucose-6-phosphatase
    c) Phosphofructokinase
    d) Pyruvate dehydrogenase

40. Which of the following processes requires ATP input in its early steps?
    a) Glycolysis
    b) Gluconeogenesis
    c) Glycogenolysis
    d) Beta-oxidation
41. Which of the following processes directly produces the highest amount of ATP in cells?
    a) Glycolysis
    b) Citric Acid Cycle
    c) Oxidative Phosphorylation
    d) Substrate-Level Phosphorylation
42. What is the primary function of ATP in the cell?
    a) Storing genetic information
    b) Acting as an enzyme
    c) Transporting oxygen
    d) Providing energy for cellular processes
43. Which of the following molecules is a direct product of glycolysis?
    a) Acetyl-CoA
    b) Pyruvate
    c) Citrate
    d) NADPH
44. During the citric acid cycle, which molecule is regenerated to allow the cycle to continue?
    a) ATP
    b) Pyruvate
    c) Oxaloacetate
    d) Glucose
45. Which molecule donates electrons to the electron transport chain?
    a) ADP
    b) NADH
    c) FAD
    d) ATP
46. In oxidative phosphorylation, ATP is synthesized by which enzyme?
    a) ATP Synthase
    b) Hexokinase
    c) Phosphofructokinase
    d) Acetyl-CoA Carboxylase
47. Which of the following is NOT a product of the citric acid cycle?
    a) NADH
    b) FADH2
    c) CO2
    d) Lactate

48. What is the role of oxygen in the electron transport chain?
    a) To transport ATP out of the mitochondria
    b) To act as the final electron acceptor
    c) To phosphorylate ADP to ATP
    d) To remove carbon dioxide from the cell
49. Which metabolic pathway is primarily responsible for the breakdown of fatty acids?
    a) Glycolysis
    b) Citric Acid Cycle
    c) Beta-Oxidation
    d) Electron Transport Chain
50. Allosteric regulation of enzymes in bioenergetic pathways typically involves which type of molecule?
    a) Hormones
    b) ATP, ADP, or AMP
    c) Nucleic acids
    d) Phospholipids
51. Which of the following statements about substrate-level phosphorylation is TRUE?
    a) It occurs only in the mitochondria
    b) It produces more ATP than oxidative phosphorylation
    c) It involves the direct transfer of a phosphate group to ADP
    d) It requires the presence of oxygen
52. The hydrolysis of ATP releases energy due to the breaking of which bonds?
    a) Glycosidic bonds
    b) Phosphodiester bonds
    c) Phosphate-phosphate bonds
    d) Peptide bonds
53. Which of the following hormones promotes the uptake of glucose into cells, regulating bioenergetic pathways?
    a) Glucagon
    b) Epinephrine
    c) Insulin
    d) Cortisol
54. Which process is primarily responsible for ATP production in the absence of oxygen?
    a) Glycolysis
    b) Oxidative Phosphorylation
    c) Electron Transport Chain
    d) Beta-Oxidation
55. The majority of ATP produced in cellular respiration is generated during which stage?
    a) Glycolysis
    b) Citric Acid Cycle

c) Electron Transport Chain and Oxidative Phosphorylation
d) Substrate-Level Phosphorylation

56. Which enzyme is responsible for catalyzing the first step in glycolysis?
    a) Pyruvate Dehydrogenase
    b) ATP Synthase
    c) Hexokinase
    d) Phosphoglycerate Kinase

57. In beta-oxidation, fatty acids are broken down into which molecule before entering the citric acid cycle?
    a) Glucose
    b) Pyruvate
    c) Acetyl-CoA
    d) Citrate

58. Which of the following is a function of NADH and FADH2 in metabolism?
    a) They transport carbon dioxide to the lungs
    b) They provide energy for muscle contraction
    c) They donate electrons to the electron transport chain
    d) They synthesize ATP directly

59. What is the effect of high levels of AMP on metabolic pathways?
    a) Inhibition of glycolysis
    b) Activation of catabolic pathways to produce more ATP
    c) Increased fatty acid synthesis
    d) Inhibition of the citric acid cycle

60. Which of the following processes occurs in the mitochondria?
    a) Glycolysis
    b) Citric Acid Cycle
    c) Fermentation
    d) Gluconeogenesis

61. Which of the following is a purine base found in both DNA and RNA?
    a) Cytosine
    b) Thymine
    c) Adenine
    d) Uracil

62. In DNA, adenine pairs with:
    a) Guanine
    b) Thymine
    c) Cytosine
    d) Uracil

63. What type of bond links the phosphate group of one nucleotide to the sugar of another in nucleic acids?
    a) Hydrogen bond
    b) Phosphodiester bond
    c) Ionic bond
    d) Covalent bond
64. Which sugar is found in the nucleotides of RNA?
    a) Deoxyribose
    b) Glucose
    c) Ribose
    d) Fructose
65. The nitrogenous base thymine is found in:
    a) Both DNA and RNA
    b) Only DNA
    c) Only RNA
    d) Neither DNA nor RNA
66. What is the primary function of DNA in a cell?
    a) Energy storage
    b) Genetic information storage
    c) Protein synthesis
    d) Catalyzing biochemical reactions
67. The 3' end of a DNA strand refers to the:
    a) End with a phosphate group attached
    b) End with a hydroxyl group attached to the 3' carbon of the sugar
    c) End where the nitrogenous base is exposed
    d) End with a ribose sugar
68. Which base replaces thymine in RNA?
    a) Cytosine
    b) Adenine
    c) Guanine
    d) Uracil
69. In the structure of DNA, the two strands are:
    a) Parallel
    b) Antiparallel
    c) Intertwined at random
    d) Unrelated in sequence
70. RNA molecules differ from DNA molecules because they:
    a) Are double-stranded
    b) Contain deoxyribose sugar
    c) Contain ribose sugar

d) Use thymine instead of uracil
71. Which of the following best describes a phosphodiester bond?
    a) It is formed between nitrogenous bases
    b) It links adjacent nucleotides in the DNA backbone
    c) It forms the hydrogen bond between base pairs
    d) It connects ribosomes to RNA
72. In DNA replication, what serves as the template for the new DNA strand?
    a) The entire chromosome
    b) One of the existing DNA strands
    c) RNA molecules
    d) Nucleotides in the cytoplasm
73. The pairing between adenine and thymine in DNA involves:
    a) Three hydrogen bonds
    b) Two hydrogen bonds
    c) One hydrogen bond
    d) No hydrogen bonds
74. The double helix structure of DNA was discovered by:
    a) Watson and Crick
    b) Hershey and Chase
    c) Avery and Griffith
    d) Chargaff and Franklin
75. Which of the following is NOT a component of a nucleotide?
    a) Nitrogenous base
    b) Phosphate group
    c) Ribosome
    d) Five-carbon sugar
76. DNA replication is described as:
    a) Conservative
    b) Semi-conservative
    c) Dispersive
    d) Fragmented
77. What feature distinguishes deoxyribose from ribose?
    a) Deoxyribose contains an extra oxygen atom
    b) Ribose lacks a hydroxyl group at the 3' position
    c) Deoxyribose lacks a hydroxyl group at the 2' position
    d) Ribose has a double bond between carbons 2 and 3
78. Which enzyme is responsible for synthesizing RNA during transcription?
    a) DNA polymerase
    b) RNA polymerase
    c) Helicase

d) Ligase
79. What is the complementary strand for a DNA sequence 5'-ATCGGTA-3'?
   a) 5'-TAGCCAT-3'
   b) 5'-UAGCCAU-3'
   c) 3'-TAGCCAT-5'
   d) 3'-UAGCCAU-5'
80. Which of the following processes converts DNA into mRNA?
   a) Translation
   b) Replication
   c) Transcription
   d) Reverse transcription
81. Which of the following molecules is the starting point for glycolysis?
   a) Acetyl-CoA
   b) Pyruvate
   c) Glucose
   d) Oxaloacetate
82. What is the primary function of NADH in cellular respiration?
   a) ATP production
   b) Electron carrier
   c) Carbon dioxide production
   d) Energy storage
83. During glycolysis, how many net ATP molecules are produced per glucose molecule?
   a) 1
   b) 2
   c) 4
   d) 6
84. Which enzyme catalyzes the conversion of pyruvate to acetyl-CoA?
   a) Pyruvate kinase
   b) Pyruvate dehydrogenase
   c) Citrate synthase
   d) Succinate dehydrogenase
85. The pentose phosphate pathway primarily produces which of the following molecules?
   a) NADH
   b) FADH2
   c) NADPH
   d) GTP
86. Fatty acid oxidation occurs in which part of the cell?
   a) Cytoplasm
   b) Nucleus
   c) Mitochondria

d) Endoplasmic reticulum
87. In the citric acid cycle, which molecule combines with acetyl-CoA to form citrate?
    a) Oxaloacetate
    b) Pyruvate
    c) Alpha-ketoglutarate
    d) Fumarate
88. Which enzyme is responsible for converting citrate to isocitrate in the citric acid cycle?
    a) Aconitase
    b) Citrate synthase
    c) Isocitrate dehydrogenase
    d) Fumarase
89. Which step of the citric acid cycle directly produces GTP?
    a) Citrate to isocitrate
    b) Alpha-ketoglutarate to succinyl-CoA
    c) Succinyl-CoA to succinate
    d) Malate to oxaloacetate
90. What is the role of FAD in the citric acid cycle?
    a) Proton donor
    b) Proton acceptor
    c) Electron carrier
    d) ATP synthase activator
91. Which of the following is NOT a product of the citric acid cycle?
    a) NADH
    b) FADH2
    c) ATP
    d) Glucose
92. Which step in the citric acid cycle produces the second molecule of carbon dioxide?
    a) Citrate to isocitrate
    b) Alpha-ketoglutarate to succinyl-CoA
    c) Succinate to fumarate
    d) Malate to oxaloacetate
93. The final product of glycolysis is _____, which is further processed in the presence of oxygen.
    a) Acetyl-CoA
    b) Pyruvate
    c) Citrate
    d) Oxaloacetate
94. Which enzyme catalyzes the conversion of succinate to fumarate in the citric acid cycle?
    a) Succinate dehydrogenase
    b) Aconitase

c) Citrate synthase
d) Fumarase

95. How many NADH molecules are generated per turn of the citric acid cycle?
    a) 1
    b) 2
    c) 3
    d) 4

96. Which of the following processes produces the highest amount of ATP?
    a) Glycolysis
    b) Citric acid cycle
    c) Fatty acid oxidation
    d) Oxidative phosphorylation

97. The electron transport chain is directly linked to which of the following pathways?
    a) Glycolysis
    b) Citric acid cycle
    c) Beta-oxidation
    d) All of the above

98. Which molecule is a key intermediate that links glycolysis and the citric acid cycle?
    a) Lactate
    b) Acetyl-CoA
    c) Glucose-6-phosphate
    d) Fructose-1,6-bisphosphate

99. During beta-oxidation, each cycle produces which of the following molecules?
    e) Pyruvate
    f) Acetyl-CoA
    g) Oxaloacetate
    h) Citrate

100. Which of the following reactions directly reduces FAD to FADH2 in the citric acid cycle?
    a) Succinate to fumarate
    b) Alpha-ketoglutarate to succinyl-CoA
    c) Isocitrate to alpha-ketoglutarate
    d) Malate to oxaloacetate

101. Which of the following best describes simple diffusion?
    a) Movement of molecules against a concentration gradient
    b) Movement of molecules down a concentration gradient without assistance
    c) Transport involving carrier proteins and ATP
    d) Transport through ion channels requiring energy

102. What type of transport protein is involved in facilitated diffusion?
    a) G-protein coupled receptor
    b) Channel proteins and carrier proteins

c) ATP-binding cassette transporter
d) Sodium-potassium pump

103. Which of the following is an example of primary active transport?
    a) Glucose uptake by cells
    b) Diffusion of oxygen across the membrane
    c) Na+/K+ pump
    d) Transport of water through aquaporins

104. In secondary active transport, energy is derived from:
    a) Hydrolysis of ATP
    b) Light energy
    c) Electrochemical gradient of another substance
    d) Breakdown of glucose

105. What is the function of the sodium-potassium pump?
    a) To transport sodium into the cell and potassium out
    b) To move glucose into cells against its gradient
    c) To maintain the electrochemical gradient by pumping sodium out and potassium in
    d) To generate ATP

106. Which molecule acts as a secondary messenger in many G-protein coupled receptor pathways?
    a) ATP
    b) cAMP
    c) Phospholipase C
    d) Calcium ions

107. Ion channels that open or close in response to changes in voltage are called:
    a) Ligand-gated ion channels
    b) Voltage-gated ion channels
    c) Mechanically-gated ion channels
    d) Constitutively open channels

108. What type of transport occurs when two substances are moved in the same direction across the membrane?
    a) Antiport
    b) Symport
    c) Uniport
    d) Passive transport

109. Which process involves receptor autophosphorylation following ligand binding?
    a) G-protein coupled receptor activation
    b) Receptor tyrosine kinase signaling
    c) Ion channel-linked signaling
    d) Secondary active transport

110. In signal transduction, which molecule is commonly involved in kinase cascades?
    a) cAMP
    b) Protein kinase A
    c) Receptor tyrosine kinase
    d) Phosphodiesterase
111. Which of the following statements about facilitated diffusion is true?
    a) It requires energy in the form of ATP.
    b) It is used to transport large, polar molecules or ions.
    c) It always occurs through gap junctions.
    d) It moves molecules against their concentration gradient.
112. What is the role of phosphatases in signal transduction?
    a) To phosphorylate target proteins
    b) To remove phosphate groups from proteins
    c) To synthesize ATP
    d) To act as secondary messengers
113. Which signal transduction pathway involves the use of GTP-binding proteins?
    a) Receptor tyrosine kinases
    b) G-protein coupled receptors
    c) Voltage-gated ion channels
    d) Ion channel-linked receptors
114. What is a major difference between passive and active transport?
    a) Active transport moves substances down their concentration gradient.
    b) Passive transport requires ATP to move substances.
    c) Active transport moves substances against their concentration gradient.
    d) Passive transport involves the movement of ions only.
115. What is the main function of secondary messengers like cAMP and calcium ions?
    a) To transport molecules across the cell membrane
    b) To amplify the signal within the cell
    c) To deactivate receptor proteins
    d) To degrade signaling molecules
116. Which of the following is a feature of receptor tyrosine kinase (RTK) signaling?
    a) It activates G-proteins.
    b) It involves ligand-gated ion channels.
    c) It triggers autophosphorylation of the receptor.
    d) It only functions in the nervous system.
117. Which transport mechanism is used by water to move across cell membranes?
    a) Active transport through pumps
    b) Simple diffusion
    c) Facilitated diffusion via aquaporins
    d) Bulk transport via vesicles

118. Which component is commonly involved in terminating a signal transduction pathway?
    a) Protein kinases
    b) Ligand degradation
    c) Receptor internalization or downregulation
    d) Increased production of secondary messengers
119. Which process is critical for moving ions during action potential propagation in neurons?
    a) Receptor-mediated endocytosis
    b) Simple diffusion
    c) Voltage-gated ion channels
    d) Signal transduction via G-protein coupled receptors
120. In secondary active transport, which molecule often provides the driving force for cotransport?
    a) Glucose
    b) Calcium
    c) Sodium
    d) ATP

Answers & Explanation

1. **C. They form disulfide bonds through peptide linkages.** – Peptide bonds form between the amino and carboxyl groups of amino acids, while disulfide bonds form between cysteine side chains and are not part of the peptide linkage itself.
2. **A. Amino and carboxyl groups.** – Peptide bonds form between the amino group of one amino acid and the carboxyl group of another, linking them together.
3. **A. Lysine.** – Lysine is a basic amino acid with a positively charged side chain at physiological pH.
4. **C. The interaction between multiple polypeptide chains.** – Quaternary structure refers to the arrangement and interaction of multiple polypeptide chains in a protein complex.
5. **A. Hydrogen bonds.** – The secondary structure of proteins, such as alpha-helices and beta-sheets, is stabilized primarily by hydrogen bonds between the backbone atoms.
6. **A. It is a coiled structure stabilized by hydrogen bonds.** – The alpha-helix is a common secondary structure in proteins, characterized by a coiled shape stabilized by hydrogen bonding between the N-H and C=O groups of the peptide backbone.
7. **B. Beta-sheets result from hydrogen bonds between backbone atoms of different strands.** – Beta-sheets are formed by hydrogen bonding between the backbone atoms of adjacent beta strands, creating a sheet-like structure.
8. **B. The sequence of amino acids.** – The primary structure of a protein is determined by its specific sequence of amino acids, which is crucial for its final three-dimensional shape and function.
9. **C. Valine.** – Valine is a nonpolar, hydrophobic amino acid typically found in the interior of proteins, where it avoids interaction with water.
10. **B. Decreasing the activation energy.** – Enzymes function by lowering the activation energy required for a reaction to proceed, making the reaction occur faster without changing the overall reaction equilibrium.
11. **B. The substrate concentration at which the reaction rate is half of Vmax.** – Km represents the substrate concentration at which the reaction velocity is half of its maximum value, and it indicates the enzyme's affinity for its substrate.
12. **C. Can be overcome by increasing substrate concentration.** – Competitive inhibitors compete with the substrate for binding to the active site, but their effects can be overcome by increasing the concentration of the substrate.
13. **C. It decreases the enzyme's Vmax.** – Noncompetitive inhibitors bind to an allosteric site on the enzyme and reduce the maximum reaction rate (Vmax) without affecting the substrate's binding affinity (Km).
14. **D. kcat/Km.** – Catalytic efficiency is represented by the ratio of kcat (the turnover number) to Km. A higher kcat/Km value indicates greater efficiency of the enzyme in converting substrate to product.

15. **A. Determine the Km and Vmax of an enzyme-catalyzed reaction.** – The Lineweaver-Burk plot is a double-reciprocal plot used to determine the Km and Vmax of enzyme-catalyzed reactions by linearizing the Michaelis-Menten equation.
16. **C. Covalent bonds like disulfide bridges.** – The tertiary structure of proteins is stabilized by various interactions, including covalent disulfide bonds between cysteine residues, which help maintain the protein's overall shape.
17. **B. The active sites of the enzyme are saturated with substrate.** – When all active sites of the enzyme are occupied by substrate molecules, the reaction rate reaches its maximum (Vmax), and increasing the substrate concentration further does not increase the rate.
18. **B. Enzyme specificity is due to the fit between the enzyme's active site and the substrate.** – Enzymes are specific to their substrates because of the precise interaction between the enzyme's active site and the substrate, often described as a "lock-and-key" fit or an induced fit.
19. **B. The number of substrate molecules converted into product per enzyme molecule per second.** – kcat, also known as the turnover number, represents the number of substrate molecules that an enzyme can convert into product per second when the enzyme is fully saturated with substrate.
20. **B. Cysteine.** – Cysteine contains a sulfhydryl (-SH) group, which can form disulfide bonds with another cysteine residue, contributing to the stabilization of protein structures.
21. **C. Glycogen.** Glycogen is the polysaccharide used for energy storage in animals, particularly in liver and muscle tissues.
22. **B. Glucose.** Glucose is the most important energy source for the human body, being the primary substrate for glycolysis.
23. **A. Saturated fatty acids.** Saturated fatty acids have no double bonds between the carbon atoms, meaning they are fully "saturated" with hydrogen atoms.
24. **C. Cell membrane.** Phospholipids are a major component of the cell membrane, where they form a bilayer that provides structural integrity and controls the movement of substances in and out of cells.
25. **C. Cholesterol.** Cholesterol is a precursor for steroid hormones such as testosterone, estrogen, and cortisol.
26. **C. Cellulose.** Cellulose is a structural polysaccharide found in plant cell walls, providing rigidity and support.
27. **A. Three fatty acids and one glycerol.** Triglycerides are formed by the esterification of three fatty acid molecules with one glycerol molecule.
28. **C. Eicosanoids.** Eicosanoids, derived from arachidonic acid (a fatty acid), are involved in cellular signaling and are precursors to molecules like prostaglandins.
29. **C. They contain one or more double bonds between carbon atoms.** Unsaturated fats have one or more double bonds between the carbon atoms in their fatty acid chains, leading to kinks that prevent tight packing, making them typically liquid at room temperature.
30. **A. Liver and muscles.** Glycogen is stored in the liver and muscles to be broken down into glucose when the body requires energy.

31. **C. Glucose-6-phosphate.** In the first step of glycolysis, glucose is phosphorylated to glucose-6-phosphate by the enzyme hexokinase.
32. **B. 2.** Glycolysis has a net gain of 2 ATP molecules per molecule of glucose after accounting for the 2 ATP used in the early steps.
33. **C. Phosphofructokinase-1 (PFK-1).** Phosphofructokinase-1 (PFK-1) catalyzes the rate-limiting step of glycolysis, converting fructose-6-phosphate to fructose-1,6-bisphosphate.
34. **C. Liver.** Gluconeogenesis primarily takes place in the liver, where glucose is synthesized from non-carbohydrate precursors.
35. **B. Lactate.** Lactate, derived from anaerobic metabolism, is one of the substrates that can be used in gluconeogenesis to produce glucose.
36. **C. Pyruvate kinase.** Pyruvate kinase is involved in glycolysis, not gluconeogenesis, and catalyzes the final step of converting phosphoenolpyruvate to pyruvate.
37. **B. Insulin.** Insulin promotes glycogenesis, the synthesis of glycogen, by stimulating the enzyme glycogen synthase in response to elevated blood glucose levels.
38. **D. Glycogenolysis.** Glycogenolysis is the process of breaking down glycogen into glucose-1-phosphate, which can then be converted into glucose for energy.
39. **A. Glycogen phosphorylase.** Glycogen phosphorylase catalyzes the breakdown of glycogen into glucose-1-phosphate, the first step in glycogenolysis.
40. **A. Glycolysis.** Glycolysis requires an input of ATP in its early steps, specifically during the phosphorylation of glucose and fructose-6-phosphate.
41. **C. Oxidative Phosphorylation** – Oxidative phosphorylation occurs in the mitochondria and produces the most ATP through the electron transport chain and chemiosmosis.
42. **D. Providing energy for cellular processes** – ATP is the main energy carrier in the cell, supplying energy for processes such as active transport, muscle contraction, and biosynthesis.
43. **B. Pyruvate** – Glycolysis breaks down glucose into two molecules of pyruvate, which can be further metabolized in the mitochondria.
44. **C. Oxaloacetate** – In the citric acid cycle, oxaloacetate is regenerated at the end of the cycle, allowing the cycle to continue with the next acetyl-CoA molecule.
45. **B. NADH** – NADH donates electrons to the electron transport chain at complex I, starting the process of ATP generation.
46. **A. ATP Synthase** – ATP synthase is the enzyme responsible for synthesizing ATP by using the proton gradient generated by the electron transport chain.
47. **D. Lactate** – Lactate is produced in anaerobic conditions during fermentation, not in the citric acid cycle.
48. **B. To act as the final electron acceptor** – Oxygen is the final electron acceptor in the electron transport chain, forming water as a byproduct.
49. **C. Beta-Oxidation** – Beta-oxidation is the process by which fatty acids are broken down into acetyl-CoA, which can then enter the citric acid cycle.
50. **B. ATP, ADP, or AMP** – Allosteric regulation often involves ATP, ADP, or AMP binding to enzymes, which affects their activity based on the cell's energy needs.

51. **C. It involves the direct transfer of a phosphate group to ADP** – Substrate-level phosphorylation involves directly transferring a phosphate group from a substrate to ADP, producing ATP without the need for oxygen.
52. **C. Phosphate-phosphate bonds** – The high-energy phosphate bonds in ATP are broken during hydrolysis, releasing energy for cellular work.
53. **C. Insulin** – Insulin promotes the uptake of glucose into cells and stimulates the storage of energy in the form of glycogen and fat.
54. **A. Glycolysis** – Glycolysis is the primary pathway for ATP production when oxygen is absent, producing ATP through substrate-level phosphorylation.
55. **C. Electron Transport Chain and Oxidative Phosphorylation** – The majority of ATP in cellular respiration is produced during oxidative phosphorylation in the mitochondria.
56. **C. Hexokinase** – Hexokinase catalyzes the first step in glycolysis, where glucose is phosphorylated to form glucose-6-phosphate.
57. **C. Acetyl-CoA** – In beta-oxidation, fatty acids are broken down into acetyl-CoA, which can then enter the citric acid cycle for further energy production.
58. **C. They donate electrons to the electron transport chain** – NADH and FADH2 carry high-energy electrons to the electron transport chain, where they help generate ATP.
59. **B. Activation of catabolic pathways to produce more ATP** – High levels of AMP signal low energy status in the cell, activating pathways like glycolysis to increase ATP production.
60. **B. Citric Acid Cycle** – The citric acid cycle occurs in the mitochondria, where it generates NADH and FADH2 for use in the electron transport chain.
61. **C. Adenine.** – Adenine is a purine base found in both DNA and RNA, while cytosine and thymine are pyrimidines, and uracil is only found in RNA.
62. **B. Thymine.** – In DNA, adenine forms two hydrogen bonds with thymine. In RNA, adenine pairs with uracil.
63. **B. Phosphodiester bond.** – A phosphodiester bond links the 5' phosphate group of one nucleotide to the 3' hydroxyl group of the next nucleotide in the sugar-phosphate backbone.
64. **C. Ribose.** – RNA contains the sugar ribose, which has a hydroxyl group at the 2' position, distinguishing it from deoxyribose found in DNA.
65. **B. Only DNA.** – Thymine is found exclusively in DNA, while uracil is present in RNA in place of thymine.
66. **B. Genetic information storage.** – The primary role of DNA is to store genetic information, which is used for protein synthesis and regulating cellular activities.
67. **B. End with a hydroxyl group attached to the 3' carbon of the sugar.** – The 3' end of a DNA strand has a free hydroxyl group attached to the 3' carbon of the deoxyribose sugar, important for DNA synthesis.
68. **D. Uracil.** – In RNA, uracil replaces thymine and pairs with adenine during base pairing.
69. **B. Antiparallel.** – In DNA, the two strands run in opposite directions; one strand runs 5' to 3', and the other runs 3' to 5'.

70. **C. Contain ribose sugar.** – RNA contains ribose sugar, which has a hydroxyl group at the 2' carbon, making RNA more reactive than DNA, which contains deoxyribose.
71. **B. It links adjacent nucleotides in the DNA backbone.** – Phosphodiester bonds form between the 5' phosphate group of one nucleotide and the 3' hydroxyl group of another, maintaining the structure of the DNA backbone.
72. **B. One of the existing DNA strands.** – DNA replication is semi-conservative, meaning each original strand serves as a template for synthesizing a new complementary strand.
73. **B. Two hydrogen bonds.** – Adenine and thymine form two hydrogen bonds in DNA, while guanine and cytosine form three hydrogen bonds.
74. **A. Watson and Crick.** – James Watson and Francis Crick are credited with discovering the double helix structure of DNA in 1953.
75. **C. Ribosome.** – Ribosomes are cellular structures where protein synthesis occurs, not components of nucleotides. A nucleotide consists of a nitrogenous base, phosphate group, and five-carbon sugar.
76. **B. Semi-conservative.** – DNA replication is semi-conservative, meaning that each new DNA molecule consists of one old strand and one newly synthesized strand.
77. **C. Deoxyribose lacks a hydroxyl group at the 2' position.** – Deoxyribose, found in DNA, lacks the hydroxyl group (-OH) at the 2' position, whereas ribose in RNA contains the hydroxyl group.
78. **B. RNA polymerase.** – RNA polymerase synthesizes RNA by reading the DNA template during transcription.
79. **C. 3'-TAGCCAT-5'.** – The complementary strand runs in the opposite direction (3' to 5') and pairs with the original strand according to base-pairing rules: A-T, C-G.
80. **C. Transcription.** – Transcription is the process where DNA is transcribed into messenger RNA (mRNA), which then undergoes translation to produce proteins.
81. **C. Glucose.** – Glycolysis begins with glucose, a six-carbon sugar, which is broken down into pyruvate, providing energy to the cell.
82. **B. Electron carrier.** – NADH acts as an electron carrier, transporting high-energy electrons to the electron transport chain for ATP production.
83. **B. 2.** – Glycolysis produces a net gain of two ATP molecules per glucose molecule, after accounting for the two ATP used in the initial steps.
84. **B. Pyruvate dehydrogenase.** – Pyruvate dehydrogenase catalyzes the conversion of pyruvate to acetyl-CoA, linking glycolysis to the citric acid cycle.
85. **C. NADPH.** – The pentose phosphate pathway generates NADPH, which is used in biosynthetic reactions and maintaining cellular redox balance.
86. **C. Mitochondria.** – Fatty acid oxidation occurs in the mitochondria, where fatty acids are broken down to produce acetyl-CoA, NADH, and FADH2.
87. **A. Oxaloacetate.** – In the first step of the citric acid cycle, oxaloacetate combines with acetyl-CoA to form citrate, catalyzed by citrate synthase.

88. **A. Aconitase.** – Aconitase is responsible for converting citrate to isocitrate through an isomerization reaction in the citric acid cycle.
89. **C. Succinyl-CoA to succinate.** – The conversion of succinyl-CoA to succinate is coupled with the production of GTP, which is equivalent to ATP in energy terms.
90. **C. Electron carrier.** – FAD is reduced to FADH2 in the citric acid cycle, which then transports electrons to the electron transport chain.
91. **D. Glucose.** – Glucose is broken down prior to the citric acid cycle, and is not a product of the cycle itself, which produces NADH, FADH2, and ATP.
92. **B. Alpha-ketoglutarate to succinyl-CoA.** – The second molecule of CO2 is released during the conversion of alpha-ketoglutarate to succinyl-CoA in the citric acid cycle.
93. **B. Pyruvate**. – Glycolysis ends with the production of pyruvate, which can enter the citric acid cycle after conversion to acetyl-CoA if oxygen is present.
94. **A. Succinate dehydrogenase.** – Succinate dehydrogenase catalyzes the oxidation of succinate to fumarate in the citric acid cycle, which also reduces FAD to FADH2.
95. **C. 3.** – Each turn of the citric acid cycle produces three molecules of NADH, which will be used in the electron transport chain to generate ATP.
96. **D. Oxidative phosphorylation.** – Oxidative phosphorylation produces the most ATP, as it uses the energy from NADH and FADH2 to drive ATP synthesis.
97. **D. All of the above.** – The electron transport chain is linked to glycolysis, the citric acid cycle, and beta-oxidation, as all three processes generate NADH or FADH2.
98. **B. Acetyl-CoA.** – Acetyl-CoA is the key intermediate that links glycolysis to the citric acid cycle, as it is produced from pyruvate and enters the cycle.
99. **B. Acetyl-CoA.** – Each cycle of beta-oxidation generates acetyl-CoA, which can enter the citric acid cycle for further energy production.
100. **A. Succinate to fumarate.** – The oxidation of succinate to fumarate is catalyzed by succinate dehydrogenase and reduces FAD to FADH2 in the citric acid cycle.
101. **B. Movement of molecules down a concentration gradient without assistance.** – Simple diffusion allows nonpolar molecules like oxygen and carbon dioxide to move directly through the lipid bilayer without energy or protein assistance, driven by the concentration gradient.
102. **B. Channel proteins and carrier proteins.** – Facilitated diffusion requires the help of channel proteins (which form pores) or carrier proteins (which change shape to transport molecules) to move large or polar molecules across the membrane.
103. **C. Na+/K+ pump.** – The sodium-potassium pump uses ATP to move sodium ions out of the cell and potassium ions into the cell, working against their concentration gradients, thus classified as primary active transport.
104. **C. Electrochemical gradient of another substance.** – Secondary active transport utilizes the energy from an electrochemical gradient, established by primary active transport, to move substances, such as glucose via the sodium-glucose symporter.

105. **C. To maintain the electrochemical gradient by pumping sodium out and potassium in.** – The Na+/K+ pump maintains the resting potential of the cell by moving three sodium ions out and two potassium ions into the cell, essential for many cellular processes.
106. **B. cAMP.** – Cyclic AMP (cAMP) acts as a common secondary messenger in GPCR pathways, amplifying the signal initiated by the ligand-receptor interaction and activating protein kinase A (PKA).
107. **B. Voltage-gated ion channels.** – Voltage-gated ion channels open or close in response to changes in the membrane potential, playing key roles in electrical signaling in neurons and muscle cells.
108. **B. Symport.** – In symport, two molecules are transported in the same direction across the membrane, as seen in sodium-glucose cotransport, where both molecules enter the cell together.
109. **B. Receptor tyrosine kinase signaling.** – Receptor tyrosine kinases (RTKs) undergo autophosphorylation after ligand binding, creating docking sites for downstream signaling proteins, triggering multiple pathways involved in cell growth and differentiation.
110. **B. Protein kinase A.** – Protein kinase A (PKA) is activated by cAMP in many signaling pathways, leading to phosphorylation of target proteins and subsequent regulation of cellular functions.
111. **B. It is used to transport large, polar molecules or ions.** – Facilitated diffusion requires transport proteins to move large or charged molecules, like glucose or ions, across the membrane down their concentration gradient without energy input.
112. **B. To remove phosphate groups from proteins.** – Phosphatases deactivate proteins by removing phosphate groups, counteracting the actions of kinases, thus playing a crucial role in terminating signal transduction.
113. **B. G-protein coupled receptors.** – GPCRs utilize GTP-binding proteins (G-proteins) to relay signals from activated receptors to downstream effectors, leading to the production of secondary messengers such as cAMP.
114. **C. Active transport moves substances against their concentration gradient.** – Active transport requires energy (usually ATP) to move substances from an area of lower concentration to higher concentration, opposite to passive transport, which follows the concentration gradient.
115. **B. To amplify the signal within the cell.** – Secondary messengers like cAMP and calcium ions are small molecules that spread the signal inside the cell by activating further components in the signaling pathway, amplifying the initial signal.
116. **C. It triggers autophosphorylation of the receptor.** – Upon ligand binding, receptor tyrosine kinases (RTKs) phosphorylate themselves on tyrosine residues, initiating downstream signaling cascades crucial for processes like cell division.

117. **C. Facilitated diffusion via aquaporins.** – Water crosses cell membranes mainly through specialized channel proteins called aquaporins, which facilitate its movement along the osmotic gradient.
118. **C. Receptor internalization or downregulation.** – Signal transduction can be terminated by the internalization of receptors or their downregulation, reducing the cell's responsiveness to further stimulation.
119. **C. Voltage-gated ion channels.** – Action potentials in neurons are propagated by the opening and closing of voltage-gated ion channels, which allow the movement of ions like sodium and potassium in and out of the cell.
120. **C. Sodium.** – In secondary active transport, the sodium ion gradient, established by the Na+/K+ pump, often provides the energy to transport other molecules such as glucose or amino acids across the membrane.

SECTION 3:
General Chemistry

Chapter 1: Atomic Structure and Periodicity

Atomic structure is fundamental to understanding the behavior of elements and their interactions. Every atom consists of a nucleus, composed of protons and neutrons, surrounded by electrons that occupy specific energy levels or orbitals. The number of protons in an atom's nucleus defines the element, while the arrangement of electrons in orbitals determines the chemical properties of the element.

Subatomic Particles

Atoms consist of three key subatomic particles: protons, neutrons, and electrons. Protons, which are positively charged, and neutrons, which have no charge, reside in the nucleus. Electrons, negatively charged, orbit the nucleus in regions called electron clouds or orbitals. The mass of the atom is concentrated in the nucleus since protons and neutrons are significantly heavier than electrons. Protons and neutrons each have a mass of approximately 1 atomic mass unit (amu), while electrons are so light that their mass is often negligible.

The number of protons in an atom's nucleus, known as the atomic number, defines the element. For instance, hydrogen has one proton, making its atomic number 1, while carbon has six protons, making its atomic number 6. The atomic number also determines the number of electrons in a neutral atom.

Neutrons help stabilize the nucleus by providing a buffer between the positively charged protons. Without neutrons, the repulsive force between protons would cause the nucleus to break apart. The number of neutrons can vary in atoms of the same element, leading to different isotopes. For example, carbon-12 and carbon-14 both have six protons, but carbon-14 has two additional neutrons, giving it different nuclear stability.

Atomic Orbitals and Electron Energy Levels

Electrons occupy specific regions of space around the nucleus called orbitals. These orbitals are grouped into energy levels, or shells, which are labeled with principal quantum numbers ($n = 1, 2, 3$, etc.). The closer an electron is to the nucleus, the lower its energy level, and the more stable it is. Each energy level can hold a certain number of electrons, determined by the formula $2n2 2n^2 2n2$, where n is the principal quantum number. The first energy level ($n = 1$) can hold 2 electrons, the second level ($n = 2$) can hold 8, the third level ($n = 3$) can hold 18, and so on. Within each energy level, electrons are further grouped into sublevels, labeled s, p, d, and f orbitals, with increasing energy.

- s orbitals are spherical and hold up to 2 electrons.
- p orbitals are dumbbell-shaped and hold up to 6 electrons.
- d orbitals are more complex in shape and hold up to 10 electrons.
- f orbitals, even more complex, can hold up to 14 electrons.

These orbitals are filled in a specific order according to the Aufbau principle, which states that electrons occupy the lowest energy orbitals first before filling higher-energy orbitals. This is crucial in determining the electronic structure of atoms and how they interact in chemical reactions.

Periodic Law and Atomic Periodicity

The arrangement of elements in the periodic table reflects their atomic structure and electron configurations. The periodic law states that when elements are arranged by increasing atomic number, their physical and chemical properties exhibit a recurring pattern or periodicity.

One of the key periodic trends is atomic radius, which generally decreases across a period (from left to right) and increases down a group (from top to bottom). As you move across a period, the number of protons in the nucleus increases, pulling the electron cloud closer to the nucleus, which results in a smaller atomic radius. However, as you move down a group, additional electron shells are added, increasing the size of the electron cloud and thus the atomic radius.

Ionization energy, the energy required to remove an electron from an atom, also follows a periodic trend. It increases across a period, as the increased nuclear charge holds the electrons more tightly, making them harder to remove. Ionization energy decreases down a group because the outermost electrons are farther from the nucleus and are shielded by inner electrons, making them easier to remove.

Electronegativity, the ability of an atom to attract electrons in a chemical bond, increases across a period and decreases down a group. This is because atoms on the right side of the periodic table (such as fluorine) have a strong pull on electrons due to their high nuclear charge and smaller atomic radii, whereas atoms on the left side (such as cesium) are less effective at attracting electrons due to their larger size and weaker nuclear pull.

Electron Configuration

Electron configuration is the distribution of electrons among the orbitals of an atom. This configuration determines the chemical behavior of an element, including its reactivity, bonding capabilities, and placement in the periodic table.

Aufbau Principle

The Aufbau principle dictates that electrons occupy the lowest energy orbitals first. The general order of filling is determined by the energy levels of the orbitals, following the sequence:

- 1s
- 2s, 2p
- 3s, 3p
- 4s, 3d, 4p
- 5s, 4d, 5p
- 6s, 4f, 5d, 6p
- 7s, 5f, 6d, 7p

For example, the electron configuration of carbon, with six electrons, is $1s^2 2s^2 2p^2$, indicating that the first two electrons occupy the 1s orbital, two electrons occupy the 2s orbital, and the remaining two electrons partially fill the 2p orbital.

Hund's Rule and Pauli Exclusion Principle

When filling orbitals of equal energy (degenerate orbitals), Hund's rule states that electrons will occupy empty orbitals singly before pairing up. This minimizes electron-electron repulsion, making the atom more stable. For example, in the case of nitrogen ($1s^2 2s^2 2p^3$), the three electrons in the 2p sublevel will occupy separate p orbitals, each with parallel spins.

The Pauli Exclusion Principle further states that no two electrons in an atom can have the same set of four quantum numbers. This means that each orbital can hold a maximum of two electrons, and these electrons must have opposite spins.

Notation and Exceptions

Electron configurations are typically written in shorthand using the noble gas core method. For instance, the electron configuration of sodium ($1s^2 2s^2 2p^6 3s^1$) is often written as $[Ne]3s^1$, where [Ne] represents the electron configuration of neon, the previous noble gas.

There are exceptions to the predicted configurations, particularly in transition metals. Elements like copper (Cu) and chromium (Cr) have electron configurations that promote an electron from the 4s orbital to the 3d orbital to achieve a more stable arrangement. For example, copper's electron configuration is $[Ar]3d^{10}4s^1$ instead of the expected $[Ar]3d^9 4s^2$

Electron Configurations and Chemical Properties

Electron configuration plays a crucial role in determining an element's chemical properties. Elements with similar configurations, particularly those in the same group, exhibit similar chemical behavior. For instance, the alkali metals (group 1) all have one electron in their outermost s orbital, making them highly reactive and prone to losing that electron to form positive ions.

In contrast, noble gases (group 18) have full outer electron shells, making them extremely stable and unreactive. Understanding electron configuration is essential for predicting the behavior of atoms during chemical reactions and the formation of compounds.

Chapter 2: Bonding and Molecular Structure

Chemical bonds form the foundation of molecular structures, playing a key role in determining how atoms combine and interact. These bonds are the result of attractions between atoms as they seek to achieve more stable electronic configurations, typically by attaining a full valence electron shell. The type of bond that forms between atoms affects a compound's physical and chemical properties, such as melting point, solubility, and conductivity. There are three primary types of chemical bonds: ionic, covalent, and metallic bonds. However, for the purposes of MCAT preparation, we will focus on covalent and ionic bonds, which are the most relevant in biological systems.

Covalent Bonds Covalent bonds form when two atoms share one or more pairs of electrons. These bonds typically occur between nonmetal atoms that have similar electronegativity values, meaning they both have a relatively equal ability to attract electrons. The shared electrons allow each atom to achieve a stable electronic configuration, resembling that of the nearest noble gas.

Covalent bonds can be single, double, or triple bonds, depending on how many pairs of electrons are shared between two atoms. A single bond shares one pair of electrons, a double bond shares two pairs, and a triple bond shares three pairs. The bond strength increases as more electrons are shared. Triple bonds are stronger and shorter than double bonds, which are stronger and shorter than single bonds.

For example:

- In a molecule of hydrogen (H_2), the two hydrogen atoms share a single pair of electrons, forming a single covalent bond.
- In a molecule of oxygen (O_2), the two oxygen atoms share two pairs of electrons, forming a double covalent bond.
- In a molecule of nitrogen (N_2), the two nitrogen atoms share three pairs of electrons, forming a triple covalent bond.

The ability of atoms to form covalent bonds is determined by their valence electrons. Valence electrons are the outermost electrons of an atom and are involved in bonding. The octet rule is a guiding principle that states that atoms tend to form bonds until they have a full valence shell, typically containing eight electrons (except for hydrogen, which requires two).

Types of Covalent Bonds There are two key types of covalent bonds: polar and nonpolar.

- Nonpolar Covalent Bonds: These occur when the electrons are shared equally between the two atoms. Nonpolar covalent bonds typically form between atoms with identical or very similar electronegativity values. For example, the bond between two hydrogen atoms in H_2 is nonpolar because both atoms exert the same pull on the shared electrons.

- Polar Covalent Bonds: These occur when the electrons are shared unequally between the two atoms due to differences in electronegativity. One atom exerts a stronger pull on the shared electrons, causing a partial negative charge (δ-) on that atom and a partial positive charge (δ+) on the other atom. For instance, in a molecule of water (H2O), oxygen is more electronegative than hydrogen, so the electrons are pulled closer to the oxygen atom, resulting in a polar bond.

Polar covalent bonds are crucial in biological systems because they create molecules with regions of partial positive and negative charge. These charges allow molecules to interact through intermolecular forces like hydrogen bonding, which are critical for maintaining the structure and function of proteins, nucleic acids, and other biomolecules.

Covalent and Ionic Bonds

Ionic Bonds Ionic bonds occur when electrons are transferred from one atom to another, resulting in the formation of ions. This type of bond typically forms between a metal and a nonmetal, where the metal donates one or more electrons to the nonmetal. The metal atom, having lost electrons, becomes a positively charged ion (cation), while the nonmetal atom, having gained electrons, becomes a negatively charged ion (anion).

The electrostatic attraction between the oppositely charged ions forms the ionic bond. For example, in sodium chloride (NaCl), sodium (Na) donates one electron to chlorine (Cl), resulting in the formation of a sodium ion (Na+) and a chloride ion (Cl-). The strong attraction between these oppositely charged ions creates the ionic bond that holds the compound together.

Ionic compounds generally have distinct properties, such as:

- High melting and boiling points: Due to the strong electrostatic forces between ions, large amounts of energy are required to break these bonds.
- Solubility in water: Ionic compounds often dissolve in water because the polar water molecules can surround the ions, stabilizing them in solution.
- Electrical conductivity: Ionic compounds conduct electricity when dissolved in water or melted, as the ions are free to move and carry charge.

Ionic bonds are typically stronger than covalent bonds, but this strength can vary depending on the charge and size of the ions involved. For example, magnesium oxide (MgO), with a +2 charge on magnesium and a -2 charge on oxygen, has a much stronger ionic bond than sodium chloride (NaCl), which has only a +1 and -1 charge.

Comparison of Ionic and Covalent Bonds While both ionic and covalent bonds are essential for molecular structure, they differ in several key ways:

- Formation: Covalent bonds form through the sharing of electrons, while ionic bonds form through the transfer of electrons.
- Types of Elements: Covalent bonds typically occur between nonmetals, whereas ionic bonds usually form between metals and nonmetals.

- Electronegativity: Covalent bonds occur between atoms with similar electronegativity, while ionic bonds form between atoms with a significant difference in electronegativity.
- Properties: Covalent compounds generally have lower melting and boiling points and are poor conductors of electricity. In contrast, ionic compounds have higher melting and boiling points and can conduct electricity when dissolved in water or melted.

Bond Polarity: The degree of ionic versus covalent character in a bond is determined by the difference in electronegativity between the two atoms. As the difference in electronegativity increases, the bond becomes more ionic in character. Bonds that fall somewhere between purely ionic and purely covalent are considered polar covalent, as they exhibit characteristics of both bond types.

For example, the bond between hydrogen and chlorine in hydrogen chloride (HCl) is polar covalent because the electronegativity difference between hydrogen and chlorine creates a partial charge separation. However, the bond is not fully ionic because the electrons are still shared, albeit unequally.

Bond Length and Bond Strength Bond length is the distance between the nuclei of two bonded atoms. In general, shorter bonds are stronger because the atoms are held together more tightly. For covalent bonds, triple bonds are the shortest and strongest, while single bonds are the longest and weakest. In ionic bonds, smaller ions and ions with higher charges tend to form stronger bonds because the electrostatic attraction is greater.

Understanding the differences between covalent and ionic bonds, as well as the factors that influence bond strength and polarity, is crucial for mastering concepts related to molecular structure and chemical reactivity. Both types of bonds are essential for the formation of compounds and play a critical role in the biological systems tested on the MCAT.

Chapter 3: States of Matter

Matter exists in three primary states: solid, liquid, and gas. Each state of matter is distinguished by the arrangement of particles, energy levels, and the forces of attraction between them. Understanding these states is crucial for grasping the fundamental principles that govern physical interactions at the molecular level.

Solids: Solids have a fixed shape and volume. The particles in a solid are tightly packed in a regular arrangement, resulting in minimal movement. These particles can vibrate, but they do not move freely. The strong intermolecular forces between the particles give solids their rigidity and structural integrity. There are two types of solids: crystalline and amorphous. Crystalline solids, like salt and diamonds, have a well-organized, repeating lattice structure. Amorphous solids, like glass and rubber, lack a long-range ordered structure, making them more flexible and capable of flowing under certain conditions.

Liquids: In liquids, particles are still close together but not as tightly packed as in solids. This allows them to move past one another, giving liquids a definite volume but no fixed shape. The particles in a liquid have more kinetic energy than those in a solid, which weakens the forces of attraction. Liquids can flow and take the shape of their container while maintaining their volume. The viscosity of a liquid, which is its resistance to flow, depends on the strength of intermolecular forces and the temperature. For example, honey is more viscous than water because of stronger intermolecular forces.

Gases: Gases have neither a definite shape nor volume. The particles in a gas are far apart and move rapidly in all directions. Because of the high kinetic energy of gas particles, the forces of attraction between them are negligible. Gases expand to fill any container they are placed in, and their volume can change easily under varying pressure and temperature conditions. The behavior of gases is best described by the ideal gas law, which relates pressure, volume, temperature, and the number of particles through the equation $PV = nRT$. Unlike solids and liquids, gases are highly compressible because the particles are widely spaced.

Gases, Liquids, and Solids
Gases

The gas state is characterized by high kinetic energy and the absence of significant intermolecular forces. Gas particles move rapidly and randomly, colliding with each other and the walls of their container. These collisions result in the gas pressure, which is the force exerted by the gas per unit area on the container walls.

Key Properties of Gases

- Pressure (P): The force that gas molecules exert when they collide with the walls of their container. It is commonly measured in units like atmospheres (atm), pascals (Pa), or torr.
- Volume (V): The space occupied by the gas. Gases expand to fill their container.
- Temperature (T): A measure of the average kinetic energy of gas particles. Temperature is directly proportional to the kinetic energy and, consequently, the speed of the particles.
- Number of Moles (n): This represents the amount of gas in a system, and it is related to the volume and pressure through the ideal gas law.

The ideal gas law, $PV=nRT$, is used to model the behavior of gases under various conditions. Here, R is the gas constant, and the equation assumes that gas particles do not interact except through elastic collisions. While this model works well under normal conditions, deviations occur at high pressures and low temperatures, where intermolecular forces become significant.

Kinetic Molecular Theory of Gases

The kinetic molecular theory explains the properties of gases by considering them as collections of particles in constant, random motion. The theory states that gas particles do not attract or repel each other, their collisions are elastic (no kinetic energy is lost), and the average kinetic energy is directly proportional to temperature. This theory helps explain why gas pressure increases with temperature or decreases with an increase in volume.

Real Gases: In reality, gases do not always behave ideally. At high pressures and low temperatures, gas particles experience attractive forces, and their volume becomes significant. The van der Waals equation accounts for these deviations by incorporating correction factors for intermolecular forces and particle volume.

Liquids:

Liquids are an intermediate state between gases and solids. They have a definite volume but no fixed shape. The particles in a liquid are in close contact, but they are not arranged in a rigid structure like solids. Instead, they have enough kinetic energy to move past each other, allowing liquids to flow and take the shape of their container.

Key Properties of Liquids

- Surface Tension: The cohesive forces between liquid molecules create surface tension, causing the surface of the liquid to contract. Surface tension explains why small objects like insects can rest on water without sinking.

- Viscosity: This refers to a liquid's resistance to flow. A more viscous liquid has stronger intermolecular forces, making it more difficult for the molecules to slide past one another. Temperature affects viscosity: higher temperatures lower viscosity by giving molecules more kinetic energy to overcome intermolecular forces.
- Vapor Pressure: When a liquid is in a closed container, some of its particles escape into the gas phase, creating vapor pressure. As temperature increases, more particles have enough energy to escape, increasing the vapor pressure.
- Boiling Point: The temperature at which a liquid's vapor pressure equals the external pressure. At this point, the liquid turns into a gas. Higher atmospheric pressures increase the boiling point, while lower pressures (as at higher altitudes) decrease it.

Intermolecular Forces in Liquids

The physical properties of liquids, such as viscosity and boiling point, depend on the strength of intermolecular forces. There are several types of intermolecular forces:

- Dipole-Dipole Interactions: These occur between polar molecules, where positive and negative ends of molecules attract each other.
- Hydrogen Bonding: A particularly strong type of dipole-dipole interaction, hydrogen bonding occurs when hydrogen is bonded to highly electronegative atoms like oxygen, nitrogen, or fluorine. This results in higher boiling points and surface tension, as seen in water.
- London Dispersion Forces: These weak forces arise from temporary dipoles in nonpolar molecules due to momentary distributions of electron density. Larger molecules have stronger dispersion forces.

Solids:

Solids have a definite shape and volume because the particles are tightly packed in a fixed structure. The motion of the particles is limited to vibrations about their fixed positions. The nature of the bonding between particles determines the properties of the solid, such as hardness, melting point, and conductivity.

Types of Solids

- Crystalline Solids: These have a highly ordered, repeating lattice structure. Common examples include table salt (sodium chloride) and diamonds (carbon). The regular arrangement of particles gives crystalline solids a defined melting point and characteristic geometric shapes.
- Amorphous Solids: These lack a well-defined structure, leading to properties more like a very thick liquid. Glass and rubber are examples of amorphous solids. Unlike crystalline solids, they do not have a sharp melting point but instead soften gradually when heated.

Properties of Solids

- Melting Point: The temperature at which a solid turns into a liquid. Solids with stronger intermolecular forces or bonds, like ionic or covalent bonds, have higher melting points.
- Electrical Conductivity: Some solids, such as metals, have free electrons that allow them to conduct electricity. In contrast, ionic solids only conduct electricity when molten or dissolved in water, as their charged particles need to move freely for electrical conductivity.

Chapter 4: Thermodynamics

Thermodynamics is a branch of physics that deals with the study of energy, heat, work, and how they interact in different systems. The fundamental focus of thermodynamics is on how energy is transferred and transformed, particularly how thermal energy is converted into other forms of energy and vice versa. The laws of thermodynamics provide a systematic framework to understand how these processes occur in nature. They govern not only physical systems like engines and refrigerators but also biological systems, chemical reactions, and even the universe's evolution.

Thermodynamics involves a few key concepts:

1. System and Surroundings:: A system refers to the specific portion of the universe being studied, while the surroundings refer to everything else outside the system. Systems can be open (where matter and energy can be exchanged with surroundings), closed (only energy is exchanged), or isolated (no exchange of energy or matter).
2. Heat (Q): Heat is the transfer of energy from one object to another due to a temperature difference. It naturally flows from hotter to colder objects.
3. Work (W): Work refers to energy transfer when an external force is applied. In thermodynamic processes, work is often done by gases expanding or contracting.
4. Internal Energy (U): The internal energy of a system represents the total energy contained within it, which includes both kinetic energy (movement of molecules) and potential energy (energy stored in chemical bonds or due to position).
5. State Functions: These are properties that depend only on the current state of the system, not on the path taken to reach that state. Examples include temperature, pressure, volume, and internal energy.
6. Enthalpy (H): Enthalpy is a state function that is useful for understanding heat changes at constant pressure. It is defined as the sum of the internal energy and the product of pressure and volume: $H = U + PV$.

Understanding these key terms sets the foundation for applying the laws of thermodynamics, which provide the principles that govern energy transformations in any system.

First Law of Thermodynamics

The First Law of Thermodynamics, also known as the Law of Energy Conservation, states that energy cannot be created or destroyed in an isolated system. The energy of a system is always conserved; it can only change forms or be transferred from one part of the system to another. This law is mathematically represented as:

$$\Delta U = Q - W$$

Where:

ΔU is the change in internal energy of the system,

Q is the heat added to the system, and

W is the work done by the system.

Key Concepts of the First Law:

1. Energy Conservation: In a closed system, the total amount of energy remains constant, though it may be transferred in the form of heat or work. For instance, when you heat a gas in a closed container, the energy supplied as heat can increase the internal energy of the gas or allow it to do work (like expanding against the walls of the container).
2. Internal Energy Changes: If heat is added to a system, it can either increase the internal energy (which might result in a temperature increase) or cause the system to do work (such as expanding a gas). Conversely, if work is done on the system (such as compressing a gas), the internal energy of the system increases.
3. Practical Application: One of the best-known applications of the First Law is in heat engines, where heat is converted into work. For example, in a car engine, the heat from burning fuel increases the internal energy of gases, which then expand and do work by moving the pistons.
4. Isolated Systems: In isolated systems, where no energy is exchanged with the surroundings, the total energy within the system remains constant. However, energy can still change forms within the system, such as the conversion of potential energy into kinetic energy.

Second Law of Thermodynamics

The Second Law of Thermodynamics introduces the concept of entropy (S), a measure of the disorder or randomness of a system. This law can be stated in several ways, but a common interpretation is that natural processes tend to move toward a state of maximum entropy or disorder.

Key Concepts of the Second Law:

1. Entropy Increase: In any spontaneous process, the total entropy of the system and its surroundings always increases. While energy is conserved (as per the First Law), the quality of that energy degrades over time. Energy transformations are never 100% efficient, and some energy is always "lost" as waste heat, increasing the system's entropy.
2. Irreversible Processes: The Second Law explains why certain processes are irreversible. For example, heat naturally flows from hot objects to cold objects, increasing the entropy of the combined system. This process cannot spontaneously reverse itself because that would require a decrease in entropy, which the Second Law forbids.
3. Heat Engines and Refrigerators: The Second Law plays a crucial role in the operation of heat engines and refrigerators. In a heat engine, such as a car engine, heat flows from a hot reservoir to a cold one, doing work in the process. However, some heat is always lost to the cold reservoir, which limits the efficiency of the engine. No engine can convert all the heat it receives into work — there is always some waste. Refrigerators, on the other hand, work by

transferring heat from a colder region to a hotter region, which requires an external input of work. The Second Law explains why energy must be expended to reduce the entropy of the cold region while increasing the entropy of the surroundings.

4. Mathematical Representation: For any reversible process, the change in entropy is given by:

$$\Delta S = \frac{Q}{T}$$

Where:

ΔS is the change in entropy,

Q is the heat exchanged, and

T is the temperature at which the heat exchange occurs.

For an irreversible process, the change in entropy is always greater than this value, indicating that entropy must increase for spontaneous processes.

5. Efficiency of Heat Engines: The efficiency η of a heat engine is defined as the ratio of the work output W to the heat input Q_{in}, and is always less than 100% due to the Second Law:

$$\eta = 1 - \frac{T_{cold}}{T_{hot}}$$

This equation shows that efficiency increases when the temperature difference between the hot and cold reservoirs is large, but it can never be perfect because of the inevitability of some heat loss.

Chapter 5: Chemical Kinetics

Chemical kinetics is the study of reaction rates and the factors that influence them. It examines how fast reactions occur, the conditions that impact this rate, and the steps or mechanisms by which reactions proceed. Understanding kinetics is essential in various fields, including biochemistry, engineering, and environmental science, as it allows us to predict and control chemical processes.

The rate of a chemical reaction refers to the speed at which reactants are converted into products. It is typically expressed as the change in concentration of a reactant or product per unit time. The general equation for the rate of a reaction can be written as:

$$\text{Rate} = -\frac{d[\text{Reactant}]}{dt} = \frac{d[\text{product}]}{dt}$$

The minus sign is used for the reactant because its concentration decreases over time, while the concentration of products increases. Reaction rates are influenced by several factors, which we will discuss below.

Factors Affecting Reaction Rates

1. Concentration of Reactants: According to the law of mass action, the rate of a chemical reaction is proportional to the concentration of the reactants. As the concentration of the reactants increases, the number of molecules or ions colliding with one another also increases, leading to a higher rate of reaction.
2. Temperature: Temperature plays a crucial role in chemical kinetics. An increase in temperature usually increases the reaction rate because molecules move faster and collide more frequently with enough energy to overcome the activation energy barrier. The relationship between temperature and reaction rate can be described by the Arrhenius equation:

$$k = A \cdot e^{-\frac{E_a}{RT}}$$

Where:

k is the rate constant,

A is the pre-exponential factor,

E_0 is the activation energy,

R is the gas constant,

T is the absolute temperature.

3. Catalysts: A catalyst is a substance that increases the rate of a reaction without being consumed in the process. It works by providing an alternative reaction pathway with a lower activation energy. Catalysts do not alter the final equilibrium of the reaction; they only make it reach equilibrium faster.
4. Surface Area: In reactions involving solids, the surface area of the solid reactant affects the rate. A larger surface area provides more sites for reaction, increasing the overall rate. This is why powdered substances react more quickly than large chunks.
5. Pressure: In reactions involving gases, increasing the pressure increases the rate of reaction. This is because higher pressure compresses the gas molecules, leading to more frequent collisions.
6. Nature of Reactants: Some substances react faster than others due to the strength of their bonds and the stability of their molecules. For example, ionic compounds in aqueous solutions often react more quickly than covalent compounds because ions move freely and can interact with one another readily.

Rate Law and Order of Reaction

The rate law of a chemical reaction expresses the relationship between the reaction rate and the concentrations of the reactants. For a reaction of the form:

The rate law might be written as:

$$aA + bB \rightarrow \text{products}$$

The rate law might be written as:

$$\text{Rate} = k[A]^m[B]^n$$

Where:

k is the rate constant,

[A] and [B] are the concentrations of the reactants,

m and n are the orders of reaction with respect to A and B, respectively.

The sum of m and n gives the overall order of the reaction. The orders of reaction are determined experimentally and cannot be inferred from the stoichiometry of the reaction. A reaction may be zero-order, first-order, second-order, or mixed-order depending on how the rate depends on the concentration of the reactants.

- Zero-order reaction: The rate is independent of the concentration of the reactants.
- First-order reaction: The rate is directly proportional to the concentration of one reactant.

- Second-order reaction: The rate is proportional to the square of the concentration of one reactant or to the product of the concentrations of two reactants.

Reaction Rates and Mechanisms

A reaction mechanism is a detailed, step-by-step description of how reactants are converted into products. It explains the sequence of elementary steps (individual reactions) that lead to the overall chemical transformation. Each elementary step involves a small number of molecules, typically one or two, and is characterized by its own rate law.

Elementary Steps and Molecularity

Elementary steps are classified based on their molecularity, which refers to the number of reactant particles involved in the step:

- Unimolecular: Involves a single reactant molecule.
- Bimolecular: Involves two reactant molecules.
- Termolecular: Involves three reactant molecules (rare due to the low probability of three molecules colliding simultaneously).

The molecularity of an elementary step determines its rate law. For example:

- A unimolecular step has a first-order rate law.
- A bimolecular step has a second-order rate law.

The overall rate law of the reaction depends on the slowest step in the mechanism, known as the rate-determining step.

Rate-Determining Step

In a multistep reaction, the rate-determining step is the slowest step and controls the overall reaction rate. It acts as a bottleneck, limiting the speed at which the entire reaction can proceed. The rate law of the rate-determining step is often used to describe the rate law of the entire reaction.

For example, consider the reaction mechanism:

1. $A + B \rightarrow C$ (fast)
2. $C + D \rightarrow E$ (slow)

Here, the second step is the rate-determining step, so the rate law of the overall reaction is based on this step.

Reaction Intermediates

Intermediates are species that are produced in one step of a reaction mechanism and consumed in a subsequent step. They do not appear in the overall balanced equation for the reaction but play a crucial role in the mechanism. Identifying reaction intermediates helps in understanding the pathway the reaction follows.

Activation Energy and Transition States

The activation energy (E_0) is the minimum energy required for a reaction to occur. During a chemical reaction, reactant molecules must collide with enough energy to overcome this energy barrier. The highest energy point along the reaction pathway is called the transition state. At the transition state, bonds are partially broken and formed, and the system can proceed to form either the products or revert to reactants.

The Arrhenius equation provides a quantitative relationship between the rate constant and activation energy:

$$k = A \cdot e^{-\frac{E_a}{RT}}$$

This equation shows that even a small increase in temperature can significantly increase the rate of reaction by providing more molecules with the energy needed to overcome the activation energy.

Catalysis and Reaction Mechanisms

Catalysts affect reaction mechanisms by providing an alternative pathway with a lower activation energy. There are two main types of catalysis:

- Homogeneous catalysis: The catalyst is in the same phase as the reactants.
- Heterogeneous catalysis: The catalyst is in a different phase (e.g., a solid catalyst with gaseous reactants).

In both cases, the catalyst lowers the activation energy and speeds up the reaction without being consumed.

Chapter 6: Equilibrium

In chemistry, equilibrium refers to a state in a reversible chemical reaction where the rate of the forward reaction equals the rate of the reverse reaction. At equilibrium, the concentrations of the reactants and products remain constant over time. It's important to note that equilibrium doesn't mean the reactants and products are present in equal amounts; rather, it means their concentrations no longer change, despite the fact that the reactions continue to occur.

Dynamic Nature of Equilibrium

Equilibrium is dynamic, meaning that both the forward and reverse reactions are still occurring, but at the same rate. This results in no net change in the concentration of reactants or products. For example, in the reaction:

$$A+B \rightleftharpoons C+D$$

Once equilibrium is reached, the rate at which A and B are converted into C and D equals the rate at which C and D are converted back into A and B.

The Equilibrium Constant (K)

The equilibrium constant,

K, is a numerical value that expresses the ratio of the concentrations of the products to the reactants, each raised to the power of their coefficients in the balanced chemical equation. For a general reaction:

$$aA+bB \rightleftharpoons cC+dD$$

The equilibrium constant expression is:

$$K = \frac{[C]^c[D]^d}{[A]^a[B]^b}$$

Here, [A], [B], [C], and [D] represent the molar concentrations of the reactants and products at equilibrium, and a, b, c, and d are the coefficients from the balanced equation.

The value of K indicates the position of equilibrium:

K>1: The reaction favors the formation of products (more products than reactants at equilibrium).

K<1: The reaction favors the formation of reactants (more reactants than products at equilibrium).

K=1: Reactants and products are present in similar amounts at equilibrium.

Factors Affecting Equilibrium

1. Concentration: Changing the concentration of reactants or products shifts the equilibrium position. If the concentration of a reactant is increased, the system will respond by producing more products to restore equilibrium.
2. Pressure: For reactions involving gases, changing the pressure can shift the equilibrium position. According to Le Chatelier's Principle (discussed later), increasing pressure favors the side of the reaction with fewer moles of gas, while decreasing pressure favors the side with more moles of gas.
3. Temperature: Changing the temperature affects the value of K and shifts the equilibrium. For exothermic reactions (which release heat), increasing temperature shifts the equilibrium toward the reactants. For endothermic reactions (which absorb heat), increasing temperature shifts the equilibrium toward the products.
4. Catalysts: While catalysts speed up both the forward and reverse reactions, they do not affect the position of equilibrium. Catalysts help the system reach equilibrium more quickly but do not change the relative concentrations of reactants and products.

Le Chatelier's Principle

Le Chatelier's Principle is a fundamental concept in chemistry that predicts how a system at equilibrium responds to disturbances. It states that if a system at equilibrium is subjected to a change (stress) in concentration, temperature, or pressure, the system will adjust itself to counteract the disturbance and restore equilibrium.

Changes in Concentration

When the concentration of a reactant or product is changed, the system responds by shifting the equilibrium to minimize the impact of the change.

Increase in Reactant Concentration: If the concentration of a reactant is increased, the system will shift the equilibrium toward the formation of more products to reduce the added reactant. For example, in the reaction:

$$A + B \rightleftharpoons C + D$$

If more A is added, the system will produce more C and D to re-establish equilibrium.

Increase in Product Concentration: If the concentration of a product is increased, the system will shift the equilibrium toward the reactants. In the above reaction, if more C is added, the reverse reaction will be favored, and more A and B will form.

Changes in Pressure (For Gaseous Reactions)

Le Chatelier's Principle also applies to systems involving gases, where changes in pressure can shift the equilibrium. Pressure affects equilibrium in reactions where the number of moles of gas differs on the reactant and product sides.

- Increase in Pressure: If the pressure on the system is increased (usually by decreasing the volume), the system shifts to the side with fewer moles of gas to reduce the pressure. For example, in the reaction:

$$N_2(g) + 3H_2(g) \rightleftharpoons 2NH_3(g)$$

There are four moles of gas on the left (1 mole of N_2 and 3 moles of H_2) and two moles of gas on the right (2 moles of NH_3). Increasing the pressure will shift the equilibrium toward the side with fewer moles of gas, in this case, the formation of NH_3

- Decrease in Pressure: If the pressure is decreased (by increasing the volume), the equilibrium will shift toward the side with more moles of gas.

Changes in Temperature

Temperature changes affect the equilibrium depending on whether the reaction is exothermic (releases heat) or endothermic (absorbs heat).

- Increase in Temperature (Exothermic Reactions): For exothermic reactions, increasing the temperature adds heat to the system. According to Le Chatelier's Principle, the system will respond by favoring the reverse reaction to consume the added heat. This shifts the equilibrium toward the reactants.
- Increase in Temperature (Endothermic Reactions): In endothermic reactions, increasing the temperature adds heat, which the system uses to drive the forward reaction. The equilibrium shifts toward the products.
- Decrease in Temperature (Exothermic Reactions): Lowering the temperature in an exothermic reaction shifts the equilibrium toward the products, as the system compensates by producing more heat.
- Decrease in Temperature (Endothermic Reactions): Lowering the temperature in an endothermic reaction shifts the equilibrium toward the reactants.

Role of Catalysts

Catalysts speed up the attainment of equilibrium but do not shift the position of the equilibrium itself. They work by lowering the activation energy required for both the forward and reverse reactions, ensuring that the system reaches equilibrium more quickly. However, they do not favor either side of the reaction.

Practical Applications of Le Chatelier's Principle

Le Chatelier's Principle is widely used in industrial chemical processes. For instance, in the Haber process for ammonia production, conditions such as temperature, pressure, and concentration are carefully controlled to maximize ammonia yield based on the shifts predicted by Le Chatelier's Principle. Another application is in the contact process for sulfuric acid production, where the principle helps in optimizing conditions for sulfur dioxide oxidation. Understanding how to shift equilibria effectively allows industries to increase efficiency and reduce costs.

Chapter 7: Acids and Bases

In chemistry, acids and bases are two fundamental categories of substances that play a crucial role in various chemical reactions, especially in aqueous solutions. Acids are substances that donate protons (H^+ ions) in a solution, while bases are substances that accept protons. This concept is based on the Brønsted-Lowry definition of acids and bases, which is widely used in chemistry. Another common definition is the Lewis definition, where acids are electron pair acceptors, and bases are electron pair donors.

Properties of Acids
- Proton donors: Acids release hydrogen ions (H^+) when dissolved in water. For example, hydrochloric acid (HCl) dissociates in water to form H^+ and Cl^- ions.
- **Sour taste:** Many acids, such as citric acid in lemons or acetic acid in vinegar, have a sour taste.
- Corrosive nature: Strong acids, like sulfuric acid (H_2SO_4), are highly corrosive and can react aggressively with metals and organic materials.
- **Electrolytes:** Acids conduct electricity in aqueous solutions because they ionize and produce charged particles.
- Reaction with metals: Acids react with certain metals to produce hydrogen gas. For instance, zinc (Zn) reacts with hydrochloric acid (HCl) to release H_2 gas.

Properties of Bases
- Proton acceptors: Bases accept hydrogen ions (H^+) when dissolved in water. A common example is sodium hydroxide (NaOH), which dissociates into Na^+ and OH^- ions in water. The hydroxide ions (OH^-) can combine with H^+ ions to form water (H_2O).
- Bitter taste: Bases generally have a bitter taste, although tasting them is not advised due to their caustic properties.
- Slippery feel: Bases like soap solutions feel slippery to the touch due to their interaction with oils and fats, forming soap molecules.
- Alkaline: A solution of a base in water is termed "alkaline." Bases turn red litmus paper blue, indicating their alkaline nature.
- Electrolytes: Similar to acids, bases also ionize in water and can conduct electricity.

Strength of Acids and Bases

The strength of an acid or base refers to how completely it dissociates in water:
- Strong acids dissociate completely in water, releasing a large concentration of H^+ ions. Examples include hydrochloric acid (HCl), sulfuric acid (H_2SO_4), and nitric acid (HNO_3).
- Weak acids partially dissociate in water, producing a lower concentration of H^+ ions. Acetic acid (CH_3COOH) and carbonic acid (H_2CO_3) are examples of weak acids.
- Strong bases dissociate completely in water to yield OH^- ions. Sodium hydroxide (NaOH) and potassium hydroxide (KOH) are strong bases.
- Weak bases partially dissociate in water and include compounds like ammonia (NH_3).

pH, pKa, and Buffers

pH

The pH scale measures the acidity or basicity of a solution and ranges from 0 to 14. It is a logarithmic scale based on the concentration of hydrogen ions (H^+) in a solution. The formula for calculating pH is:

$$pH = -\log[H^+]$$

- **pH < 7:** The solution is acidic, meaning there is a higher concentration of H^+ ions compared to OH^- ions. Examples include lemon juice (pH ≈ 2) and vinegar (pH ≈ 3).
- **pH = 7:** The solution is neutral, indicating equal concentrations of H^+ and OH^- ions. Pure water, at 25°C, has a neutral pH of 7.
- **pH > 7:** The solution is basic or alkaline, meaning there is a lower concentration of H^+ ions compared to OH^- ions. Common bases like baking soda (pH ≈ 9) and bleach (pH ≈ 12) have high pH values.

Since the pH scale is logarithmic, a change of one pH unit represents a tenfold change in H^+ concentration. For example, a solution with a pH of 3 is ten times more acidic than a solution with a pH of 4.

pKa

The pKa is the negative logarithm of the acid dissociation constant (Ka) of a weak acid:

$$pKa = -\log Ka$$

The **Ka** represents how easily an acid donates a proton, with a larger Ka indicating a stronger acid. The pKa value provides insight into the strength of an acid:

- A **lower pKa** means a stronger acid, which dissociates more in solution.
- A **higher pKa** corresponds to a weaker acid, which dissociates less.

For instance, acetic acid (CH_3COOH) has a pKa of 4.76, indicating that it is a weak acid. Hydrochloric acid (HCl), with a pKa of -6.3, is a much stronger acid.

The relationship between pH and pKa is crucial in determining the dissociation of weak acids. According to the Henderson-Hasselbalch equation:

$$pH = pKa + \log\left(\frac{[A^-]}{[HA]}\right)$$

Where:
- A^- is the concentration of the conjugate base.
- **HA** is the concentration of the acid.

This equation helps in calculating the pH of buffer solutions and understanding how the pH changes when an acid or base is added.

Buffers

A **buffer** is a solution that resists changes in pH when small amounts of acid or base are added. Buffers are composed of a weak acid and its conjugate base (or a weak base and its conjugate acid). They are essential in biological systems and chemical reactions where pH stability is necessary.

For example, in the human body, the bicarbonate buffer system maintains blood pH within a narrow range (around 7.35-7.45) by using carbonic acid (H_2CO_3) and bicarbonate (HCO_3^-):

$$H_2CO_3 \rightleftharpoons H^+ + HCO_3^-$$

Buffers work by neutralizing added acids or bases:
- When an acid (H^+) is added to a buffer, the conjugate base (A^-) reacts with it, minimizing the pH change.
- When a base (OH^-) is added, the weak acid (HA) donates protons (H^+) to neutralize the OH^-.

Buffer Capacity

Buffer capacity refers to the ability of a buffer to maintain pH when acids or bases are added. A buffer is most effective when the pH of the solution is close to the pKa of the acid. The buffer capacity depends on the concentrations of the acid and its conjugate base:
- Higher concentrations of the buffer components result in greater capacity to resist pH changes.
- Buffers are less effective when the pH differs significantly from the pKa of the acid.

Buffers are used in various applications, including maintaining the pH of biological fluids, controlling pH in fermentation processes, and preparing chemical solutions in laboratories.

Chapter 8: Electrochemistry

Electrochemistry is a branch of chemistry that deals with the relationship between electrical energy and chemical reactions. It involves the study of how chemical reactions can generate electricity and how electrical energy can drive chemical reactions. The two main types of electrochemical processes are those that involve spontaneous reactions (galvanic or voltaic cells) and those that involve non-spontaneous reactions driven by external energy sources (electrolytic cells). Understanding electrochemistry is crucial for a wide range of applications, from batteries to corrosion prevention.

Basic Concepts of Electrochemistry

1. **Redox Reactions (Oxidation-Reduction Reactions)** Electrochemical processes are governed by redox reactions, which involve the transfer of electrons between chemical species. In a redox reaction, one species loses electrons (oxidation), and another gains electrons (reduction). The substance that loses electrons is called the reducing agent, while the one that gains electrons is the oxidizing agent.

   A typical redox reaction can be represented as:
   - Oxidation: $A \rightarrow A^{n+} + ne^-$
   - Reduction: $B^{m+} + me^- \rightarrow B$

   Here, A is oxidized by losing electrons, and B is reduced by gaining electrons. The overall reaction is a combination of these oxidation and reduction processes.

2. **Galvanic (Voltaic) Cells** A galvanic cell is a device that converts chemical energy into electrical energy through spontaneous redox reactions. These cells consist of two half-cells, each containing an electrode immersed in an electrolyte solution. The half-cells are connected by a wire and a salt bridge, which allows ions to flow between them, maintaining electrical neutrality.

   In a galvanic cell:
   - The **anode** is the electrode where oxidation occurs. Electrons are released from the oxidized species and flow through the external circuit to the cathode.
   - The **cathode** is the electrode where reduction occurs. Electrons enter the cathode and reduce the species in the solution.

The flow of electrons from the anode to the cathode through the external circuit creates an electric current. The voltage (also called electromotive force, EMF) of the cell depends on the nature of the chemical reactions occurring at the electrodes.

A common example of a galvanic cell is the **Daniell cell**, which uses a zinc anode and a copper cathode:

$$Zn(s) \rightarrow Zn^{2+}(aq) + 2e^- \quad \text{(anode reaction)}$$

$$Cu^{2+}(aq) + 2e^- \rightarrow Cu(s) \quad \text{(cathode reaction)}$$

The overall cell reaction is:

$$Zn(s) + Cu^{2+}(aq) \rightarrow Zn^{2+}(aq) + Cu(s)$$

3. **Electrolytic Cells** Electrolytic cells operate by using electrical energy to drive a non-spontaneous chemical reaction. These cells are the opposite of galvanic cells in that they require an external power source (like a battery) to force electrons to move in the desired direction.

   In an electrolytic cell:
   - The **anode** is still the site of oxidation, but electrons are now pulled from the anode by the external power source.
   - The **cathode** is where reduction occurs, and electrons are supplied by the power source to reduce the species at the cathode.

   A key application of electrolytic cells is **electrolysis**, where electrical energy is used to decompose chemical compounds. For instance, the electrolysis of water can split water into hydrogen and oxygen gases:

   $$2H_2O(l) \rightarrow 2H_2(g) + O_2(g)$$

   This reaction is non-spontaneous and requires an external energy input to occur.

4. **Cell Potentials (E° values)** The potential difference between the anode and the cathode in a cell is called the **cell potential** or **electromotive force (EMF)**. It is measured in volts (V) and is a measure of the driving force behind the electron flow. The standard cell potential ($E°_{cell}$) can be calculated using the standard reduction potentials ($E°$) of the half-reactions occurring at the electrodes.

   The formula for calculating the standard cell potential is:

   $$E°_{cell} = E°_{cathode} - E°_{anode}$$

   The Positive $E°_{cell}$ values indicate a spontaneous reaction, while negative values indicate non-spontaneous reactions.

   Standard reduction potentials are determined under standard conditions (1 M concentration, 25°C, and 1 atm pressure). For example, the standard reduction potential for the copper half-reaction is: $E°_{Cu^{2+}/Cu} = +0.34\ V$, while for zinc, it is $E°_{Zn^{2+}/Zn} = -0.76\ V$.

   To calculate the cell potential for the Daniell cell:

   $$E°_{cell} = 0.34\ V - (-0.76\ V) = 1.10\ V$$

   This positive value indicates that the Daniell cell operates spontaneously under standard conditions.

5. **Nernst Equation** The Nernst equation allows us to calculate the cell potential under non-standard conditions. As the concentrations of the reactants and products change, so does the cell potential. The Nernst equation is expressed as:

   $$E = E° - \frac{RT}{nF} \ln Q$$

Where:
- E is the cell potential under non-standard conditions.
- $E°$ is the standard cell potential.

- R is the gas constant (8.314 J/mol·K).
- T is the temperature in Kelvin.
- n is the number of moles of electrons transferred in the reaction.
- F is the Faraday constant (96,485 C/mol).
- Q is the reaction quotient, which is the ratio of the concentrations of the products to the reactants.

This equation helps in determining how the cell potential changes as the reaction progresses.

6. **Faraday's Laws of Electrolysis** Faraday's laws quantify the relationship between the amount of substance produced or consumed at an electrode and the quantity of electricity passed through the electrolyte.
    - **First Law**: The amount of chemical change produced at an electrode is directly proportional to the quantity of electricity passed through the cell.

    $$m = \frac{Q}{F} \cdot (\text{molar mass})/(\text{number of electrons})$$

    - **Second Law**: The amounts of different substances liberated by the same quantity of electricity are proportional to their equivalent weights.

These principles of electrochemistry form the foundation of many technologies, including batteries, fuel cells, electroplating, and more. Understanding the flow of electrons and the energetic changes involved in these reactions is essential for applying electrochemical concepts in both industrial and laboratory settings.

Practical Question For Section 3:

1. Which of the following particles is located in the nucleus of an atom?

   a) Electron
   b) Proton
   c) Photon
   d) Neutrino

2. What is the charge of a neutron?

   a) Positive
   b) Negative
   c) Neutral
   d) Variable

3. The atomic number of an element is defined by the number of which subatomic particle?

   a) Neutrons
   b) Protons
   c) Electrons
   d) Positrons

4. Which principle dictates that electrons occupy the lowest available energy orbitals first?

   a) Pauli Exclusion Principle
   b) Hund's Rule
   c) Aufbau Principle
   d) Heisenberg Uncertainty Principle

5. The maximum number of electrons that can occupy the second energy level (n=2) is:

   a) 2
   b) 6
   c) 8
   d) 10

6. What is the electron configuration of oxygen (atomic number 8)?

   a) $1s^2\ 2s^2\ 2p^4$
   b) $1s^2\ 2s^2\ 2p^2$
   c) $1s^2\ 2s^1\ 2p^5$
   d) $1s^2\ 2s^2\ 2p^6$

7. Which of the following elements has the smallest atomic radius?

   a) Sodium

b) Magnesium
c) Fluorine
d) Chlorine

8. Which of the following trends is observed across a period from left to right?

    a) Atomic radius increases
    b) Ionization energy decreases
    c) Electronegativity decreases
    d) Ionization energy increases

9. What is the shape of a p-orbital?

    a) Spherical
    b) Dumbbell-shaped
    c) Clover-shaped
    d) Circular

10. How many orbitals are present in a d-subshell?

    a) 2
    b) 3
    c) 5
    d) 7

11. Which electron configuration corresponds to the element with atomic number 11?

    a) $1s^2\ 2s^2\ 2p^6$
    b) $1s^2\ 2s^2\ 2p^6\ 3s^1$
    c) $1s^2\ 2s^2\ 2p^6\ 3p^1$
    d) $1s^2\ 2s^2\ 2p^6\ 3s^2$

12. Which of the following elements has a partially filled d-subshell in its ground state?

    a) Neon
    b) Carbon
    c) Iron
    d) Potassium

13. Which of the following is an exception to the predicted electron configuration due to increased stability?

    a) Carbon
    b) Chromium
    c) Nitrogen
    d) Oxygen

14. The first ionization energy is the energy required to:

    a) Add an electron to a neutral atom
    b) Remove an electron from a neutral atom
    c) Split the nucleus of an atom
    d) Create an ion with multiple charges

15. Which principle explains that no two electrons in an atom can have the same set of four quantum numbers?

    a) Hund's Rule
    b) Pauli Exclusion Principle
    c) Heisenberg Principle
    d) Dalton's Law

16. What is the correct electron configuration for a neutral atom of sulfur (atomic number 16)?

    a) $1s^2\ 2s^2\ 2p^6\ 3s^2\ 3p^4$
    b) $1s^2\ 2s^2\ 2p^6\ 3s^1\ 3p^5$
    c) $1s^2\ 2s^2\ 2p^6\ 3s^2\ 3p^3$
    d) $1s^2\ 2s^2\ 2p^6\ 3s^2\ 3p^6$

17. In which period of the periodic table would you find an element with the electron configuration [Ne] $3s^2\ 3p^1$?

    a) Period 1
    b) Period 2
    c) Period 3
    d) Period 4

18. Which of the following has the greatest electronegativity?

    a) Lithium
    b) Sodium
    c) Chlorine
    d) Fluorine

19. What happens to atomic size as you move down a group in the periodic table?

    a) It increases
    b) It decreases
    c) It stays the same
    d) It first increases, then decreases

20. Which subshell fills after the 4s subshell according to the Aufbau principle?

    a) 3d
    b) 4p
    c) 5s
    d) 4d

21. Which type of bond involves the equal sharing of electrons between two atoms?

    a) Polar covalent bond
    b) Nonpolar covalent bond
    c) Ionic bond
    d) Hydrogen bond

22. What type of bond is formed between sodium (Na) and chlorine (Cl) in NaCl?

    a) Nonpolar covalent bond
    b) Polar covalent bond
    c) Ionic bond
    d) Metallic bond

23. Which of the following compounds is most likely to have a polar covalent bond?

    a) H2
    b) O2
    c) CO2
    d) H2O

24. Which of the following is true about ionic compounds?

    a) They have low melting points
    b) They conduct electricity in their solid state
    c) They are generally soluble in water
    d) They form between two nonmetals

25. The octet rule states that atoms tend to bond in such a way that they:

    a) Lose all their electrons
    b) Gain or share eight valence electrons
    c) Attain the configuration of noble gases
    d) Have six electrons in their outer shell

26. Which of the following molecules contains a double covalent bond?

    a) CH4
    b) O2

c) N2
d) HCl

27. In which bond is there the greatest difference in electronegativity between the atoms?

   a) H-H
   b) H-F
   c) Cl-Cl
   d) H-O

28. Which of the following statements about ionic bonds is true?

   a) They form between atoms with similar electronegativities
   b) They involve the transfer of electrons
   c) They only form between nonmetals
   d) They always result in nonpolar molecules

29. Which molecule has the longest bond length?

   a) H2
   b) O2
   c) N2
   d) Cl2

30. Which of the following best describes the bond between carbon and hydrogen in methane (CH4)?

   a) Polar covalent
   b) Nonpolar covalent
   c) Ionic
   d) Metallic

31. What type of bond is present in a molecule of carbon dioxide (CO2)?

   a) Single covalent bonds
   b) Double covalent bonds
   c) Ionic bonds
   d) Triple covalent bonds

32. Which compound is most likely to form hydrogen bonds with water?

   a) CH4
   b) NH3
   c) NaCl
   d) CO2

33. Which of the following bonds has the highest bond energy?

   a) Single bond
   b) Double bond
   c) Triple bond
   d) Ionic bond

34. In a molecule of nitrogen (N2), the nitrogen atoms are held together by:

   a) A single covalent bond
   b) A double covalent bond
   c) A triple covalent bond
   d) Ionic bonds

35. Which of the following statements about covalent bonds is false?

   a) They can involve the sharing of two, four, or six electrons
   b) They form between atoms of different electronegativities
   c) They can be polar or nonpolar
   d) They are usually formed between nonmetal atoms

36. Which of the following is a property of covalent compounds?

   a) High melting point
   b) High electrical conductivity in solid state
   c) Poor electrical conductivity in water
   d) Typically soluble in water

37. What type of bond is most likely to form between two elements with a large difference in electronegativity?

   a) Nonpolar covalent
   b) Polar covalent
   c) Ionic
   d) Metallic

38. What happens to the bond length as the bond order increases from single to double to triple?

   a) Bond length increases
   b) Bond length decreases
   c) Bond length remains the same
   d) Bond length is not affected by bond order

39. Which of the following is most likely to form an ionic compound?

   a) Carbon and hydrogen

b) Magnesium and oxygen
c) Nitrogen and oxygen
d) Hydrogen and chlorine

40. Which of the following bonds has the lowest polarity?

    a) C-H
    b) H-F
    c) H-Cl
    d) O-H

41. Which of the following states of matter has a definite shape and volume?

    a) Solid
    b) Liquid
    c) Gas
    d) Plasma

42. In which state of matter do particles have the highest kinetic energy?

    a) Solid
    b) Liquid
    c) Gas
    d) Plasma

43. What is the term used to describe the resistance of a liquid to flow?

    a) Surface tension
    b) Viscosity
    c) Density
    d) Pressure

44. Which law relates pressure, volume, temperature, and the number of moles for an ideal gas?

    a) Boyle's Law
    b) Charles's Law
    c) Ideal Gas Law
    d) Dalton's Law

45. What type of intermolecular force is present between nonpolar molecules?

    a) Hydrogen bonding
    b) Dipole-dipole interaction
    c) London dispersion forces
    d) Ionic bonding

46. Which of the following is true about the particles in a solid?

    a) They move freely past each other.
    b) They vibrate in fixed positions.
    c) They have a negligible volume.
    d) They have the highest kinetic energy.

47. What happens to the boiling point of a liquid at higher altitudes where the atmospheric pressure is lower?

    a) The boiling point increases.
    b) The boiling point decreases.
    c) The boiling point remains constant.
    d) The liquid does not boil.

48. Which of the following best describes a crystalline solid?

    a) Particles arranged randomly
    b) A definite melting point
    c) Lack of long-range order
    d) Soft and malleable structure

49. The temperature at which a solid turns into a liquid is known as the:

    a) Boiling point
    b) Melting point
    c) Freezing point
    d) Sublimation point

50. Which property of gases allows them to fill any container, regardless of the container's shape?

    a) Surface tension
    b) Compressibility
    c) Expansibility
    d) Viscosity

51. What is the pressure exerted by a gas in a closed container due to?

    a) Intermolecular forces
    b) Collisions of gas molecules with the container walls
    c) The weight of gas molecules
    d) Temperature of the gas

52. Which of the following is NOT an intermolecular force?

    a) Ionic bonding

b) Hydrogen bonding
c) Dipole-dipole interaction
d) London dispersion forces

53. How do gas molecules behave according to the kinetic molecular theory?

    a) They attract each other strongly.
    b) They have negligible volume.
    c) They move in straight lines without colliding.
    d) Their average kinetic energy is independent of temperature.

54. Which phase change occurs when a gas turns into a liquid?

    a) Melting
    b) Freezing
    c) Condensation
    d) Sublimation

55. What is the unit of pressure commonly used in the ideal gas law?

    a) Joules
    b) Pascals
    c) Moles
    d) Meters

56. Which statement is true about liquids compared to solids?

    a) Liquids have a definite shape.
    b) Liquids have fixed particles in a rigid structure.
    c) Liquids can flow and take the shape of their container.
    d) Liquids are incompressible and have a definite volume.

57. The volume of a gas is inversely proportional to its pressure at constant temperature, according to:

    a) Charles's Law
    b) Boyle's Law
    c) Dalton's Law
    d) Avogadro's Law

58. Which type of solid has no definite crystalline structure?

    a) Amorphous solid
    b) Ionic solid
    c) Covalent solid
    d) Crystalline solid

59. Which force is responsible for the high boiling point of water compared to other similar-sized molecules?

   a) Dipole-dipole forces
   b) Hydrogen bonding
   c) London dispersion forces
   d) Van der Waals forces

60. When a solid change directly into a gas without passing through the liquid state, the process is called:

   a) Freezing
   b) Melting
   c) Vaporization
   d) Sublimation

61. Which of the following statements best describes the First Law of Thermodynamics?

   a) Energy can be created and destroyed.
   b) The total energy of an isolated system is constant.
   c) Entropy always increases in an isolated system.
   d) Heat always flows from cold to hot bodies.

62. Which term refers to the measure of disorder or randomness in a system?

   a) Enthalpy
   b) Entropy
   c) Work
   d) Heat

63. In the equation $\Delta U = Q - W$, what does W represent?

   a) Heat transferred to the system
   b) Work done by the system
   c) Work done on the system
   d) Change in internal energy

64. Which of the following is a consequence of the Second Law of Thermodynamics?

   a) Heat flows from cold to hot bodies.
   b) All energy can be converted into work.
   c) Energy transformations are 100% efficient.
   d) The entropy of the universe always increases.

65. Which process does the Second Law of Thermodynamics say is irreversible?

    a) Heat flow from hot to cold objects
    b) Compression of a gas
    c) Expansion of a gas
    d) Spontaneous heat flow from cold to hot objects

66. Which equation represents the efficiency of a heat engine?

    a) $N = 1 - \dfrac{T cold}{T hot}$

    b) $N = 1 - \dfrac{T cold}{T hot}$

    c) $N = \dfrac{T cold}{T hot}$

    d) $N = \dfrac{T cold}{T hot} - 1$

67. What is the unit of entropy?

    a) Joules per Kelvin (J/K)
    b) Joules (J)
    c) Kelvin (K)
    d) Watts (W)

68. Which of the following is true for an isolated system?

    a) The system can exchange energy but not matter.
    b) The system can exchange both energy and matter.
    c) The system cannot exchange energy or matter.
    d) The system exchanges only heat with its surroundings.

69. In thermodynamics, what is meant by a "reversible process"?

    a) A process where the system and surroundings return to their original states.
    b) A process that occurs without the transfer of heat.
    c) A process that only increases entropy.
    d) A process that involves no work.

70. What does the First Law of Thermodynamics suggest about energy in a closed system?

   a) Energy is constantly created and destroyed.
   b) Energy remains constant but can change forms.
   c) Heat and work are always equal.
   d) Entropy decreases in a closed system.

71. What does the symbol Q typically represent in thermodynamic equations?

   a) Pressure
   b) Volume
   c) Work
   d) Heat

72. Which of the following is a valid interpretation of the Second Law of Thermodynamics?

   a) Energy can be destroyed in isolated systems.
   b) It is impossible to convert all heat into work.
   c) The entropy of a system always decreases.

D) Heat flows from cold to hot spontaneously.

73. What is the significance of the term "enthalpy" in thermodynamics?

   a) It measures the total energy of a system.
   b) It is a measure of work done by a system.
   c) It represents the heat content at constant pressure.
   d) It represents the internal energy change of a system.

74. What type of system allows for the exchange of energy but not matter?

   a) Open system
   b) Closed system
   c) Isolated system
   d) Adiabatic system

75. Which of the following does the Second Law of Thermodynamics predict about heat engines?

   a) Heat engines can be 100% efficient.
   b) All heat added to the engine is converted to work.
   c) Some energy is always lost as heat.
   d) Heat engines do not obey the laws of thermodynamics.

76. Which of the following is true at equilibrium in a chemical reaction?

    a) The concentration of reactants is higher than the concentration of products.
    b) The concentration of products is higher than the concentration of reactants.
    c) The rates of the forward and reverse reactions are equal.
    d) The forward reaction has stopped completely.

77. The equilibrium constant for a reaction is expressed as which of the following?

    a) The ratio of the concentration of reactants to products.
    b) The ratio of the concentration of products to reactants.
    c) The sum of the concentrations of reactants and products.

D) The difference between the concentrations of products and reactants.

78. In the equilibrium expression $K = \frac{[C]^c[D]^d}{[A]^a[B]^b}$, what does [A] represent?

    a) The initial concentration of reactants.
    b) The equilibrium concentration of product A.
    c) The equilibrium concentration of reactant A.
    d) The rate of the reverse reaction.

79. If the equilibrium constant K is less than 1, which statement is correct?

    a) The forward reaction is favored.
    b) The reverse reaction is favored.
    c) The reaction is at equilibrium.
    d) The reaction will not occur.

80. According to Le Chatelier's Principle, how does a system at equilibrium respond to an increase in the concentration of a reactant?

    a) The equilibrium shifts to the left to consume more products.
    b) The equilibrium shifts to the right to produce more products.
    c) The equilibrium remains unchanged.
    d) The reaction stops completely.

81. In a gaseous reaction, how will an increase in pressure affect a system where there are more moles of gas on the reactant side?

    a) The equilibrium will shift toward the products.
    b) The equilibrium will shift toward the reactants.
    c) The equilibrium will remain unchanged.
    d) The reaction rate will decrease.

82. In the reaction $N_2(g) + 3H_2(g) \rightleftharpoons 2NH_3(g)$, how will a decrease in pressure affect the system?

   a) The equilibrium will shift to the left, toward the reactants.
   b) The equilibrium will shift to the right, toward the products.
   c) The equilibrium will remain unchanged.
   d) The reaction will stop.

83. If a reaction is endothermic, how does an increase in temperature affect the equilibrium?

   a) The equilibrium shifts toward the reactants.
   b) The equilibrium shifts toward the products.
   c) The equilibrium remains unchanged.
   d) The rate of the reverse reaction decreases.

84. Which of the following changes will not affect the position of equilibrium in a chemical reaction?

   a) Changing the concentration of a reactant.
   b) Changing the pressure of a gaseous system.
   c) Adding a catalyst.
   d) Changing the temperature.

85. In an exothermic reaction, what is the effect of lowering the temperature on the equilibrium?

   a) The equilibrium shifts toward the products.
   b) The equilibrium shifts toward the reactants.
   c) The equilibrium remains unchanged.
   d) The forward reaction stops.

86. 11. If the equilibrium constant K for a reaction increases with temperature, what type of reaction is it?

   a) Exothermic.
   b) Endothermic.
   c) Both exothermic and endothermic.
   d) Neither exothermic nor endothermic.

87. What happens to the equilibrium when a product is removed from the system?

   a) The equilibrium shifts to the left to produce more reactants.
   b) The equilibrium shifts to the right to produce more products.
   c) The equilibrium remains unchanged.
   d) The forward and reverse reactions stop.

88. How does adding an inert gas to a gaseous reaction mixture at constant volume affect the equilibrium?

   a) The equilibrium shifts toward the products.
   b) The equilibrium shifts toward the reactants.
   c) The equilibrium remains unchanged.
   d) The reaction rate increases.

89. In the reaction $2SO_2(g) + O_2(g) \rightleftharpoons 2SO_3(g)$, (g), increasing the concentration of SO_2 will have what effect?

   a) The equilibrium will shift to the right.
   b) The equilibrium will shift to the left.
   c) The equilibrium will remain unchanged.
   d) The reverse reaction will stop.

90. Which of the following correctly describes the role of a catalyst in a chemical reaction?

   a) It increases the equilibrium constant.
   b) It shifts the equilibrium toward the reactants.
   c) It speeds up both the forward and reverse reactions.
   d) It increases the yield of products at equilibrium.

91. Which of the following is a property of a strong acid?
   a) It fully dissociates in water.
   b) It has a high pKa value.
   c) It resists changes in pH.
   d) It is only slightly ionized in solution.

92. What is the pH of a solution with a hydrogen ion concentration of 1×10^{-3} M?
   a) 1
   b) 3
   c) 7
   d) 9

93. Which of the following substances can act as a buffer?
   a) HCl and NaCl
   b) CH_3COOH and CH_3COONa
   c) H_2SO_4 and NaOH
   d) NaCl and NaOH

94. The pH of a solution is 4. What is the hydrogen ion concentration [H^+]?
   a) 1×10^{-1} M
   b) 1×10^{-2} M
   c) 1×10^{-4} M
   d) 1×10^{-6} M

95. Which of the following describes a solution with a pH of 9?
    a) Acidic
    b) Neutral
    c) Basic
    d) Highly acidic
96. What happens when a small amount of a strong acid is added to a buffer solution?
    a) The pH changes drastically.
    b) The buffer neutralizes the acid, and the pH changes slightly.
    c) The pH increases significantly.
    d) The buffer is destroyed, and the solution becomes neutral.
97. If the pKa of an acid is 5, at what pH will the acid be 50% dissociated?
    a) 2
    b) 5
    c) 7
    d) 10
98. What is the function of a buffer system in biological fluids?
    a) To maintain a constant temperature.
    b) To prevent fluctuations in ionic concentration.
    c) To resist changes in pH.
    d) To facilitate acid dissociation.
99. A solution has a pH of 2. What can be inferred about the solution?
    a) It is basic.
    b) It is neutral.
    c) It is acidic.
    d) It has a high pKa.
100. Which equation relates pH, pKa, and the concentrations of the acid and its conjugate base?
    a) Henderson-Hasselbalch equation
    b) Boyle's law
    c) Ideal gas law
    d) Van der Waals equation
101. What is the pKa of a weak acid if the pH of a solution where $[A^-] = [HA]$ is 7?
    a) 1
    b) 4
    c) 7
    d) 10
102. Which of the following pairs would form a buffer solution?
    a) NaOH and NaCl
    b) HCl and H_2O
    c) NH_4Cl and NH_3
    d) H_2SO_4 and HNO_3
103. Which of the following is true for a weak base?
    a) It has a low pKa.
    b) It fully dissociates in solution.
    c) It partially accepts protons in water.

d) It does not affect pH.
104. What would happen to the pH of a buffer solution if a small amount of strong base is added?
   a) The pH would decrease significantly.
   b) The pH would remain constant.
   c) The pH would increase slightly.
   d) The buffer would be destroyed immediately.
105. What is the main role of the bicarbonate buffer system in the human body?
   a) To regulate oxygen transport.
   b) To maintain a constant pH in blood.
   c) To promote glucose metabolism.
   d) To regulate electrolyte balance

Answers & Explanations

1. b) Proton – Protons are positively charged particles located in the nucleus of an atom, along with neutrons. Electrons, on the other hand, are found in orbitals surrounding the nucleus.
2. c) Neutral – Neutrons carry no charge. They are neutral particles that exist in the nucleus, where they contribute to the atom's mass but not its charge.
3. b) Protons – The atomic number of an element is defined by the number of protons in its nucleus. This number is unique to each element and determines its identity.
4. c) Aufbau Principle – The Aufbau principle states that electrons fill the lowest energy orbitals first before occupying higher energy ones, helping define the electron configuration of atoms.
5. c) 8 – The second energy level (n=2) consists of the 2s and 2p sublevels, which together can hold a maximum of 8 electrons (2 in the 2s orbital and 6 in the 2p orbitals).
6. a) $1s^2\ 2s^2\ 2p^4$ – Oxygen has 8 electrons, and its electron configuration shows 2 electrons in the 1s orbital, 2 electrons in the 2s orbital, and 4 electrons in the 2p orbital.
7. c) Fluorine – Atomic radius decreases across a period from left to right due to increasing nuclear charge. Fluorine, being further to the right in the period, has a smaller atomic radius compared to sodium, magnesium, and chlorine.
8. d) Ionization energy increases – Across a period, the number of protons increases, pulling electrons closer and making them harder to remove. Thus, ionization energy increases from left to right across a period.
9. b) Dumbbell-shaped – p-orbitals have a dumbbell shape. Each p sublevel contains three p-orbitals, oriented at 90 degrees to each other.
10. c) 5 – A d-subshell contains 5 orbitals. Each orbital can hold 2 electrons, allowing the d-subshell to hold a total of 10 electrons.
11. b) $1s^2\ 2s^2\ 2p^6\ 3s^1$ – Sodium (atomic number 11) has 11 electrons. Its electron configuration fills the 1s, 2s, and 2p orbitals, followed by a single electron in the 3s orbital.
12. c) Iron – Iron (Fe), a transition metal, has a partially filled d-subshell. Its electron configuration includes electrons in the 3d sublevel.
13. b) Chromium – Chromium (Cr) is an exception to the expected electron configuration. Instead of following the expected pattern, one electron from the 4s orbital is promoted to the 3d orbital for increased stability: $[Ar]3d^5 4s^1$
14. b) Remove an electron from a neutral atom – The first ionization energy is the energy required to remove one electron from a neutral atom, resulting in the formation of a positively charged ion.
15. b) Pauli Exclusion Principle – The Pauli Exclusion Principle states that no two electrons in an atom can have the same four quantum numbers, meaning each orbital can hold a maximum of two electrons with opposite spins.
16. a) $1s^2\ 2s^2\ 2p^6\ 3s^2\ 3p^4$ – Sulfur (atomic number 16) has 16 electrons. Its electron configuration shows full 1s, 2s, and 2p sublevels, and the 3s sublevel with 2 electrons and 3p sublevel with 4 electrons.
17. c) Period 3 – The electron configuration [Ne] $3s^2\ 3p^1$ corresponds to an element in the third period of the periodic table, since it has electrons in the 3rd energy level.
18. d) Fluorine – Fluorine has the highest electronegativity of all elements because of its small size and high nuclear charge, making it highly effective at attracting electrons.
19. a) It increases – Atomic size increases down a group because additional electron shells are added, increasing the distance between the nucleus and the outermost electrons.

20. a) 3d – After filling the 4s orbital, the next subshell to fill is 3d according to the Aufbau principle
21. B) Nonpolar covalent bond - In a nonpolar covalent bond, electrons are shared equally between the atoms because they have similar electronegativity.
22. C) Ionic bond - In sodium chloride (NaCl), sodium donates an electron to chlorine, forming an ionic bond due to the transfer of electrons.
23. D) H2O - Water (H2O) is polar because the oxygen atom is more electronegative than the hydrogen atoms, leading to an unequal sharing of electrons.
24. C) They are generally soluble in water - Ionic compounds tend to dissolve in polar solvents like water due to the interaction between ions and water molecules.
25. B) Gain or share eight valence electrons - According to the octet rule, atoms bond to complete their outer electron shell with eight electrons.
26. B) O2 - In a molecule of oxygen (O2), two oxygen atoms share two pairs of electrons, forming a double bond.
27. B) H-F - The electronegativity difference between hydrogen and fluorine is large, making the bond highly polar.
28. B) They involve the transfer of electrons - Ionic bonds form when one atom transfers electrons to another, resulting in the formation of ions.
29. D) Cl2 - The bond between two chlorine atoms (Cl2) is longer because they are larger atoms compared to hydrogen, oxygen, and nitrogen.
30. B) Nonpolar covalent - The bond between carbon and hydrogen in methane (CH4) is nonpolar covalent because the electronegativity difference is minimal.
31. B) Double covalent bonds - In carbon dioxide (CO2), each oxygen atom forms a double bond with the carbon atom, involving the sharing of two pairs of electrons.
32. B) NH3 - Ammonia (NH3) can form hydrogen bonds with water due to its lone pair on nitrogen and the polar nature of the N-H bonds.
33. C) Triple bond - A triple bond has the highest bond energy because it involves the sharing of three pairs of electrons, making it stronger than single or double bonds.
34. C) A triple covalent bond - In nitrogen gas (N2), the two nitrogen atoms share three pairs of electrons, forming a triple covalent bond.
35. B) They form between atoms of different electronegativities - Covalent bonds typically form between atoms with similar electronegativities, not significantly different ones, which would form ionic bonds.
36. C) Poor electrical conductivity in water - Covalent compounds do not conduct electricity in water because they do not form ions, unlike ionic compounds.
37. C) Ionic - A large difference in electronegativity between two atoms typically results in the formation of an ionic bond, where electrons are transferred.
38. B) Bond length decreases - As bond order increases (from single to triple bonds), the bond length decreases because the atoms are held more tightly together.
39. B) Magnesium and oxygen - Magnesium (a metal) and oxygen (a nonmetal) are likely to form an ionic bond due to the transfer of electrons from magnesium to oxygen.
40. A) C-H - The C-H bond has the lowest polarity because carbon and hydrogen have similar electronegativities, making the bond nearly nonpolar.

41. a) Solid. – Solids have a definite shape and volume because the particles are closely packed and arranged in a fixed structure.
42. c) Gas. – In the gaseous state, particles have the highest kinetic energy because they move rapidly and freely in all directions.
43. b) Viscosity. – Viscosity refers to a liquid's resistance to flow, which depends on the strength of intermolecular forces and temperature.
44. c) Ideal Gas Law. – The ideal gas law, PV=nRT, relates pressure (P), volume (V), temperature (T), and the number of moles (n) of a gas.
45. c) London dispersion forces. – London dispersion forces are weak intermolecular forces present between nonpolar molecules due to temporary dipoles.
46. b) They vibrate in fixed positions. – In solids, particles vibrate but remain in fixed positions due to strong intermolecular forces.
47. b) The boiling point decreases. – At higher altitudes, the atmospheric pressure is lower, so less energy is needed for the liquid to reach its boiling point.
48. b) A definite melting points. – Crystalline solids have a well-ordered structure, which gives them a sharp, defined melting point.
49. b) Melting point. – The melting point is the temperature at which a solid turn into a liquid as the particles gain enough energy to move freely.
50. c) Expansibility. – Gases expand to fill any container because the particles move freely and have negligible intermolecular forces.
51. b) Collisions of gas molecules with the container walls. – Gas pressure results from collisions between the gas molecules and the walls of the container.
52. a) Ionic bonding. – Ionic bonding is not an intermolecular force; it is a strong chemical bond between ions, whereas intermolecular forces occur between molecules.
53. b) They have negligible volume. – According to the kinetic molecular theory, gas particles have negligible volume compared to the space they occupy.
54. c) Condensation. – Condensation is the process where a gas turns into a liquid when it loses energy and the particles slow down.
55. b) Pascals. – Pressure in the ideal gas law is typically measured in Pascals (Pa) or atmospheres (atm), depending on the system of units used.
56. c) Liquids can flow and take the shape of their container. – Liquids do not have a definite shape, but they have a definite volume and can flow to fit the container.
57. b) Boyle's Law. – Boyle's law states that the volume of a gas is inversely proportional to its pressure when temperature is constant.
58. a) Amorphous solid. – Amorphous solids lack a well-defined crystalline structure, which gives them unique properties compared to crystalline solids.
59. b) Hydrogen bonding. – Hydrogen bonding between water molecules results in a higher boiling point compared to other molecules of similar size.
60. d) Sublimation. – Sublimation is the phase change where a solid turns directly into a gas without passing through the liquid state, as seen in dry ice.
61. B. The total energy of an isolated system is constant. – The First Law of Thermodynamics states that energy cannot be created or destroyed, only transferred or converted. Therefore, the total energy of an isolated system remains constant.
62. B. Entropy. – Entropy is a measure of disorder or randomness in a system, and it tends to increase in natural processes according to the Second Law of Thermodynamics.

63. B. Work done by the system. – In the equation ΔU=Q−W, W represents the work done by the system, which decreases the system's internal energy.
64. D. The entropy of the universe always increases. – The Second Law of Thermodynamics states that the entropy of the universe tends to increase over time, reflecting a move towards disorder.
65. D. Spontaneous heat flow from cold to hot objects. – The Second Law of Thermodynamics implies that heat cannot spontaneously flow from a colder body to a hotter one; such processes are irreversible.
66. $N = 1 - \dfrac{T_{cold}}{T_{hot}}$. This equation represents the efficiency of a heat engine, where T_{cold} and T_{hot} are the temperatures of the cold and hot reservoirs, respectively.
67. A. Joules per Kelvin (J/K). – Entropy is measured in units of joules per kelvin (J/K), reflecting energy per degree of temperature.
68. C. The system cannot exchange energy or matter. – An isolated system is defined as one that does not exchange energy or matter with its surroundings.
69. A. A process where the system and surroundings return to their original states. – A reversible process is one that can be reversed, returning both the system and surroundings to their initial conditions, with no net change in entropy.
70. B. Energy remains constant but can change forms. – According to the First Law of Thermodynamics, energy is conserved in a closed system but can be transformed from one form (like heat) to another (like work).
71. D. Heat. – The symbol Q in thermodynamic equations typically represents heat transferred into or out of a system.
72. B. It is impossible to convert all heat into work. – The Second Law of Thermodynamics states that no process can be 100% efficient, as some energy will always be lost as waste heat.
73. C. It represents the heat content at constant pressure. – Enthalpy (H) is the measure of the total heat content of a system at constant pressure, which is used to analyze heat exchanges in chemical reactions.
74. B. Closed system. – A closed system allows energy to be exchanged with the surroundings but does not allow the transfer of matter.
75. C. Some energy is always lost as heat. – The Second Law of Thermodynamics predicts that heat engines are never 100% efficient because some energy will always be lost as unusable heat during the conversion process.
76. C. The rates of the forward and reverse reactions are equal.– At equilibrium, the rate of the forward reaction equals the rate of the reverse reaction, resulting in no net change in the concentrations of reactants and products.
77. B. The ratio of the concentration of products to reactants.– The equilibrium constant K is defined as the ratio of the concentrations of products to reactants, each raised to the power of their respective coefficients in the balanced chemical equation.
78. C. The equilibrium concentration of reactant A.– In the equilibrium expression, [A] refers to the concentration of reactant A at equilibrium.
79. B. The reverse reaction is favored.– When K<1, the reverse reaction is favored, meaning that at equilibrium, the concentration of reactants is greater than that of products.
80. B. The equilibrium shifts to the right to produce more products.– According to Le Chatelier's Principle, increasing the concentration of a reactant will shift the equilibrium to the right, favoring the forward reaction to produce more products.

81. A. The equilibrium will shift toward the products.– An increase in pressure will shift the equilibrium toward the side with fewer moles of gas. If there are more moles of gas on the reactant side, the equilibrium will shift toward the products.
82. A. The equilibrium will shift to the left, toward the reactants.– A decrease in pressure will favor the side with more moles of gas. Since there are more moles of gas on the reactant side in this reaction, the equilibrium will shift toward the reactants.
83. 8. B. The equilibrium shifts toward the products. – In an endothermic reaction, increasing the temperature adds heat, favoring the forward reaction and shifting the equilibrium toward the products.
84. C. Adding a catalyst.– A catalyst speeds up both the forward and reverse reactions equally but does not affect the position of the equilibrium.
85. A. The equilibrium shifts toward the products. – In an exothermic reaction, lowering the temperature removes heat, favoring the forward reaction and shifting the equilibrium toward the products.
86. B. Endothermic .– If the equilibrium constant K increases with temperature, it indicates that the reaction is endothermic, as higher temperatures favor the forward reaction in endothermic processes.
87. B. The equilibrium shifts to the right to produce more products. – Removing a product from the system will shift the equilibrium toward the right, favoring the forward reaction to produce more of the removed product.
88. C. The equilibrium remains unchanged. – Adding an inert gas at constant volume does not affect the equilibrium position, as it doesn't change the concentration of the reactants or products.
89. A. The equilibrium will shift to the right.– Increasing the concentration of SO_2 will shift the equilibrium to the right, producing more SO_3 to balance the disturbance according to Le Chatelier's Principle.
90. C. It speeds up both the forward and reverse reactions. – A catalyst lowers the activation energy for both the forward and reverse reactions, allowing the system to reach equilibrium faster without changing the position of the equilibrium.
91. A. It fully dissociates in water. – Strong acids completely dissociate into ions in aqueous solutions, releasing all their hydrogen ions (H^+), resulting in high conductivity and lower pH.
92. B. 3. – pH is calculated as the negative logarithm of the hydrogen ion concentration. A hydrogen ion concentration of 1×10^{-3} M corresponds to a pH of 3.
93. B. CH_3COOH and CH_3COONa. – A buffer is made of a weak acid and its conjugate base. Acetic acid (CH_3COOH) and sodium acetate (CH_3COONa) form a common buffer system.
94. C. 1×10^{-4} M. – The pH is the negative logarithm of the hydrogen ion concentration. A pH of 4 corresponds to an H^+ concentration of 1×10^{-4} M.
95. C. Basic. – A pH above 7 indicates a basic (alkaline) solution. pH 9 is considered weakly basic.
96. B. The buffer neutralizes the acid, and the pH changes slightly. – Buffers work by neutralizing small amounts of added acid or base, maintaining a relatively stable pH.
97. B. 5. – At the pKa, the concentration of the acid and its conjugate base is equal, meaning the acid is 50% dissociated. Therefore, at a pKa of 5, the pH is also 5.
98. C. To resist changes in pH. – Buffers maintain a stable pH in biological systems by neutralizing added acids or bases, essential for maintaining homeostasis.

99. C. It is acidic. – A pH of 2 indicates a high concentration of hydrogen ions (H⁺), making the solution strongly acidic.
100. A. Henderson-Hasselbalch equation. – This equation relates the pH, pKa, and the ratio of the concentration of the conjugate base ([A⁻]) to the weak acid ([HA]) in a buffer system.
101. C. 7. – When [A⁻] equals [HA], the pH is equal to the pKa. Therefore, if the pH is 7, the pKa must also be 7.
102. C. NH_4Cl and NH_3. – Ammonium chloride (NH_4Cl) and ammonia (NH_3) form a buffer system, as NH_4Cl is a weak acid (NH_4^+) and NH_3 is its conjugate base.
103. C. It partially accepts protons in water. – Weak bases only partially accept protons (H⁺) in solution, leading to partial ionization and a higher pH than strong bases.
104. C. The pH would increase slightly. – When a small amount of strong base is added to a buffer, the weak acid component neutralizes it, causing only a slight increase in pH.
105. B. To maintain a constant pH in blood. – The bicarbonate buffer system is critical for maintaining the pH of blood within the narrow range necessary for proper physiological function (7.35-7.45).

SECTION 4:
Organic Chemistry

Chapter 1: Structure, Nomenclature, and Properties of Organic Molecules

Organic molecules are compounds mainly made up of carbon atoms in combination with elements like hydrogen, oxygen, nitrogen, and others. The unique ability of carbon to form stable bonds with other carbon atoms, as well as with different elements, allows the creation of a vast array of organic compounds with diverse structures and properties.

Carbon Bonding in Organic Molecules

Carbon atoms are tetravalent, meaning they can form four covalent bonds. This bonding behavior leads to various structures such as chains, rings, and networks. Organic molecules can exist as straight chains, branched chains, or rings, and their three-dimensional arrangements define their chemical reactivity and physical properties.

1. The simplest organic molecules, called hydrocarbons, consist solely of carbon and hydrogen. These can be classified into several categories based on the type of bonding:
2. Alkanes: Contain only single bonds between carbon atoms.
3. Alkenes: Contain at least one double bond between carbon atoms.
4. Alkynes: Contain at least one triple bond between carbon atoms.

Each type of hydrocarbon has distinct properties due to the nature of the bonds between carbon atoms, affecting factors like reactivity and stability.

Nomenclature of Organic Molecules

The naming system for organic molecules is based on rules set by the International Union of Pure and Applied Chemistry (IUPAC). Proper nomenclature allows chemists to communicate clearly about the structure and composition of compounds. The IUPAC system follows specific steps:

1. Identify the Parent Chain: The longest continuous chain of carbon atoms in the molecule forms the base name (e.g., "meth-" for one carbon, "eth-" for two, "prop-" for three, and so on).
2. Identify Substituents: Groups attached to the parent chain are considered substituents, and their position on the chain is indicated by a number corresponding to the carbon atom to which they are attached.
3. Number the Carbon Chain: The carbon atoms in the parent chain are numbered in such a way that substituents receive the lowest possible numbers.
4. Name the Compound: Combine the names of the substituents with the base name of the parent chain, along with any prefixes (such as di-, tri-, etc.) indicating the number of identical substituents.

For example, "2-methylpropane" refers to a three-carbon alkane (propane) with a methyl group (-CH_3) attached to the second carbon atom.

Properties of Organic Molecules

Organic molecules display a wide range of physical and chemical properties. These properties are determined by factors like molecular structure, the nature of the bonds between atoms, and the presence of functional groups (specific groups of atoms that impart particular reactivity to a molecule).

- Physical Properties: These include boiling and melting points, solubility, and density. The molecular size, polarity, and intermolecular forces (such as hydrogen bonding and van der Waals forces) all contribute to these properties. For example, hydrocarbons with longer carbon chains generally have higher boiling points due to stronger van der Waals forces.
- Chemical Properties: The chemical reactivity of organic molecules is influenced by the types of bonds present and the functional groups. For instance, alkanes are relatively unreactive compared to alkenes and alkynes, which contain double and triple bonds that are more susceptible to chemical reactions like addition reactions.

Alkanes, Alkenes, Alkynes

Hydrocarbons are fundamental organic molecules consisting of only carbon and hydrogen atoms. They are categorized into three primary groups based on the types of bonds between carbon atoms: alkanes, alkenes, and alkynes. Each group exhibits distinct structural features and chemical behaviors, making them important building blocks in organic chemistry.

Alkanes

Alkanes, also known as saturated hydrocarbons, contain only single covalent bonds between carbon atoms. This means that each carbon atom is bonded to the maximum number of hydrogen atoms possible. The general formula for alkanes is C_nH_{2n+2}, where "n" represents the number of carbon atoms.

- Structure: Alkanes can exist as straight chains or branched chains. In straight-chain alkanes, the carbon atoms are arranged in a linear sequence, whereas branched alkanes have one or more carbon atoms attached to the main chain in a non-linear fashion.
- Nomenclature: The names of alkanes are derived from the number of carbon atoms in the longest chain, followed by the suffix "-ane." For example, methane (CH_4) is the simplest alkane with one carbon atom, and ethane (C_2H_6) has two.
- Properties: Alkanes are relatively non-polar molecules, which makes them insoluble in water but soluble in organic solvents. Their boiling points increase with the length of the carbon chain due to the increase in van der Waals forces. Chemically, alkanes are quite stable and exhibit low reactivity, making them suitable as fuels. They undergo combustion and halogenation reactions.

Alkenes

Alkenes are unsaturated hydrocarbons that contain at least one double bond between carbon atoms. The general formula for alkenes is C_nH_{2n}. The presence of a double bond gives alkenes distinct chemical properties compared to alkanes.

- Structure: The carbon atoms involved in the double bond are sp^2 hybridized, leading to a planar structure around the double bond. This planar geometry restricts rotation around the bond, giving rise to cis-trans (geometric) isomerism. In cis isomers, the substituents are on the same side of the double bond, while in trans isomers, they are on opposite sides.
- Nomenclature: Alkenes are named similarly to alkanes, but the suffix "-ene" is used to indicate the presence of a double bond. The position of the double bond is specified by

numbering the carbon chain from the end nearest the double bond. For example, "but-2-ene" refers to a four-carbon chain with a double bond between the second and third carbons.
- Properties: Alkenes are more reactive than alkanes due to the electron-rich nature of the double bond. This makes them susceptible to electrophilic addition reactions, where atoms or groups of atoms are added across the double bond. Alkenes are also involved in polymerization reactions, where small alkene molecules (monomers) link together to form long chains (polymers), as seen in the production of plastics like polyethylene.

Alkynes

Alkynes are another class of unsaturated hydrocarbons, distinguished by the presence of a triple bond between carbon atoms. The general formula for alkynes is C_nH_{2n-2}. The triple bond imparts unique structural and chemical properties to alkynes.
- Structure: The carbon atoms in a triple bond are sp hybridized, resulting in a linear geometry. This bond structure leads to a straight arrangement of atoms in alkynes, unlike the more flexible structures of alkanes and alkenes.
- Nomenclature: Alkynes are named similarly to alkanes and alkenes, with the suffix "-yne" indicating the presence of a triple bond. The position of the triple bond is also indicated by numbering the carbon chain from the nearest end. For example, "but-1-yne" refers to a four-carbon alkyne with a triple bond between the first and second carbon atoms.
- Properties: Alkynes are even more reactive than alkenes due to the presence of the triple bond. They participate in a variety of addition reactions, where atoms are added to the carbon atoms involved in the triple bond. Alkynes are also important in organic synthesis, serving as precursors to many other types of compounds.

Chapter 2: Stereochemistry

Stereochemistry is a branch of chemistry focused on the spatial arrangement of atoms in molecules. The 3D configuration of molecules plays a significant role in determining their physical and chemical properties, particularly in biological systems. Even molecules that share the same molecular formula can exhibit different behaviors if their atoms are arranged differently in space. This difference often becomes critical in organic chemistry and biochemistry, as seen in the biological activity of molecules like drugs, where one arrangement might be active and another inactive or even harmful.

Stereochemistry is mainly concerned with stereoisomers, molecules that have the same molecular formula and connectivity of atoms but differ in the arrangement of those atoms in space. The spatial arrangement can influence the molecule's interaction with biological systems, giving rise to distinct physical and chemical properties. Stereochemistry is important in reactions like addition, substitution, and elimination, where the stereochemical outcome can vary based on the reaction mechanism.

There are two primary types of stereoisomers: enantiomers and diastereomers. Enantiomers are stereoisomers that are non-superimposable mirror images of each other, while diastereomers are not mirror images. The classification into these categories arises from the molecule's chiral centers and overall symmetry.

Chirality and Isomers

Chirality

Chirality is a key concept in stereochemistry. A molecule is said to be chiral if it cannot be superimposed on its mirror image. This non-superimposability is analogous to the difference between left and right hands; no matter how you orient them, your left hand cannot be placed on top of your right hand to perfectly match it. In chemistry, this asymmetry arises when a carbon atom (often referred to as a chiral center) is bonded to four different substituents. This configuration leads to two distinct molecules that are mirror images of each other, known as enantiomers.

Chiral molecules exhibit optical activity, meaning they rotate plane-polarized light. Each enantiomer rotates light in opposite directions: one rotates light to the right (dextrorotatory, denoted as "+"), and the other to the left (levorotatory, denoted as "−"). The magnitude of this rotation is measured using a polarimeter. In many biological systems, chirality is critical. Enzymes, receptors, and other biological molecules are chiral, and their interactions with other chiral molecules, such as drugs, can differ dramatically depending on the enantiomer involved.

For example, the drug thalidomide is a famous case where chirality played a crucial role. One enantiomer was effective for morning sickness in pregnant women, while the other caused severe birth defects. This case highlights the importance of understanding and controlling chirality in pharmaceutical development.

Isomers
Isomers are compounds with the same molecular formula but different structural arrangements of atoms. Isomers are classified into two main types: structural isomers and stereoisomers.
- Structural Isomers: These differ in the connectivity of atoms, meaning that the atoms are linked in different sequences. Structural isomers include chain isomers, position isomers, and functional group isomers.
- Stereoisomers: As mentioned earlier, stereoisomers have the same connectivity of atoms but differ in their spatial arrangement. There are two primary types of stereoisomers:
  - Enantiomers: These are non-superimposable mirror images of each other. They are chiral and have opposite configurations at every chiral center.
  - Diastereomers: Unlike enantiomers, diastereomers are not mirror images of each other. Diastereomers occur when there are two or more stereocenters in a molecule, and the configuration at one or more of these centers differs between the isomers, but not all.

Within diastereomers, we also encounter geometric isomers, which arise from restricted rotation around a bond, usually in alkenes or cyclic compounds. For example, in alkenes, we can have cis and trans isomers depending on the relative positions of substituents around the double bond. In cyclic compounds, cis and trans refer to the positioning of substituents relative to the ring structure.

Enantiomers
Enantiomers are characterized by their chirality, as discussed earlier. They have identical physical properties (such as melting point and boiling point) in an achiral environment but differ in the way they interact with other chiral entities, including polarized light. The biological effects of enantiomers can vary significantly because biological systems are chiral by nature. A classic example is the interaction of chiral drugs with enzymes and receptors, where one enantiomer may have a therapeutic effect, while the other may have no effect or cause adverse reactions.

Diastereomers
Diastereomers, unlike enantiomers, have different physical properties, such as melting points, boiling points, and solubilities. This makes it easier to separate diastereomers using conventional techniques like distillation or recrystallization. They also differ in their chemical reactivity, making them distinguishable in various chemical reactions. Diastereomers are common in compounds with multiple stereocenters, and the complexity of their behavior adds to the importance of stereochemistry in organic synthesis.

An example of diastereomers is the relationship between glucose and galactose. Both are hexoses with the same molecular formula, but they differ in the spatial arrangement of atoms at a single chiral center, making them diastereomers. These subtle differences in structure lead to their unique properties and roles in metabolism.

Geometric Isomers
Geometric isomers are another category of stereoisomers, typically arising in molecules with restricted rotation, such as alkenes or cyclic compounds. In alkenes, geometric isomers result from the positioning of substituents around a double bond. When the substituents are on the same side of the double bond, the isomer is called cis; when they are on opposite sides, it is called trans.

For example, 2-butene exists in both cis and trans forms, with different physical properties like boiling points. The trans isomer is usually more stable due to reduced steric hindrance between substituents, leading to a lower energy configuration.

Importance of Stereochemistry in Biological Systems

Stereochemistry is crucial in understanding how molecules interact in biological systems. Enzymes, receptors, and other biomolecules are highly specific to the stereochemistry of the molecules they interact with. This specificity arises because biological macromolecules are chiral themselves. Therefore, the 3D arrangement of atoms in a molecule can influence its binding affinity, reactivity, and overall effect within a biological context.

For instance, the interactions between hormones and their receptors are often stereospecific. Only one enantiomer of a hormone might effectively bind to a receptor, triggering a biological response, while the other enantiomer could be inactive or even harmful. This specificity is also seen in neurotransmitters and their receptors, where small changes in stereochemistry can result in significant changes in biological activity.

Chapter 3: Reactivity and Mechanisms

Reactivity in organic chemistry refers to how readily a substance undergoes a chemical reaction, while a mechanism explains the step-by-step process through which this reaction occurs. Understanding reactivity and mechanisms is crucial in predicting how molecules interact in organic reactions. Several factors influence reactivity, such as the nature of the reactants, the type of bonds involved, and external conditions like temperature and solvents.

Factors Affecting Reactivity:

1. Electronegativity: Atoms with high electronegativity, such as oxygen and nitrogen, tend to withdraw electron density from neighboring atoms. This withdrawal creates partial charges that can make certain atoms or functional groups more reactive. For example, in carbonyl compounds (C=O), the oxygen is more electronegative than carbon, making the carbon electrophilic and susceptible to nucleophilic attack.
2. Resonance: Delocalization of electrons across a molecule through resonance can stabilize or destabilize certain intermediates or reactants, thus influencing reactivity. For instance, the stability of carbocations in electrophilic addition reactions can be enhanced by resonance, making the reaction proceed more efficiently.
3. Inductive Effects: The inductive effect is the transmission of charge through a chain of atoms in a molecule, affecting reactivity. Electron-withdrawing groups (like halogens) pull electron density away, making nearby carbon atoms more electrophilic, while electron-donating groups (like alkyl groups) push electron density toward a reactive center, reducing electrophilicity.
4. Steric Effects: The spatial arrangement of atoms can either hinder or enhance the reactivity of a molecule. Bulky groups near a reactive center can prevent access to attacking reagents, slowing down or preventing reactions. Steric hindrance is particularly relevant in substitution reactions where large substituents block nucleophiles.
5. Solvent Effects: Polar solvents, such as water or alcohols, stabilize charged intermediates (like carbocations or carbanions), facilitating reactions that proceed through ionic intermediates. Non-polar solvents, on the other hand, are often used in reactions where ionic intermediates are not stable or desired.

Reactivity is often described through reaction mechanisms, which are detailed descriptions of the steps a reaction takes. These mechanisms often involve breaking and forming bonds, leading to the formation of intermediates, which may be stabilized by various factors. Two common types of mechanisms in organic chemistry are electrophilic addition and nucleophilic substitution.

Electrophilic Addition

Electrophilic addition reactions occur when an electrophile, a species that seeks electrons, attacks a region of high electron density, such as a double or triple bond in alkenes or alkynes. These reactions are typical of compounds containing pi bonds, which are more reactive than sigma bonds due to their exposed nature.

Example: Addition of HBr to an Alkene

In the addition of hydrogen bromide (HBr) to an alkene, the alkene's double bond acts as a nucleophile (donates electrons), while the proton (H^+) from HBr serves as the electrophile (accepts electrons). The reaction proceeds as follows:

1. Step 1: Protonation of the Double Bond The double bond between the carbon atoms of the alkene is broken, and a bond is formed between one of the carbon atoms and the proton (H^+) from HBr. This creates a carbocation on the adjacent carbon atom. The location of the carbocation is influenced by Markovnikov's rule, which states that the more stable carbocation (usually the one attached to more alkyl groups) will form.
2. Step 2: Nucleophilic Attack by Bromide Once the carbocation is formed, the bromide ion (Br^-) acts as a nucleophile, attacking the positively charged carbon atom to form the final product, an alkyl halide.

The overall reaction can be summarized as:

$$RCH=CH_2 + HBr \rightarrow RCHBr\text{-}CH_3$$

This two-step mechanism is a hallmark of electrophilic addition reactions. The stability of the carbocation intermediate is crucial for determining the reaction rate, and the stereochemistry of the final product can also be affected if the alkene is asymmetric.

Factors Influencing Electrophilic Addition:
- Carbocation Stability: More substituted carbocations (those attached to more carbon atoms) are more stable due to hyperconjugation and inductive effects.
- Markovnikov's Rule: In unsymmetrical alkenes, the proton (H^+) adds to the carbon that is already bonded to more hydrogen atoms, ensuring that the more stable carbocation forms.
- Stereochemistry: The addition of the nucleophile can lead to stereoisomers depending on the configuration of the initial alkene.

Nucleophilic Substitution

Nucleophilic substitution reactions involve the replacement of a leaving group (a group capable of departing with an electron pair) by a nucleophile (a species that donates an electron pair). These reactions typically occur at saturated carbon atoms (sp^3 hybridized) and are classified as S_n1 or S_n2 mechanisms based on the reaction pathway.

S_n1 Mechanism (Unimolecular Nucleophilic Substitution):

The S_n1 mechanism involves a two-step process where the rate-determining step is the dissociation of the leaving group, leading to the formation of a carbocation intermediate.

1. Step 1: Formation of Carbocation The bond between the leaving group and the carbon atom breaks, resulting in the formation of a carbocation. This step is slow and determines the overall reaction rate.
2. Step 2: Nucleophilic Attack Once the carbocation forms, the nucleophile attacks the positively charged carbon atom, forming the final product. Since the carbocation is planar, the nucleophile can attack from either side, often leading to a racemic mixture of products if the carbon is chiral.

The S_n1 mechanism is favored by:
- Stable Carbocations: Tertiary carbocations are more stable and therefore more likely to undergo S_n1 reactions.
- Weak Nucleophiles: Since the rate-determining step is the formation of the carbocation, the nucleophile does not need to be particularly strong.
- Polar Solvents: Polar solvents stabilize the carbocation intermediate through solvation.

S_n2 Mechanism (Bimolecular Nucleophilic Substitution):

The S_n2 mechanism involves a one-step, concerted process where the nucleophile attacks the carbon atom at the same time that the leaving group departs. There is no formation of a carbocation intermediate.

1. Single Step: Nucleophilic Attack and Departure of Leaving Group The nucleophile attacks the carbon from the opposite side of the leaving group, pushing the leaving group off and inverting the configuration of the carbon atom (if chiral).

The S_n2 mechanism is favored by:
- Strong Nucleophiles: Since the nucleophile directly participates in the rate-determining step, stronger nucleophiles increase the reaction rate.
- Less Steric Hindrance: Primary carbons are more likely to undergo S_n2 reactions due to minimal steric hindrance, while tertiary carbons are too crowded for the nucleophile to effectively attack.
- Aprotic Solvents: Aprotic solvents do not solvate nucleophiles as strongly as polar solvents, leaving the nucleophile more reactive.

Chapter 4: Functional Groups

Functional groups are specific groups of atoms within molecules that have characteristic properties, regardless of the other atoms present in a molecule. These groups play a crucial role in determining the reactivity, polarity, and phase of organic compounds. Understanding functional groups is essential for predicting chemical reactions and behavior in organic chemistry.

1. Hydroxyl Group (-OH) The hydroxyl group is characteristic of alcohols. It consists of an oxygen atom bonded to a hydrogen atom. The presence of a hydroxyl group in a molecule increases its polarity, making alcohols soluble in water. Hydroxyl groups can participate in hydrogen bonding, contributing to higher boiling points of alcohols compared to hydrocarbons of similar molecular weight.
2. Carbonyl Group (C=O) The carbonyl group, a carbon atom double-bonded to an oxygen atom, is found in aldehydes, ketones, carboxylic acids, and their derivatives. The carbonyl group's polarity makes compounds containing it reactive with nucleophiles. Its reactivity plays a key role in organic synthesis and biochemical reactions.
3. Carboxyl Group (-COOH) The carboxyl group is a combination of a carbonyl group and a hydroxyl group attached to the same carbon atom. This functional group is characteristic of carboxylic acids, which are weak acids and can donate a proton (H+) in solution. Carboxylic acids form strong hydrogen bonds, leading to higher melting and boiling points.
4. Amino Group (-NH2) The amino group contains a nitrogen atom bonded to two hydrogen atoms. It is characteristic of amines and amino acids. The nitrogen atom has a lone pair of electrons, making it a basic functional group capable of accepting a proton. Amino groups can participate in hydrogen bonding, influencing solubility and reactivity.
5. Ester Group (-COOR) Esters are derived from carboxylic acids by replacing the hydroxyl group (-OH) with an alkoxy group (-OR). Esters are known for their pleasant fragrances and are widely used in flavors and perfumes. In biochemistry, esters are found in fats and oils, which are triesters of glycerol and fatty acids.
6. Amide Group (-CONH2) Amides are formed by the reaction of carboxylic acids with amines. The amide group consists of a carbonyl group bonded to a nitrogen atom. Amides are prevalent in proteins, where they form peptide bonds between amino acids. Amides have high boiling points due to hydrogen bonding and are less reactive than esters.

Alcohols, Aldehydes, Ketones, Carboxylic Acids

Alcohols, aldehydes, ketones, and carboxylic acids are four fundamental classes of organic compounds that contain distinct functional groups. Each class has its unique chemical properties and plays a vital role in various chemical reactions, biological processes, and industrial applications.

Alcohols

Alcohols are organic compounds that contain one or more hydroxyl groups (-OH) attached to a carbon atom. The general formula for alcohols is R-OH, where R represents an alkyl or aryl group.

1. Classification of Alcohols

Alcohols are classified based on the carbon to which the hydroxyl group is attached:
- Primary alcohols (1°) have the hydroxyl group attached to a carbon atom that is bonded to only one other carbon atom.
- Secondary alcohols (2°) have the hydroxyl group attached to a carbon atom bonded to two other carbons.
- Tertiary alcohols (3°) have the hydroxyl group attached to a carbon atom bonded to three other carbons.

2. Properties of Alcohols
- The presence of the hydroxyl group makes alcohols polar molecules capable of forming hydrogen bonds, resulting in higher boiling points than hydrocarbons of similar molecular weight. Alcohols are also miscible in water, especially lower molecular weight alcohols, due to their polarity.

3. Reactions of Alcohols

Alcohols undergo various reactions, including:
- Oxidation: Primary alcohols can be oxidized to aldehydes and further to carboxylic acids, while secondary alcohols are oxidized to ketones. Tertiary alcohols do not undergo oxidation easily.
- Dehydration: Alcohols can lose a molecule of water to form alkenes in the presence of a strong acid.
- Substitution: Alcohols can be converted to alkyl halides by substitution reactions.

Aldehydes

Aldehydes contain the carbonyl group (C=O) at the end of a carbon chain, with the general formula R-CHO, where R is an alkyl or aryl group. The carbonyl carbon is bonded to at least one hydrogen atom.

1. Properties of Aldehydes
- The carbonyl group makes aldehydes polar, giving them higher boiling points than hydrocarbons but lower than alcohols. Aldehydes are often reactive due to the partial positive charge on the carbonyl carbon, which is susceptible to nucleophilic attack.

2. Reactions of Aldehydes

Aldehydes undergo several important reactions:
- Oxidation: Aldehydes can be easily oxidized to carboxylic acids using mild oxidizing agents.
- Reduction: Aldehydes can be reduced to primary alcohols using reducing agents like sodium borohydride ($NaBH_4$) or lithium aluminum hydride ($LiAlH_4$).
- Nucleophilic addition: Aldehydes are reactive toward nucleophiles, undergoing addition reactions to form a variety of products, such as hemiacetals and acetals.

Ketones

Ketones, like aldehydes, contain the carbonyl group, but in ketones, the carbonyl carbon is bonded to two other carbon atoms. The general formula for ketones is R-CO-R', where R and R' are alkyl or aryl groups.

1. Properties of Ketones
   - The carbonyl group in ketones also makes them polar. Ketones have higher boiling points than alkanes but lower than alcohols. Unlike aldehydes, ketones are not as easily oxidized, making them relatively more stable.
2. Reactions of Ketones

Ketones undergo similar reactions to aldehydes, including:
   - Reduction: Ketones are reduced to secondary alcohols using reducing agents like NaBH4 or LiAlH4.
   - Nucleophilic addition: Ketones react with nucleophiles in addition reactions to form products like alcohols or derivatives such as imines and hydrazones.

Carboxylic Acids

Carboxylic acids contain both a carbonyl group and a hydroxyl group attached to the same carbon atom. The general formula for carboxylic acids is R-COOH, where R is an alkyl or aryl group.

1. Properties of Carboxylic Acids
   - Carboxylic acids are highly polar due to the presence of both the carbonyl and hydroxyl groups. They can form strong hydrogen bonds, which result in high boiling points. Carboxylic acids are weak acids, dissociating in water to produce H+ ions.
2. Reactions of Carboxylic Acids

Carboxylic acids participate in a wide variety of chemical reactions:
   - Reduction: Carboxylic acids can be reduced to primary alcohols using powerful reducing agents like LiAlH4.
   - Formation of esters: Carboxylic acids react with alcohols in the presence of an acid catalyst to form esters in a process known as esterification.
   - Acid-base reactions: Carboxylic acids can react with bases to form carboxylate salts.

Chapter 5: Aromatic Compounds

Aromatic compounds are a class of organic compounds that contain one or more benzene rings. These rings are characterized by a unique stability due to a phenomenon called aromaticity, which arises from the delocalization of electrons within the ring structure. Aromaticity is a key concept in understanding why benzene and other aromatic compounds behave differently from other unsaturated hydrocarbons like alkenes or alkynes. The term "aromatic" was originally used because many compounds in this category have distinct smells, although today the term refers specifically to their electronic structure.

Criteria for Aromaticity

Aromatic compounds must satisfy several criteria to be classified as aromatic. These include:
1. Cyclic Structure: The compound must be cyclic, meaning it forms a closed loop.
2. Planarity: The atoms in the ring must be arranged in a flat (planar) structure to allow for continuous overlapping of p-orbitals.
3. Conjugated System: The compound must have alternating single and double bonds, forming a conjugated system where p-orbitals can overlap.
4. Hückel's Rule: The compound must follow Hückel's rule, which states that for a molecule to be aromatic, it must have $4n+2$ pi electrons (where n is a non-negative integer). For example, benzene has 6 pi electrons, satisfying the $4n+2$ rule with $n=1$.

Structure of Benzene

Benzene, the simplest aromatic compound, consists of a six-membered carbon ring with alternating single and double bonds between carbon atoms. However, these bonds are not localized as single or double bonds. Instead, the electrons involved in the double bonds are delocalized, meaning they are shared equally across all six carbon atoms in the ring. This delocalization of electrons is what gives benzene its stability and makes it less reactive than typical alkenes.

Each carbon atom in benzene is sp^2 hybridized, meaning that three of its four valence electrons are involved in sigma bonds (two with neighboring carbon atoms and one with a hydrogen atom), while the fourth electron occupies a p-orbital. The overlap of the p-orbitals across the ring allows for the formation of a delocalized pi system.

Physical and Chemical Properties of Aromatic Compounds

Aromatic compounds are generally non-polar and hydrophobic. They tend to have higher boiling points compared to alkanes or alkenes of similar molecular weight because of the delocalized pi electrons that provide added stability. Benzene, for example, has a boiling point of 80°C, higher than many aliphatic hydrocarbons.

In terms of chemical reactivity, aromatic compounds do not undergo addition reactions typical of alkenes. Instead, they participate in substitution reactions. This difference is due to the stability of the aromatic ring, which would be lost if addition reactions occurred. The most common reactions for aromatic compounds are electrophilic aromatic substitution (EAS) reactions, where an electrophile replaces one of the hydrogen atoms attached to the ring.

Examples of Aromatic Compounds
Aside from benzene, other well-known aromatic compounds include:
- Toluene (Methylbenzene): A benzene ring with a methyl group attached.
- Naphthalene: Consists of two fused benzene rings.
- Phenol: A benzene ring with a hydroxyl (-OH) group attached.

These compounds display similar chemical properties due to their aromatic rings but can have variations based on their functional groups.

Benzene and Substitution Reactions

Benzene undergoes substitution reactions rather than addition reactions. This is due to the stability of its aromatic system, which is preserved in substitution reactions. The most common type of reaction that benzene and its derivatives undergo is Electrophilic Aromatic Substitution (EAS). In these reactions, an electrophile replaces a hydrogen atom on the aromatic ring.

Mechanism of Electrophilic Aromatic Substitution (EAS)

1. Generation of Electrophile: The reaction typically begins with the generation of a strong electrophile. This can be a cation or a neutral species that is electron-deficient and capable of accepting electron pairs from the aromatic ring. Common electrophiles include NO_2^+ (from nitric acid and sulfuric acid for nitration), SO_3H^+ (from sulfuric acid for sulfonation), and halogen cations ($Br^+ Cl^+$) in halogenation reactions.

2. Attack on the Electrophile: The benzene ring, which is rich in pi-electrons, donates electron density to the electrophile, forming a sigma complex (also called the arenium ion). This step temporarily breaks the aromaticity of the ring, creating a positively charged intermediate where one carbon atom is no longer sp^2 hybridized.

3. Restoration of Aromaticity: To restore the aromatic nature of the compound, a proton is removed from the carbon that formed the bond with the electrophile. This proton is typically abstracted by a base or counter-ion present in the reaction mixture. The result is the substitution of a hydrogen atom with the electrophile, while maintaining the stability of the aromatic ring.

Types of Electrophilic Aromatic Substitution

1. Nitration: In this reaction, a nitro group (NO_2) is introduced onto the benzene ring using a mixture of concentrated nitric acid and sulfuric acid. The electrophile in this case is NO_2^+, formed by protonation of nitric acid.

$$\text{Example: } C_6H_6 + HNO_3 \longrightarrow C_6H_5NO_2 + H_2O$$

2. Halogenation: Benzene reacts with halogens (like chlorine or bromine) in the presence of a Lewis acid catalyst (such as $AlCl_3$ or $FeBr_3$) to form halogen-substituted benzene derivatives.

$$\text{Example: } C_6H_6 + Br_2 \longrightarrow C_6H_5Br + HBr$$

3. Friedel-Crafts Alkylation: In this reaction, an alkyl group is added to the benzene ring using an alkyl halide and a Lewis acid catalyst. The electrophile is an alkyl cation generated by the reaction between the alkyl halide and the Lewis acid.

$$\text{Example: } C_6H_6 + RCl \longrightarrow C_6H_5R + HCl$$

4. Friedel-Crafts Acylation: Similar to alkylation, this reaction involves the addition of an acyl group (RCO-) to the benzene ring. The acylium ion (RCO$^+$) is the electrophile in this case.

$$\text{Example: } C_6H_6 + RCOCl \longrightarrow C_6H_5COR + HCl$$

5. Sulfonation: This reaction involves the introduction of a sulfonic acid group (SO$_3$H) onto the benzene ring. The electrophile is sulfur trioxide (SO$_3$) generated by the reaction of concentrated sulfuric acid.

$$\text{Example: } C_6H_6 + SO_3 \longrightarrow C_6H_5SO_3H$$

Substituent Effects on EAS

Substituents on a benzene ring can influence the rate and position of further substitution reactions. Groups that donate electron density to the ring, such as alkyl groups and hydroxyl groups, are activating and direct new electrophiles to the ortho and para positions. Electron-withdrawing groups, such as nitro and carboxyl groups, deactivate the ring and direct substitution to the meta position.

Chapter 6: Biological Molecules

Biological molecules are essential components that make up cells and are involved in the structure and function of living organisms. These molecules are primarily composed of carbon, hydrogen, oxygen, nitrogen, phosphorus, and sulfur. The major categories of biological molecules include carbohydrates, lipids, proteins, and nucleic acids. Each plays a unique role in cellular activities, from providing structural support to carrying out metabolic functions.

1. Carbohydrates: Carbohydrates are organic compounds made of carbon, hydrogen, and oxygen in a ratio of 1:2:1. They are classified into monosaccharides, disaccharides, and polysaccharides based on the number of sugar units. Monosaccharides like glucose and fructose serve as a primary energy source for cells, while polysaccharides such as starch and glycogen act as storage molecules. In addition to energy, carbohydrates are essential for cell recognition and signaling processes, especially through glycoproteins and glycolipids on cell surfaces.

2. Lipids: Lipids are hydrophobic molecules that include fats, oils, phospholipids, and steroids. They play a critical role in storing energy, forming cell membranes, and signaling. Triglycerides, composed of glycerol and three fatty acid chains, are the primary form of stored energy in adipose tissue. Phospholipids, with a hydrophilic head and two hydrophobic tails, form the bilayer of cell membranes, maintaining the integrity and functionality of cells. Steroids, such as cholesterol, are involved in cell membrane fluidity and serve as precursors for hormones like estrogen and testosterone.

3. Proteins: Proteins are composed of amino acids and are vital to the structure and function of cells. They act as enzymes, structural components, and signaling molecules. Proteins have diverse roles, including catalyzing metabolic reactions, providing cellular structure, and aiding in cell communication. The unique sequence of amino acids determines a protein's three-dimensional structure and, consequently, its function. For example, enzymes lower the activation energy of biochemical reactions, facilitating various cellular processes. Proteins like hemoglobin transport oxygen, while antibodies in the immune system help defend against pathogens.

4. Nucleic Acids: Nucleic acids, such as DNA and RNA, store and transmit genetic information. They consist of nucleotides, which are made up of a sugar, a phosphate group, and a nitrogenous base. DNA holds the genetic blueprint for protein synthesis, while RNA plays a role in translating this information into functional proteins. Nucleic acids are also involved in cellular regulation, such as gene expression and signal transduction.

Amino Acids and Nucleic Acids

Amino Acids

Amino acids are the building blocks of proteins, and they play a critical role in virtually all biological processes. There are 20 standard amino acids, each having an amino group (-NH2), a carboxyl group (-COOH), and a unique side chain (R-group) attached to a central carbon atom. The side chain determines the properties of each amino acid, such as whether it is hydrophobic, hydrophilic, acidic, or basic.

1. Classification of Amino Acids Amino acids can be classified based on the nature of their side chains:
   - Nonpolar (hydrophobic): These include amino acids like alanine, valine, leucine, and phenylalanine. They are typically found in the interior of proteins, away from water.
   - Polar (hydrophilic): Amino acids like serine, threonine, and glutamine are polar and tend to interact with water or form hydrogen bonds with other polar molecules.
   - Acidic and Basic: Acidic amino acids, such as aspartic acid and glutamic acid, have negatively charged side chains, while basic amino acids like lysine and arginine have positively charged side chains. These charges enable ionic interactions, which are important in protein folding and function.
2. Peptide Bonds and Protein Structure Amino acids link together through peptide bonds to form polypeptides. This bond occurs between the carboxyl group of one amino acid and the amino group of another, releasing a molecule of water in the process (a dehydration reaction). Proteins have four levels of structure:
   - Primary Structure: The linear sequence of amino acids in a polypeptide chain.
   - Secondary Structure: Local folding patterns, such as alpha-helices and beta-sheets, stabilized by hydrogen bonds.
   - Tertiary Structure: The three-dimensional structure of a single polypeptide, formed by interactions between side chains.
   - Quaternary Structure: The assembly of multiple polypeptide subunits into a functional protein complex.
3. Functions of Amino Acids Amino acids are not only essential for building proteins but also play other critical roles:
   - Neurotransmitters: Some amino acids, such as glutamate and glycine, act as neurotransmitters in the nervous system, transmitting signals between nerve cells.
   - Metabolic Precursors: Amino acids are precursors to various biomolecules, including hormones (e.g., thyroxine derived from tyrosine) and nucleotides (e.g., purines and pyrimidines from glycine and aspartate).
   - Energy Source: During periods of fasting or intense exercise, amino acids can be broken down and used as an energy source via gluconeogenesis, where amino acids are converted into glucose.

Nucleic Acids

Nucleic acids are long chains of nucleotides that form the backbone of genetic material in living organisms. The two main types of nucleic acids are DNA (deoxyribonucleic acid) and RNA (ribonucleic acid).

1. DNA Structure and Function: DNA is a double-stranded helix composed of nucleotides, which include a phosphate group, a deoxyribose sugar, and a nitrogenous base (adenine, thymine, cytosine, or guanine). The strands run antiparallel, with complementary base pairing between adenine (A) and thymine (T), and between cytosine (C) and guanine (G). DNA's main function is to store genetic information that guides the synthesis of proteins and the replication of cells.

- Replication: DNA replicates through a semi-conservative mechanism, where each new DNA molecule consists of one original strand and one newly synthesized strand. Enzymes like DNA polymerase are crucial for this process.
- Transcription and Translation: DNA serves as a template for RNA synthesis in transcription. The RNA is then translated into proteins by ribosomes in the process of translation, where the sequence of nucleotides is decoded into an amino acid sequence.

2. RNA Structure and Function: RNA differs from DNA in that it is single-stranded, contains ribose sugar, and uses uracil (U) instead of thymine. There are several types of RNA, each with distinct functions:
   - Messenger RNA (mRNA): Carries the genetic code from DNA to the ribosome for protein synthesis.
   - Transfer RNA (tRNA): Helps decode mRNA into a protein by bringing the correct amino acid to the ribosome during translation.
   - Ribosomal RNA (rRNA): A structural component of ribosomes, which are the sites of protein synthesis.
3. Nucleic Acid Functions: Beyond their role in genetics and protein synthesis, nucleic acids also serve regulatory and catalytic functions. RNA molecules like ribozymes act as enzymes to catalyze biological reactions. Nucleotides such as ATP (adenosine triphosphate) serve as energy currency within the cell, fueling many biochemical processes.

Chapter 7: Spectroscopy and Analysis

Spectroscopy is an essential tool in organic chemistry used to determine the structure and properties of molecules. It involves the interaction of light (or other electromagnetic radiation) with matter to provide detailed information about molecular composition, structure, and dynamics. The most common forms of spectroscopy used in organic analysis are infrared (IR) spectroscopy, nuclear magnetic resonance (NMR) spectroscopy, and mass spectrometry (MS). Each of these techniques offers unique insights and is frequently used in combination to provide a complete picture of a molecule's structure.

1. Infrared (IR) Spectroscopy

Infrared (IR) spectroscopy is primarily used to identify functional groups in organic molecules. The IR region of the electromagnetic spectrum falls between visible light and microwaves, with wavelengths ranging from about 700 nm to 1 mm. When molecules are exposed to infrared radiation, their chemical bonds vibrate, and each type of bond absorbs infrared light at characteristic frequencies.

How IR Spectroscopy Works

In IR spectroscopy, a sample is irradiated with infrared light, and the energy is absorbed by molecular vibrations, such as stretching, bending, or twisting of bonds. Different functional groups absorb at specific wavelengths, making IR spectroscopy an effective way to identify key functional groups within a compound. For example, the O-H stretch in alcohols and carboxylic acids shows a broad absorption band around 3200-3600 cm^{-1}, while carbonyl groups (C=O) exhibit sharp absorption around 1700 cm^{-1}.

Key Absorption Frequencies

- O-H (Alcohols): 3200-3600 cm^{-1} (broad)
- N-H (Amines): 3300-3500 cm^{-1} (sharp)
- C=O (Carbonyls): 1650-1750 cm^{-1} (sharp)
- C-H (Alkanes): 2850-2960 cm^{-1} (sharp)
- C≡C (Alkynes): 2100-2260 cm^{-1} (sharp)
- C=C (Alkenes): 1620-1680 cm^{-1}

By comparing the observed IR spectrum with known reference spectra, organic chemists can identify specific functional groups in a molecule.

2. Nuclear Magnetic Resonance (NMR) Spectroscopy

NMR spectroscopy is one of the most powerful tools in organic chemistry for elucidating the structure of organic compounds. It involves the interaction of atomic nuclei with a strong magnetic field and radiofrequency radiation, leading to transitions between different nuclear spin states. The most common types of NMR used in organic chemistry are proton NMR (^{1}H NMR) and carbon-13 NMR (^{13}C NMR).

How NMR Spectroscopy Works

In a magnetic field, certain atomic nuclei (such as ^{1}H or ^{13}C) can absorb radiofrequency energy, resulting in transitions between their spin states. The frequency at which a nucleus absorbs energy depends on its chemical environment, which is influenced by nearby electrons and neighboring atoms. This results in a highly detailed spectrum, where each peak corresponds to a specific chemical environment within the molecule.

¹H NMR (Proton NMR)

¹H NMR is used to study the hydrogen atoms (protons) within a molecule. Key features of a ¹H NMR spectrum include:
- Chemical Shift (δ): Indicates the environment of the hydrogen atoms. Proton signals appear at specific chemical shifts depending on their surroundings (e.g., alkyl protons appear between 0-3 ppm, aromatic protons around 6-8 ppm).
- Integration: The area under each peak correlates with the number of protons contributing to that signal.
- Multiplicity (Splitting): Peaks are split into multiple sub-peaks due to the interactions between neighboring protons. This splitting follows the n+1 rule, where n is the number of adjacent protons.

¹³C NMR (Carbon-13 NMR)

¹³C NMR provides information about the carbon atoms in a molecule. While less sensitive than proton NMR, it gives valuable insight into the carbon skeleton of an organic compound. Carbon signals are observed at chemical shifts ranging from 0-200 ppm, with carbonyl carbons appearing between 160-220 ppm and alkyl carbons between 10-40 ppm. Unlike proton NMR, ¹³C NMR spectra are usually recorded without splitting due to decoupling techniques that simplify the interpretation of the spectrum.

3. **Mass Spectrometry (MS)**

Mass spectrometry is a technique used to determine the molecular weight and structure of a compound by ionizing the sample and analyzing the resulting ions based on their mass-to-charge ratio (m/z). It provides highly precise information about the molecular formula of a compound, fragment ions, and sometimes structural details.

How Mass Spectrometry Works

The mass spectrometer ionizes the sample, typically by electron impact (EI), chemical ionization (CI), or electrospray ionization (ESI). The ions produced are then accelerated in a magnetic or electric field, and their m/z values are measured. The resulting spectrum consists of peaks representing the different ions, with the most intense peak being the base peak, and the peak corresponding to the intact molecule being the molecular ion (M^+).

Key Features of Mass Spectra
- Molecular Ion (M^+): This peak represents the intact molecule and gives the molecular weight of the compound.
- Base Peak: The most intense peak in the spectrum, which corresponds to the most stable fragment ion.
- Fragmentation Patterns: The molecule often breaks apart during ionization, producing smaller ions that give clues about the structure of the molecule. These fragment ions can indicate which bonds within the molecule are weaker and more likely to break under ionization.

Mass spectrometry can also be coupled with chromatography techniques such as gas chromatography (GC-MS) or liquid chromatography (LC-MS) to separate complex mixtures before analysis, providing a powerful tool for the identification of unknown compounds.

IR, NMR, and Mass Spectrometry: Comparison and Complementarity

While each of these techniques—IR, NMR, and MS—provides valuable information about molecular structure, they are often used in combination to fully characterize organic compounds.

- IR Spectroscopy helps identify functional groups through characteristic bond vibrations.
- ^{1}H NMR and ^{13}C NMR Spectroscopy provide detailed information about the structure and environment of hydrogen and carbon atoms, revealing the molecule's carbon skeleton and the connectivity of atoms.
- Mass Spectrometry gives the molecular weight and fragmentation pattern, which can confirm the molecular formula and provide insights into the compound's structure.

Together, these techniques allow chemists to confidently determine the complete structure of an unknown compound, verify the purity of synthesized materials, and elucidate complex molecular architectures. For example, by using IR to identify functional groups, NMR to understand connectivity, and MS to determine the molecular weight, chemists can cross-check the results to confirm the accuracy of their conclusions.

This combination of methods is crucial in research, drug development, and forensic analysis, where precise identification of compounds is essential.

Practical Question For Section 4:

1. What is the general formula for alkanes?

A) C_nH_{2n+2}

B) C_nH_{2n-2}

C) C_nH_{2n}

D) C_nH_{2n-4}

2. What type of hybridization is found in carbon atoms involved in a triple bond?

A) sp

B) sp^2

C) sp^3

D) sp^3d

3. Which of the following is an example of an alkane?

A) Ethene

B) Ethane

C) Propyne

D) Butene

4. Which IUPAC name corresponds to the structure $CH_3\text{-}CH=CH\text{-}CH_3$?

A) 1-butene

B) 2-butene

C) butane

D) propene

5. Alkynes are characterized by what type of bond?

A) Single bond

B) Double bond

C) Triple bond

D) Quadruple bond

6. Which of the following is true about alkanes?

A) They are unsaturated hydrocarbons.

B) They contain double bonds.

C) They contain single bonds only.

D) They are reactive to electrophilic addition.

7. What is the molecular formula of propane?

A) C_4H_{10}

B) C_3H_8

C) C_2H_6

D) C_5H_{12}

8. What is the hybridization of the carbon atoms in ethene (C_2H_4)?

A) sp

B) sp^2

C) sp^3

D) sp^3d

9. Which alkane has the highest boiling point?

A) Methane

B) Propane

C) Pentane

D) Ethane

10. What is the correct name for CH₃-C≡C-CH₃?

A) Butyne

B) 1-butyne

C) 2-butyne

D) Butane

11. What is the molecular geometry around a carbon atom in an alkene?

A) Tetrahedral

B) Trigonal planar

C) Linear

D) Bent

12. Which of the following is a characteristic of cis-trans isomerism in alkenes?

A) Rotation around the single bond

B) Rotation around the double bond

C) Restricted rotation around the double bond

D) Free rotation around the triple bond

13. Which of these is an unsaturated hydrocarbon?

A) Propane

B) Methane

C) Ethyne

D) Pentane

14. What is the name of the compound with the formula C_2H_2?

A) Ethane

B) Ethene

C) Ethyne

D) Propane

15. Which compound has a higher reactivity in addition reactions?

A) Ethane

B) Propane

C) Ethene

D) Butane

16. Which of the following is a saturated hydrocarbon?

A) Ethene

B) Ethyne

C) Methane

D) Butene

17. What is the correct name for a molecule with a triple bond between the second and third carbons in a four-carbon chain?

A) 2-butene

B) 1-butyne

C) 2-butyne

D) butadiene

18. Which type of hybridization is found in the carbon atoms of methane (CH_4)?

A) sp

B) sp^2

C) sp^3

D) sp^3d

19. What is the structure of 2-methylpropane?

A) CH$_3$-CH$_2$-CH$_3$

B) CH$_3$-CH$_2$-CH=CH$_2$

C) CH$_3$-CH=CH-CH$_3$

D) (CH$_3$)$_2$CH-CH$_3$

20. Which alkene has the molecular formula C$_4$H$_8$?

A) Butane

B) Butyne

C) Butene

D) Propene

21. What is the correct IUPAC name for CH$_3$CH$_2$CH$_2$CH$_3$?

A) Methane

B) Propane

C) Butane

D) Pentane

22. Which of the following hydrocarbons undergoes combustion to produce carbon dioxide and water?

A) Ethane

B) Ethene

C) Ethyne

D) All of the above

23. Which of the following represents an alkane with five carbon atoms?

A) C$_3$H$_6$

B) C$_5$H$_{12}$

C) C₄H₈

D) C₂H₄

24. In which of the following is the bond length between carbon atoms the shortest?

A) Ethane

B) Ethene

C) Ethyne

D) Propane

25. Which of the following processes can be used to convert an alkene to an alkane?

A) Hydration

B) Halogenation

C) Hydrogenation

D) Dehydration

26. Which of the following is true about chiral molecules?

A) They have a plane of symmetry

B) They are superimposable on their mirror images

C) They rotate plane-polarized light

D) They have two identical substituents

27. What is the term for molecules that are non-superimposable mirror images of each other?

A) Structural Isomers

B) Diastereomers

C) Enantiomers

D) Geometric Isomers

28. Which of the following does not exhibit chirality?

A) A carbon atom attached to four different groups

B) A carbon atom in a double bond

C) A carbon atom in a ring structure with identical groups

D) A carbon atom attached to a hydrogen atom and three different groups

29. Which of the following statements is true regarding enantiomers?

A) They have different molecular formulas

B) They have identical physical properties in a chiral environment

C) They have identical chemical properties in an achiral environment

D) They do not rotate plane-polarized light

30. What term describes molecules that differ in spatial arrangement but not in connectivity?

A) Functional Isomers

B) Stereoisomers

C) Chain Isomers

D) Positional Isomers

31. Which of the following is a type of stereoisomerism?

A) Chain isomerism

B) Geometric isomerism

C) Functional group isomerism

D) Tautomerism

32. What type of isomerism is exhibited by cis- and trans-2-butene?

A) Enantiomerism

B) Functional group isomerism

C) Geometric isomerism

D) Structural isomerism

33. Which of the following is an example of a pair of diastereomers?

A) Glucose and fructose

B) D-glucose and L-glucose

C) D-glucose and D-galactose

D) Cis-2-butene and trans-2-butene

34. Which type of stereoisomer does not have a mirror image relationship?

A) Enantiomers

B) Diastereomers

C) Structural isomers

D) Chain isomers

35. Which of the following would be optically inactive?

A) A chiral molecule with one chiral center

B) A racemic mixture of two enantiomers

C) An achiral molecule with a chiral center

D) A pure sample of a single enantiomer

36. How do enantiomers differ from each other?

A) In their chemical reactivity

B) In their physical properties such as melting point

C) In the direction they rotate plane-polarized light

D) In their molecular formula

37. What is the significance of a chiral center in a molecule?

A) It leads to the formation of geometric isomers

B) It creates the possibility for enantiomerism

C) It has only three substituents

D) It ensures the molecule is achiral

38. Which of the following is true about diastereomers?

A) They are mirror images of each other

B) They have identical chemical properties in all reactions

C) They differ in physical properties like boiling point

D) They are non-chiral compounds

39. Which of the following methods is commonly used to separate enantiomers?

A) Filtration

B) Crystallization

C) Chromatography with a chiral stationary phase

D) Distillation

40. A molecule that has two or more stereocenters but is superimposable on its mirror image is called a:

A) Chiral molecule

B) Racemic mixture

C) Meso compound

D) Diastereomer

41. What is a racemic mixture?

A) A mixture containing only one enantiomer

B) A mixture with two diastereomers

C) A 50:50 mixture of two enantiomers

D) A mixture of geometric isomers

42. Which property is different between two enantiomers?

A) Boiling point

B) Solubility in water

C) Specific rotation of light

D) Molecular weight

43. In which situation would geometric isomerism arise?

A) When a molecule has a single chiral center

B) When rotation around a double bond is restricted

C) When atoms are connected differently

D) When a carbon atom is bonded to four identical groups

44. Which of the following can exhibit both enantiomerism and diastereomerism?

A) A molecule with one stereocenter

B) A molecule with two or more stereocenters

C) A molecule with no stereocenters

D) A planar molecule

45. What happens to the optical activity of a racemic mixture?

A) It becomes twice as strong as a single enantiomer

B) It is zero because the rotations cancel out

C) It shows only levorotatory activity

D) It rotates light in both directions equally

46. Which of the following factors increases the reactivity of a carbocation?

a) Electronegativity of neighboring atoms

b) Presence of electron-donating groups

c) Steric hindrance

d) Lack of resonance stabilization

47. What is the first step in an electrophilic addition reaction involving an alkene?

a) Formation of a carbocation

b) Nucleophilic attack

c) Protonation of the double bond

d) Breaking of the C-H bond

48. Which type of intermediate is formed during an S_n1 reaction?

a) Carbanion

b) Carbocation

c) Radical

d) None of the above

49. In electrophilic addition reactions, the addition of hydrogen halides (HX) to unsymmetrical alkenes follows:

a) Zaitsev's Rule

b) Anti-Markovnikov's Rule

c) Markovnikov's Rule

d) Hoffmann's Rule

50. Which solvent is most suitable for an S_n2 reaction mechanism?

a) Water

b) Acetic acid

c) DMSO

d) Ethanol

51. In an S_n2 reaction, what happens to the stereochemistry of the carbon atom being attacked?

a) Retains configuration

b) Undergoes racemization

c) Inverts configuration

d) Becomes a mixture of enantiomers

52. What is the rate-determining step in an S_n1 mechanism?

a) Nucleophilic attack

b) Formation of carbocation

c) Loss of a proton

d) Attack by the electrophile

53. Which of the following nucleophiles would react fastest in an S_n2 reaction?

a) Water (H_2O)

b) Hydroxide (OH^-)

c) Ammonia (NH_3)

d) Methanol (CH_3OH)

54. Which of the following statements is true about electrophilic addition reactions?

a) Electrophiles attack nucleophilic centers

b) Nucleophiles attack electrophilic centers

c) Both a and b are true

d) None of the above

55. The nucleophile in a nucleophilic substitution reaction typically donates:

a) Protons

b) Electrons

c) Neutrons

d) None of the above

56. In the addition of HBr to propene, which intermediate is formed?

a) A free radical

b) A carbanion

c) A carbocation

d) A bromonium ion

57. Which of the following halides undergoes an S_n2 reaction most rapidly?

a) Tertiary halide

b) Secondary halide

c) Primary halide

d) Quaternary halide

58. The reactivity of alkenes in electrophilic addition reactions is primarily due to:

a) The strong sigma bond

b) The weak pi bond

c) Steric hindrance

d) The inductive effect

59. Which of the following is an example of a leaving group in nucleophilic substitution?

a) Hydroxide (OH^-)

b) Chloride (Cl^-)

c) Ethyl group ($C_2H_5^+$)

d) Ammonia (NH_3)

60. During an S_n1 reaction, the nucleophile attacks:

a) The leaving group

b) The carbocation intermediate

c) The nucleophile

d) None of the above

61. In which of the following solvents would an S_n1 reaction occur fastest?

a) Methanol

b) Hexane

c) Ether

d) Benzene

62. Which of the following factors affects the stability of a carbocation?

a) Hyperconjugation

b) Inductive effects

c) Resonance stabilization

d) All of the above

63. Which of the following factors makes a nucleophile stronger in S_n2 reactions?

a) High electronegativity

b) Large atomic size

c) Presence of a positive charge

d) Strong negative charge

64. What is the outcome of an S_n2 reaction involving a chiral carbon center?

a) Racemization

b) Retention of configuration

c) Inversion of configuration

d) No change in stereochemistry

65. In electrophilic addition of H₂O to an alkene, the reaction typically proceeds through the formation of a:

a) Halonium ion

b) Carbocation

c) Carbanion

d) Hydronium ion

66. Which functional group is characteristic of alcohols?

A) -COOH

B) -OH

C) -NH2

D) -COO-

67. Which of the following is a primary alcohol?

A) 2-Propanol

B) 1-Butanol

C) 2-Butanol

D) tert-Butanol

68. Which of the following reactions converts an alcohol to an alkene?

A) Oxidation

B) Dehydration

C) Esterification

D) Reduction

69. What is the general formula for an aldehyde?

A) R-COOH

B) R-CHO

C) R-CO-R'

D) R-OH

70. Which functional group is present in carboxylic acids?

A) -NH2

B) -OH

C) -COOH

D) -CHO

71. Which of the following statements about ketones is correct?

A) They contain a carbonyl group attached to a hydrogen atom.

B) They are easily oxidized to carboxylic acids.

C) They contain a carbonyl group bonded to two carbon atoms.

D) They are more reactive than aldehydes.

72. Which of the following reactions results in the formation of a carboxylic acid from an aldehyde?

A) Oxidation

B) Reduction

C) Dehydration

D) Hydrolysis

73. In which reaction do carboxylic acids react with alcohols to form esters?

A) Saponification

B) Esterification

C) Hydrogenation

D) Hydration

74. Which reagent is commonly used to reduce aldehydes to primary alcohols?

A) NaBH4

B) H2SO4

C) KMnO4

D) HCl

75. What is the characteristic functional group of ketones?

A) -CHO

B) -OH

C) -CO-

D) -COOH

76. Which of the following functional groups contains both a carbonyl and hydroxyl group?

A) Ester

B) Carboxyl

C) Amino

D) Alkyl

77. Which of the following will produce a carboxylic acid when oxidized?

A) Primary alcohol

B) Secondary alcohol

C) Ketone

D) Tertiary alcohol

78. Which of the following is a product of the oxidation of a primary alcohol?

A) Ether

B) Ketone

C) Aldehyde

D) Ester

79. Aldehydes are more reactive than ketones due to which of the following reasons?

A) Aldehydes have a larger dipole moment.

B) Aldehydes are less sterically hindered than ketones.

C) Ketones are less polar than aldehydes.

D) Ketones have more resonance structures.

80. Which of the following reactions can produce a secondary alcohol?

A) Reduction of an aldehyde

B) Reduction of a ketone

C) Oxidation of a primary alcohol

D) Dehydration of a secondary alcohol

81. Which reagent is typically used to reduce carboxylic acids to primary alcohols?

A) NaBH4

B) LiAlH4

C) H2/Pt

D) Br2/FeBr3

82. Which of the following functional groups is the most acidic?

A) Hydroxyl

B) Amino

C) Carboxyl

D) Carbonyl

83. Which of the following is a product of the reaction between a carboxylic acid and a strong base?

A) Alcohol

B) Carboxylate salt

C) Ketone

D) Aldehyde

84. Which of the following is a property of carboxylic acids?

A) They are strong bases.

B) They do not form hydrogen bonds.

C) They have high boiling points due to hydrogen bonding.

D) They are nonpolar molecules.

85. Which of the following can be classified as a nucleophile in a nucleophilic addition reaction with an aldehyde?

A) H+

B) H2O

C) OH-

D) Cl2

86. Which of the following compounds is aromatic?

A) Cyclohexane

B) Benzene

C) Ethylene

D) Propane

87. What is the number of pi electrons in a benzene molecule?

A) 2

B) 4

C) 6

D) 8

88. Which of the following reactions does benzene primarily undergo?

A) Addition reactions

B) Substitution reactions

C) Elimination reactions

D) Rearrangement reactions

89. What is the electrophile in the nitration of benzene?

A) NO_2

B) NO_2^+

C) H_2SO_4

D) HNO_3

90. In an electrophilic aromatic substitution, the intermediate formed is called a:

A) Free radical

B) Carbocation

C) Sigma complex

D) Carbanion

91. Which of the following is NOT a requirement for aromaticity according to Hückel's rule?

A) Planarity

B) Cyclic structure

C) 4n pi electrons

D) Conjugated system

92. Which reagent is necessary for the bromination of benzene?

A) Br₂ and AlCl₃

B) H₂ and Pt

C) HBr

D) Br₂ and sunlight

93. Which position does an -OH group direct incoming electrophiles to in electrophilic substitution reactions of phenol?

A) Ortho and meta

B) Ortho and para

C) Meta and para

D) Only ortho

94. What type of reaction is the Friedel-Crafts alkylation?

A) Electrophilic addition

B) Electrophilic substitution

C) Nucleophilic substitution

D) Nucleophilic addition

95. Which compound will deactivate a benzene ring towards electrophilic substitution?

A) -OH

B) -NO₂

C) -CH₃

D) -NH₂

96. What is the major product of the reaction of benzene with CH₃Cl in the presence of AlCl₃?

A) Methylbenzene

B) Ethylbenzene

C) Chlorobenzene

D) Phenol

97. In the sulfonation of benzene, which reagent is used to generate the electrophile?

A) H₂SO₄

B) SO₃

C) HNO₃

D) AlCl₃

98. Which of the following is NOT an example of an electrophilic aromatic substitution reaction?

A) Nitration

B) Halogenation

C) Hydrolysis

D) Sulfonation

99. What type of bond is involved in the delocalization of electrons in an aromatic compound?

A) Sigma bond

B) Pi bond

C) Ionic bond

D) Hydrogen bond

100. What is the molecular formula of benzene?

A) C₅H₆

B) C₆H₆

C) C₇H₆

D) C₆H₈

101. Which of the following functional groups increases the reactivity of the benzene ring in electrophilic substitution?

A) Nitro (-NO₂)

B) Methyl (-CH₃)

C) Carboxyl (-COOH)

D) Nitrile (-CN)

102. Which of the following positions will a nitro group direct further substitution to on a benzene ring?

A) Ortho

B) Meta

C) Para

D) Both ortho and para

103. Which of the following is true about the structure of benzene?

A) It has alternating single and double bonds.

B) It has localized pi bonds.

C) All carbon-carbon bonds are of equal length.

D) It has no conjugation of pi electrons.

104. Which product is formed when benzene reacts with concentrated nitric acid in the presence of sulfuric acid?

A) Nitrobenzene

B) Chlorobenzene

C) Toluene

D) Aniline

105. What is the role of AlCl₃ in the Friedel-Crafts acylation reaction?

A) It is the nucleophile

B) It acts as a catalyst

C) It is the reducing agent

D) It is the oxidizing agent

106. Which of the following is NOT a component of a nucleotide in nucleic acids?

A) Phosphate group

B) Nitrogenous base

C) Glycerol

D) Pentose sugar

107. What type of bond links amino acids together to form proteins?

A) Hydrogen bond

B) Ionic bond

C) Peptide bond

D) Phosphodiester bond

108. Which of the following amino acids is considered essential, meaning it must be obtained from the diet?

A) Glycine

B) Alanine

C) Lysine

D) Glutamine

109. The primary structure of a protein refers to:

A) The 3D folding pattern of the polypeptide chain

B) The sequence of amino acids

C) The association of multiple polypeptide chains

D) The hydrogen bonding between amino acid side chains

110. **In DNA, adenine (A) pairs with which nitrogenous base?**

A) Uracil (U)

B) Guanine (G)

C) Cytosine (C)

D) Thymine (T)

111. **Which of the following types of RNA is responsible for carrying amino acids to the ribosome during protein synthesis?**

A) Messenger RNA (mRNA)

B) Ribosomal RNA (rRNA)

C) Transfer RNA (tRNA)

D) Small interfering RNA (siRNA)

112. **Which of the following is a hydrophobic (nonpolar) amino acid?**

A) Serine

B) Valine

C) Lysine

D) Glutamate

113. **In DNA replication, the enzyme responsible for synthesizing the new DNA strand is:**

A) RNA polymerase

B) DNA helicase

C) DNA polymerase

D) Ligase

114. Which of the following is NOT a function of proteins in the cell?

A) Catalyzing biochemical reactions

B) Serving as a template for RNA synthesis

C) Transporting molecules across membranes

D) Acting as structural components

115. Which of the following statements about the secondary structure of proteins is correct?

A) It refers to the sequence of amino acids in a polypeptide chain.

B) It involves the interaction between multiple polypeptide chains.

C) It includes alpha-helices and beta-sheets formed by hydrogen bonding.

D) It is stabilized by covalent bonds between amino acid side chains.

116. Which of the following regions in an IR spectrum is associated with the absorption of O-H bonds in alcohols?

a) 2800-3000 cm^{-1}

b) 3200-3600 cm^{-1}

c) 1700-1800 cm^{-1}

d) 2100-2260 cm^{-1}

117. In ^{1}H NMR spectroscopy, which feature of the spectrum indicates the number of hydrogen atoms in a particular chemical environment?

a) Chemical shift

b) Integration

c) Splitting pattern

d) Coupling constant

118. Which of the following represents the molecular ion peak in a mass spectrum?

a) The peak with the smallest m/z ratio

b) The base peak

c) The peak with the highest m/z ratio

d) The fragment ion peak

119. In ^{1}H NMR spectroscopy, what is the splitting pattern for a proton with two neighboring equivalent protons?

a) Singlet

b) Doublet

c) Triplet

d) Quartet

120. Which functional group typically shows an absorption peak around 1700 cm^{-1} in an IR spectrum?

a) Alcohol

b) Carbonyl

c) Amine

d) Alkane

121. In mass spectrometry, what is the primary purpose of the ionization process?

a) To measure molecular weight

b) To break down the molecule into smaller fragments

c) To generate ions from the molecule

d) To separate ions based on their polarity

122. Which NMR technique is commonly used to analyze the carbon skeleton of organic compounds?

a) ^{1}H NMR

b) ^{13}C NMR

c) ^{2}H NMR

d) ³¹P NMR

123. In mass spectrometry, what does the base peak in a spectrum represent?

a) The heaviest ion

b) The molecular ion

c) The most stable fragment

d) The ion with the lowest m/z ratio

124. Which of the following is true about the relationship between chemical shift and electron density in NMR?

a) Higher electron density leads to a lower chemical shift

b) Lower electron density leads to a lower chemical shift

c) Chemical shift is independent of electron density

d) Chemical shift decreases with increasing electron density

125. In IR spectroscopy, a sharp absorption around 3300-3500 cm⁻¹ would most likely indicate the presence of which functional group?

a) Alkene

b) Amine

c) Alkane

d) Ether

Answers & Explanation

1. C_nH_{2n+2} – The general formula for alkanes, which are saturated hydrocarbons, is C_nH_{2n+2}, meaning each carbon atom is single-bonded to other atoms, providing the maximum number of hydrogen atoms.
2. A. sp – Carbon atoms involved in a triple bond are sp hybridized, meaning one s orbital and one p orbital mix to form two sp orbitals, resulting in a linear geometry.
3. B. Ethane – Ethane (C_2H_6) is an alkane, meaning it consists of only single bonds between carbon atoms and is fully saturated with hydrogen atoms.
4. B. 2-butene – 2-butene has a double bond between the second and third carbons in a four-carbon chain, following IUPAC rules for naming alkenes.
5. C. Triple bond – Alkynes are characterized by the presence of at least one triple bond between two carbon atoms.
6. C. They contain single bonds only. – Alkanes consist solely of single bonds between carbon atoms, making them saturated hydrocarbons with a relatively low reactivity.
7. B. C_3H_8 – The molecular formula for propane is C_3H_8, where three carbon atoms form single bonds with hydrogen atoms.
8. B. sp^2 – In ethene (C_2H_4), the carbon atoms involved in the double bond are sp^2 hybridized, giving the molecule a trigonal planar shape.
9. C. Pentane – Pentane (C_5H_{12}) has the highest boiling point among the given options due to the increased van der Waals forces associated with its larger molecular size.
10. C. 2-butyne – 2-butyne has a triple bond between the second and third carbons in a four-carbon chain.
11. B. Trigonal planar – In alkenes, the carbon atoms involved in the double bond are sp^2 hybridized, resulting in a trigonal planar geometry around the double bond.
12. C. Restricted rotation around the double bond – In alkenes, the presence of a double bond restricts rotation, leading to cis-trans isomerism.
13. C. Ethyne – Ethyne is an unsaturated hydrocarbon due to the presence of a triple bond between its carbon atoms.
14. C. Ethyne – The molecular formula C_2H_2 corresponds to ethyne, an alkyne with a triple bond between its two carbon atoms.
15. C. Ethene – Ethene (C_2H_4) is more reactive in addition reactions because the double bond can be easily broken, allowing other atoms or groups to add across the bond.
16. C. Methane – Methane (CH_4) is a saturated hydrocarbon with only single bonds between carbon and hydrogen atoms.
17. C. 2-butyne – 2-butyne is an alkyne with a triple bond between the second and third carbons in a four-carbon chain.
18. C. sp^3 – In methane (CH_4), the carbon atom is sp^3 hybridized, resulting in a tetrahedral geometry where the four hydrogen atoms are bonded to the carbon.

19. D. (CH$_3$)$_2$CH-CH$_3$ – 2-methylpropane is a branched alkane where a methyl group (-CH$_3$) is attached to the second carbon of a three-carbon chain.
20. C. Butene – Butene (C$_4$H$_8$) is an alkene with a double bond in a four-carbon chain.
21. C. Butane – Butane (C$_4$H$_{10}$) is the IUPAC name for a four-carbon alkane with single bonds between the carbon atoms.
22. D. All of the above – Ethane, ethene, and ethyne all undergo combustion reactions to produce carbon dioxide and water.
23. B. C$_5$H$_{12}$ – The molecular formula C$_5$H$_{12}$ corresponds to an alkane with five carbon atoms, which is pentane.
24. C. Ethyne – The triple bond in ethyne results in the shortest bond length between carbon atoms compared to single bonds (ethane) and double bonds (ethene).
25. C. Hydrogenation – Hydrogenation is the process of converting an alkene to an alkane by adding hydrogen atoms across the double bond
26. C. They rotate plane-polarized light. – Chiral molecules lack internal symmetry and are optically active, which means they can rotate plane-polarized light.
27. C. Enantiomers. – Enantiomers are non-superimposable mirror images of each other, differing only in the way they interact with polarized light.
28. B. A carbon atom in a double bond. – A carbon atom in a double bond cannot be chiral because it is connected to only three different groups, not four.
29. C. They have identical chemical properties in an achiral environment. – Enantiomers have the same chemical properties in an achiral environment but may differ in a chiral environment or in the way they rotate light.
30. B. Stereoisomers. – Stereoisomers have the same molecular connectivity but differ in the spatial arrangement of their atoms.
31. B. Geometric isomerism. – Geometric isomerism occurs when there is restricted rotation around a bond, such as in alkenes, leading to cis and trans forms.
32. C. Geometric isomerism. – Cis and trans isomers in 2-butene differ in the spatial arrangement of substituents around the double bond, which is a form of geometric isomerism.
33. C. D-glucose and D-galactose. – These two sugars differ in the configuration around a single carbon atom, making them diastereomers.
34. B. Diastereomers. – Diastereomers are stereoisomers that are not mirror images of each other, unlike enantiomers.
35. B. A racemic mixture of two enantiomers. – A racemic mixture contains equal amounts of two enantiomers, which cancel out each other's optical activity, making the mixture optically inactive.
36. C. In the direction they rotate plane-polarized light. – Enantiomers rotate plane-polarized light in opposite directions, even though their other physical properties are identical in an achiral environment.
37. B. It creates the possibility for enantiomerism. – A chiral center leads to the possibility of enantiomers, as the carbon atom is attached to four different groups.

38. C. They differ in physical properties like boiling point. – Diastereomers have different physical properties, making it easier to separate them using methods like distillation or recrystallization.
39. C. Chromatography with a chiral stationary phase. – Enantiomers can be separated using chromatography with a chiral stationary phase, which interacts differently with each enantiomer.
40. C. Meso compound. – A meso compound has two or more stereocenters but is superimposable on its mirror image due to an internal plane of symmetry, making it achiral.
41. C. A 50:50 mixture of two enantiomers. – A racemic mixture consists of equal amounts of two enantiomers, which cancel out each other's optical activity, making the mixture optically inactive.
42. C. Specific rotation of light. – The specific rotation of light is different between enantiomers, even though their other physical properties, like boiling point and solubility, are the same in an achiral environment.
43. B. When rotation around a double bond is restricted. – Geometric isomerism arises when there is restricted rotation, as in double bonds or rings, leading to cis and trans isomers.
44. B. A molecule with two or more stereocenters. – A molecule with two or more stereocenters can exhibit both enantiomerism and diastereomerism, depending on how the stereocenters are arranged.
45. B. It is zero because the rotations cancel out. – In a racemic mixture, the optical activity of each enantiomer cancels out, resulting in no overall rotation of plane-polarized light.
46. b) Presence of electron-donating groups. - Electron-donating groups stabilize carbocations by pushing electron density toward the positively charged carbon, increasing reactivity.
47. c) Protonation of the double bond. - In electrophilic addition, the first step involves protonation of the double bond, generating a carbocation intermediate.
48. b) Carbocation. - In an S_n1 reaction, the rate-determining step is the formation of a carbocation intermediate after the leaving group departs.
49. c) Markovnikov's Rule. - Markovnikov's Rule states that in the addition of HX to an unsymmetrical alkene, the hydrogen attaches to the carbon with more hydrogens.
50. c) DMSO. - Dimethyl sulfoxide (DMSO) is an aprotic solvent that does not stabilize nucleophiles, making them more reactive for S_n2 reactions.
51. c) Inverts configuration. - S_n2 reactions proceed through backside attack, causing inversion of the stereochemistry at the carbon center (Walden inversion).
52. b) Formation of carbocation. - The slowest step in the S_n1 reaction is the dissociation of the leaving group and the formation of a carbocation.
53. b) Hydroxide (OH^-). - Hydroxide is a strong nucleophile due to its negative charge and small size, making it very reactive in S_n2 reactions.
54. a) Electrophiles attack nucleophilic centers. - Electrophiles, which seek electrons, target nucleophilic centers with high electron density, like pi bonds in alkenes.

55. b) Electrons. - Nucleophiles are electron-rich species and donate electrons during a reaction to form a bond with an electrophilic center.
56. c) A carbocation. - During the addition of HBr to propene, the proton adds first, forming a carbocation intermediate, which is then attacked by the bromide ion.
57. c) Primary halide. - Primary halides are less sterically hindered, making them more reactive in S_n2 reactions compared to secondary or tertiary halides.
58. b) The weak pi bond. - The pi bond in alkenes is weaker and more reactive than sigma bonds, making alkenes susceptible to electrophilic addition.
59. b) Chloride (Cl^-). - Chloride is a good leaving group in nucleophilic substitution because it can stabilize the negative charge after leaving.
60. b) The carbocation intermediate. - In an S_n1 reaction, after the leaving group departs, the nucleophile attacks the carbocation intermediate to form the product.
61. a) Methanol. - Methanol is a polar protic solvent that stabilizes the carbocation intermediate and promotes the S_n1 mechanism.
62. d) All of the above. - Hyperconjugation, inductive effects, and resonance stabilization all contribute to the stability of carbocations, making them more reactive.
63. d) Strong negative charge. - A nucleophile with a strong negative charge is more reactive in S_n2 reactions because it can more effectively attack the electrophilic carbon.
64. c) Inversion of configuration. - In S_n2 reactions, the nucleophile attacks from the opposite side of the leaving group, leading to inversion of the configuration.
65. b) Carbocation. - The addition of water to an alkene proceeds through the formation of a carbocation intermediate, followed by nucleophilic attack by water.
66. B. -OH. - The hydroxyl group (-OH) is characteristic of alcohols. It consists of an oxygen atom bonded to a hydrogen atom and is responsible for the properties of alcohols.
67. B. 1-Butanol. - 1-Butanol is a primary alcohol because the hydroxyl group is attached to a carbon that is bonded to only one other carbon atom.
68. B. Dehydration. - Dehydration of an alcohol involves the loss of a water molecule, resulting in the formation of an alkene.
69. B. R-CHO. - The general formula for aldehydes is R-CHO, where R represents a hydrocarbon chain and -CHO is the aldehyde functional group.
70. C. -COOH. - The carboxyl group (-COOH) is characteristic of carboxylic acids, which consist of a carbonyl group and a hydroxyl group attached to the same carbon atom.
71. C. They contain a carbonyl group bonded to two carbon atoms. - Ketones have a carbonyl group (C=O) in which the carbon is bonded to two other carbon atoms, distinguishing them from aldehydes.
72. A. Oxidation. - Aldehydes are oxidized to carboxylic acids when they react with oxidizing agents, such as potassium permanganate (KMnO4).
73. B. Esterification. - In esterification, carboxylic acids react with alcohols in the presence of an acid catalyst to form esters and water.

74. A. NaBH4. - Sodium borohydride (NaBH4) is a reducing agent that reduces aldehydes to primary alcohols.
75. C. -CO-. - The functional group of ketones is the carbonyl group (-CO-) bonded to two other carbon atoms.
76. B. Carboxyl. - The carboxyl group (-COOH) contains both a carbonyl (C=O) and a hydroxyl (-OH) group, found in carboxylic acids.
77. A. Primary alcohol. - When oxidized, primary alcohols first form aldehydes, which can be further oxidized to carboxylic acids.
78. C. Aldehyde. - The oxidation of a primary alcohol produces an aldehyde, which can then be further oxidized to a carboxylic acid.
79. B. Aldehydes are less sterically hindered than ketones. - Aldehydes are more reactive than ketones because the carbonyl carbon in aldehydes is less hindered by surrounding groups, making it more accessible to nucleophiles.
80. B. Reduction of a ketone. - Reduction of a ketone using reducing agents like NaBH4 results in the formation of a secondary alcohol.
81. B. LiAlH4. - Lithium aluminum hydride (LiAlH4) is a strong reducing agent used to reduce carboxylic acids to primary alcohols.
82. C. Carboxyl. - The carboxyl group (-COOH) is the most acidic functional group because it can donate a proton (H+) to form a carboxylate ion (-COO-).
83. B. Carboxylate salt. - A carboxylic acid reacts with a strong base to form a carboxylate salt, where the acidic proton is replaced by a metal ion from the base.
84. C. They have high boiling points due to hydrogen bonding. - Carboxylic acids form strong hydrogen bonds, leading to higher boiling points compared to other functional groups of similar molecular weight.
85. C. OH-. - Hydroxide ion (OH-) is a strong nucleophile that can attack the carbonyl carbon in nucleophilic addition reactions with aldehydes.
86. B. Benzene – Benzene is an aromatic compound due to its cyclic structure, planar geometry, and the delocalization of 6 pi electrons, following Hückel's rule.
87. C. 6 – Benzene contains 6 pi electrons, which are delocalized over the ring and contribute to its aromaticity.
88. B. Substitution reactions – Benzene primarily undergoes substitution reactions because addition reactions would disrupt the aromatic stability of the ring.
89. B. NO_2^+ – The nitronium ion (NO_2^+) is the electrophile in the nitration of benzene, generated from nitric acid in the presence of sulfuric acid.
90. C. Sigma complex – During electrophilic aromatic substitution, the intermediate formed is a sigma complex, where the aromaticity is temporarily lost.
91. C. 4n pi electrons – According to Hückel's rule, an aromatic compound must have 4n+2 pi electrons, not simply 4n.
92. A. Br$_2$ and AlCl$_3$ – Bromination of benzene requires a halogen (Br$_2$) and a Lewis acid catalyst (AlCl$_3$) to generate the electrophilic bromonium ion.

93. B. Ortho and para – The -OH group is an electron-donating group, which activates the benzene ring and directs electrophiles to the ortho and para positions.
94. B. Electrophilic substitution – Friedel-Crafts alkylation is an electrophilic substitution reaction where an alkyl group is added to the benzene ring.
95. B. $-NO_2$ – The nitro group is electron-withdrawing and deactivates the benzene ring, making it less reactive towards electrophilic substitution and directing substituents to the meta position.
96. A. Methylbenzene – Methylbenzene (toluene) is the product of the reaction between benzene and methyl chloride in the presence of $AlCl_3$.
97. B. SO_3 – Sulfur trioxide (SO_3) is the electrophile in the sulfonation of benzene, which reacts with sulfuric acid to produce benzenesulfonic acid.
98. C. Hydrolysis – Hydrolysis is not an electrophilic aromatic substitution reaction; it involves the breaking of bonds with water, not substitution on an aromatic ring.
99. B. Pi bond – Delocalization of pi electrons occurs in the p-orbitals of the aromatic ring, contributing to the overall stability of the compound.
100. B. C_6H_6 – Benzene has a molecular formula of C_6H_6, consisting of six carbon and six hydrogen atoms.
101. B. Methyl ($-CH_3$) – The methyl group is an electron-donating group that increases the reactivity of the benzene ring toward electrophilic substitution reactions.
102. B. Meta – The nitro group is an electron-withdrawing group that deactivates the ring and directs substitution to the meta position.
103. C. All carbon-carbon bonds are of equal length – In benzene, all carbon-carbon bonds are of equal length due to the delocalization of pi electrons.
104. A. Nitrobenzene – Nitration of benzene with nitric acid and sulfuric acid results in the formation of nitrobenzene.
105. B. It acts as a catalyst – $AlCl_3$ acts as a Lewis acid catalyst in the Friedel-Crafts acylation reaction by facilitating the formation of the acylium ion, which is the electrophile in the reaction.
106. C. Glycerol. - Glycerol is not a component of nucleotides. Nucleotides are made up of a phosphate group, a nitrogenous base, and a pentose sugar (ribose in RNA and deoxyribose in DNA).
107. C. Peptide bond. - Peptide bonds are the covalent bonds that link amino acids together in a polypeptide chain, formed between the carboxyl group of one amino acid and the amino group of another.
108. C. Lysine. - Lysine is an essential amino acid, meaning it must be obtained from the diet as the body cannot synthesize it.
109. B. The sequence of amino acids. - The primary structure of a protein refers to its linear sequence of amino acids, which determines how the protein will fold into its secondary, tertiary, and quaternary structures.
110. D. Thymine (T). - In DNA, adenine (A) forms complementary base pairs with thymine (T) through two hydrogen bonds.

111. C. Transfer RNA (tRNA). - tRNA is responsible for carrying specific amino acids to the ribosome, where they are added to the growing polypeptide chain during translation.
112. B. Valine. - Valine is a hydrophobic (nonpolar) amino acid, which tends to be located in the interior of proteins, away from water.
113. C. DNA polymerase. - DNA polymerase is the enzyme responsible for synthesizing the new DNA strand by adding nucleotides in a sequence complementary to the template strand during DNA replication.
114. B. Serving as a template for RNA synthesis. - Proteins do not serve as templates for RNA synthesis; DNA acts as the template during transcription. Proteins, however, perform various functions like catalyzing reactions, transporting molecules, and providing structure.
115. C. It includes alpha-helices and beta-sheets formed by hydrogen bonding. - The secondary structure of proteins involves local folding patterns like alpha-helices and beta-sheets, which are stabilized by hydrogen bonds between the backbone atoms of the polypeptide chain.
116. B. 3200-3600 cm^{-1}. - The O-H bond in alcohols absorbs in the range of 3200-3600 cm^{-1} in an IR spectrum. This broad peak is characteristic of hydrogen bonding.
117. B. Integration. - In ^{1}H NMR spectroscopy, integration measures the area under a peak, which corresponds to the number of hydrogen atoms in a particular environment.
118. C. The peak with the highest m/z ratio. - The molecular ion peak in a mass spectrum represents the ionized form of the entire molecule, typically with the highest m/z ratio, reflecting the molecular weight.
119. C. Triplet. - In ^{1}H NMR, a proton with two neighboring equivalent protons follows the n+1 rule, leading to a triplet splitting pattern.
120. B. Carbonyl. - The carbonyl group (C=O) typically shows a sharp absorption peak around 1700 cm^{-1} in an IR spectrum.
121. C. To generate ions from the molecule. - The primary goal of the ionization process in mass spectrometry is to convert neutral molecules into charged ions so that they can be analyzed based on their mass-to-charge ratio (m/z).
122. B. ^{13}C NMR. - ^{13}C NMR is used to analyze the carbon framework of organic compounds, providing information on the number and environment of carbon atoms.
123. C. The most stable fragment. - The base peak in a mass spectrum is the most intense peak, representing the most stable ion fragment produced during the ionization process.
124. A. Higher electron density leads to a lower chemical shift. - In NMR spectroscopy, nuclei in regions of higher electron density experience shielding, resulting in a lower chemical shift (upfield).
125. B. Amine. - A sharp absorption around 3300-3500 cm^{-1} in an IR spectrum is characteristic of N-H stretching in amines.

SECTION 5: Physics

Chapter 1: Mechanics

Mechanics is the branch of physics that deals with the motion of objects and the forces that affect them. This field is fundamental to understanding the behavior of objects in both everyday and complex systems, from simple projectiles to planetary motion. Mechanics is typically divided into two main categories: kinematics and dynamics.

Kinematics focuses on describing motion without considering the causes of that motion. It deals with concepts like displacement, velocity, and acceleration. Dynamics, on the other hand, involves the study of forces and how they influence the motion of objects.

Mechanics provides the foundation for a broad range of applications, including engineering, automotive systems, aerospace technologies, and more. A deep understanding of mechanical principles allows you to solve real-world problems where predicting and controlling motion is critical.

Motion, Forces, and Newton's Laws

Motion

Motion refers to the change in the position of an object over time. To describe motion, you need to understand several key concepts: displacement, velocity, and acceleration.

- Displacement is a vector quantity that represents the change in position of an object. It has both magnitude and direction. It differs from distance, which only considers the total path covered, whereas displacement focuses on the shortest path between two points.
- Velocity is the rate of change of displacement over time. It's also a vector quantity, which means it includes both speed and direction. Average velocity can be calculated by dividing the total displacement by the total time taken. Instantaneous velocity refers to the velocity at a specific point in time.
- Acceleration refers to the rate of change of velocity over time. Positive acceleration indicates an increase in velocity, while negative acceleration (or deceleration) means a decrease in velocity. Like velocity, acceleration is also a vector quantity.

Motion can be either uniform or non-uniform. Uniform motion refers to movement at a constant velocity, meaning there is no change in speed or direction. Non-uniform motion involves changes in velocity, either in magnitude or direction, which means the object is accelerating.

Forces

A force is a vector quantity that causes an object to undergo a change in speed, direction, or shape. In simple terms, a force is a push or pull acting on an object. Forces can be categorized into two main types: contact forces and non-contact forces.

- Contact forces require physical contact between two objects. Examples include friction, tension, and normal forces.
- Non-contact forces act over a distance without direct physical contact. These include gravitational, electromagnetic, and nuclear forces.

The net force acting on an object is the vector sum of all the forces acting upon it. If the net force is zero, the object remains in its current state of motion (either at rest or moving at constant velocity). If the net force is non-zero, the object will accelerate in the direction of the net force. Common forces include:
- Frictional force: This is the force that opposes the relative motion of two surfaces in contact. Friction depends on the nature of the surfaces and the force pressing them together. It can be static (preventing motion) or kinetic (resisting ongoing motion).
- Gravitational force: This is the attractive force between two masses. On Earth, gravity gives weight to objects and causes them to fall toward the ground when dropped.
- Tension: This is the pulling force transmitted through a string, rope, cable, or similar object when it is pulled tight by forces acting from opposite ends.
- Normal force: This is the perpendicular force exerted by a surface to support the weight of an object resting on it.

Newton's Laws of Motion

Newton's First Law (The Law of Inertia)
Newton's First Law states that an object at rest will remain at rest, and an object in motion will continue in motion at a constant velocity, unless acted upon by a net external force. This concept is known as inertia—the tendency of an object to resist changes in its motion.

For example, a book resting on a table will stay at rest until someone applies a force to move it. Similarly, a soccer ball kicked on a smooth field would keep moving indefinitely if it weren't for forces like friction and air resistance gradually slowing it down.

Inertia depends on an object's mass. The greater the mass, the greater the inertia, meaning more force is required to change the object's motion.

Newton's Second Law (Force and Acceleration)
Newton's Second Law quantitatively describes how forces affect motion. It states that the acceleration of an object is directly proportional to the net force acting on it and inversely proportional to its mass. The mathematical representation of this law is:
$$F=ma$$
Where: F is the net force applied to the object,
m is the mass of the object,
a is the acceleration of the object.

This equation shows that a larger force results in a greater acceleration, assuming the mass is constant. Conversely, for the same force, a more massive object will experience less acceleration. For example, if you push a shopping cart, the force you apply determines how quickly the cart speeds up. The heavier the cart, the harder you need to push to achieve the same acceleration.

Newton's Third Law (Action and Reaction)
Newton's Third Law states that for every action, there is an equal and opposite reaction. This means that when one object exerts a force on another, the second object exerts a force of equal magnitude but in the opposite direction on the first object.

A common example is the interaction between your foot and the ground when walking. As you push backward on the ground with your foot (action), the ground pushes you forward (reaction). This law explains how objects interact with one another, even in systems where multiple objects are in contact.

Applications of Newton's Laws

Understanding Newton's Laws is crucial in analyzing various physical situations. These laws are applied in solving problems related to:
- Projectile motion: Objects in free fall, such as a thrown ball, experience only the force of gravity acting on them after being released.
- Inclined planes: The motion of objects on a slope can be analyzed using Newton's laws, accounting for forces like gravity, normal force, and friction.
- Circular motion: Objects moving in a circular path require a centripetal force to maintain their motion. Newton's Second Law can be applied to determine the required centripetal force based on the object's mass, speed, and radius of the circle.

Chapter 2: Work and Energy

Work and energy are fundamental concepts in physics that describe how forces cause changes in motion and how energy is transferred or transformed. These concepts are deeply intertwined and are essential to understanding mechanical systems.

Definition of Work

In physics, work is defined as the transfer of energy that occurs when a force is applied to an object and causes it to move in the direction of the force. Mathematically, work (W) is expressed as:

$$W = F \cdot d \cdot \cos(\theta)$$

Where:
- F is the magnitude of the applied force,
- d is the displacement of the object,
- θ is the angle between the direction of the force and the displacement.

For work to be done, a force must cause displacement. If no movement occurs, no work is done, regardless of how much force is applied. This definition implies that even if you push against a wall with all your might, if the wall does not move, the work done is zero.

Units of Work

The SI unit of work is the joule (J), where one joule is equal to one newton-meter (N·m). This unit reflects the fact that work is a form of energy transfer. For instance, when a force of 1 newton moves an object 1 meter in the direction of the force, 1 joule of work is done.

Types of Work

Work can be categorized into different types depending on the nature of the force and displacement:

1. Positive Work: When the force and displacement are in the same direction, the work done is positive. For example, when you lift a box upward, the force applied (upward) is in the same direction as the displacement (upward).
2. Negative Work: When the force and displacement are in opposite directions, the work done is negative. This occurs, for instance, when friction slows down a sliding object.
3. Zero Work: If the force is perpendicular to the displacement or there is no displacement, no work is done. For example, holding a book stationary in the air results in zero work, even though you are exerting a force to keep it up.

Energy

Energy is the ability to do work. Like work, energy is measured in joules. Energy exists in different forms, such as kinetic energy, potential energy, thermal energy, and chemical energy. In the context of mechanical systems, the two most important forms of energy are kinetic and potential energy.

Kinetic and Potential Energy

Kinetic Energy

Kinetic energy (KE) is the energy an object possesses due to its motion. The amount of kinetic energy an object has depends on its mass and velocity. The formula for kinetic energy is:

$$KE = \frac{1}{2}mv^2$$

Where:
- m is the mass of the object,
- v is the velocity of the object.

The greater the mass and the faster the velocity of an object, the more kinetic energy it has. For example, a moving car has kinetic energy because of its mass and speed. If the car speeds up, its kinetic energy increases, while if it slows down, its kinetic energy decreases.

Kinetic energy is a scalar quantity, meaning it only has magnitude and no direction. When work is done on an object to accelerate it, the object's kinetic energy changes. This change in kinetic energy is related to the work done on the object, as expressed in the Work-Energy Theorem:

$$W = \Delta KE$$

This theorem states that the net work done on an object is equal to the change in its kinetic energy. If the net work is positive, the object's kinetic energy increases. If the net work is negative, the object's kinetic energy decreases.

Potential Energy

Potential energy (PE) is the energy stored in an object due to its position in a force field, such as gravity or electromagnetism. The most commonly discussed form of potential energy in physics is gravitational potential energy, which depends on an object's height above a reference point. The formula for gravitational potential energy is:

$$PE = mgh$$

Where:
- m is the mass of the object,
- g is the acceleration due to gravity (9.8 m/s² near Earth's surface),
- h is the height of the object above a reference level.

For example, when you lift a book to a higher shelf, you are increasing its gravitational potential energy. If the book falls, the potential energy is converted into kinetic energy.

Potential energy is also a scalar quantity. In addition to gravitational potential energy, other types of potential energy include elastic potential energy, which is stored in objects like stretched springs, and chemical potential energy, stored in chemical bonds.

Relationship Between Kinetic and Potential Energy

In many physical systems, energy is continuously transferred between kinetic and potential forms. This energy transformation is particularly evident in conservative systems, where no energy is lost to friction or other non-conservative forces. A classic example of this energy transfer is a pendulum.

At the highest point of its swing, the pendulum has maximum potential energy and zero kinetic energy. As it falls, its potential energy decreases while its kinetic energy increases, reaching maximum kinetic energy and minimum potential energy at the lowest point of the swing. As the pendulum rises again, kinetic energy is converted back into potential energy.

The total mechanical energy in a conservative system is constant, as long as no energy is lost to non-conservative forces like friction or air resistance. This is expressed by the conservation of mechanical energy:

$$E_{total} = KE + PE = constant$$

This principle is vital in understanding how energy transfers between objects and systems.

Practical Applications

1. Roller Coasters: A roller coaster converts potential energy into kinetic energy as it descends from a height. At the top of a hill, the cars have high potential energy, and as they fall, that energy is converted into kinetic energy, causing them to speed up. As they climb the next hill, the kinetic energy is converted back into potential energy.

2. Hydroelectric Dams: Water stored behind a dam has gravitational potential energy. As it flows down through turbines, this potential energy is converted into kinetic energy, which is then used to generate electricity.

3. Projectile Motion: When an object is launched into the air, its kinetic energy decreases as it rises, while its potential energy increases. At the peak of its flight, it has maximum potential energy and minimal kinetic energy. As it falls back down, potential energy is converted back into kinetic energy.

Chapter 3: Waves and Sound

In physics, waves are disturbances that transfer energy from one point to another without transferring matter. Waves can be categorized broadly into two types: mechanical waves and electromagnetic waves. Mechanical waves, like sound waves, require a medium (air, water, solids) to travel through, whereas electromagnetic waves, like light, do not require a medium and can propagate through a vacuum.

Sound waves are mechanical waves, meaning they rely on the vibration of particles in a medium, like air. When an object vibrates, it creates compressions (areas of high pressure) and rarefactions (areas of low pressure) in the surrounding medium. These compressions and rarefactions travel through the medium, forming a longitudinal wave, which is how sound propagates. In longitudinal waves, the direction of particle vibration is parallel to the direction of wave propagation.

A key property of sound waves is that they can be characterized by various measurable parameters, including frequency, amplitude, wavelength, and velocity. Each of these characteristics defines a specific aspect of how sound is experienced and how it behaves in different environments.

The speed of sound depends on the medium it is traveling through. In air at room temperature, sound travels at approximately 343 meters per second. In water and solids, sound travels faster because particles in these media are more tightly packed, allowing energy to transfer more efficiently between particles.

Frequency, Amplitude, and Resonance

Frequency refers to the number of oscillations or vibrations that occur per second in a wave and is measured in hertz (Hz). In sound, the frequency determines the pitch we hear. For example, a high-frequency wave corresponds to a high-pitched sound (like a whistle), while a low-frequency wave corresponds to a low-pitched sound (like a bass drum). Human hearing typically ranges from about 20 Hz to 20,000 Hz, though this range can decrease with age or exposure to loud noises. Frequency is directly related to the wavelength of the sound wave, with higher frequencies having shorter wavelengths and vice versa.

Mathematically, frequency (f) is related to the speed (v) of the wave and its wavelength (λ) by the equation:

$$f = \frac{v}{\lambda}$$

This relationship shows that for a given wave speed, increasing the wavelength decreases the frequency and vice versa.

Amplitude refers to the maximum displacement of particles from their equilibrium position as the wave passes through the medium. In the context of sound waves, amplitude correlates with the loudness or volume of the sound. A wave with a larger amplitude will produce a louder sound, while a wave with a smaller amplitude will produce a softer sound. Amplitude is often measured in units of pressure (pascals) or as a relative measure of intensity (decibels, dB). The decibel scale is logarithmic, meaning a small increase in decibels represents a large increase in the sound's power.

For example, a 10 dB increase means the sound is ten times more powerful. The threshold of hearing (the quietest sound the average human can hear) is defined as 0 dB, while sounds above 120 dB can cause immediate hearing damage.

The resonance phenomenon occurs when a system is driven by an external force at its natural frequency. Every object has a natural frequency of vibration, and when the frequency of a sound wave matches this natural frequency, the object will resonate, leading to a dramatic increase in the amplitude of the vibrations. This is why resonance can cause objects to vibrate strongly when exposed to certain frequencies.

A classic example of resonance is the breaking of a wine glass when exposed to a specific high-pitched note. If the frequency of the sound matches the natural frequency of the glass, the vibrations grow in amplitude until the structural integrity of the glass is compromised, causing it to shatter.

In musical instruments, resonance is used to amplify sound. For example, in a guitar, the strings produce sound waves that resonate within the hollow body of the guitar, amplifying the sound that reaches our ears. The length and shape of the instrument body influence the resonance frequencies, which is why different instruments produce unique sounds.

In medical imaging, resonance plays a critical role in magnetic resonance imaging (MRI), where magnetic fields and radio waves resonate with atoms in the body to produce detailed images of internal structures.

Chapter 4: Electricity and Magnetism

Electricity and magnetism are fundamental forces that govern the behavior of charged particles and magnetic fields. These two fields are closely related through the principles of electromagnetism, where electric charges generate electric fields and moving charges (currents) create magnetic fields. Understanding the relationship between electricity and magnetism is essential in various technological applications, including electronics, power generation, and medical equipment.

Electric Charge

Electric charge is a fundamental property of matter that causes particles to experience a force when placed in an electric or magnetic field. There are two types of electric charges: positive and negative. Like charges repel, while opposite charges attract each other. The unit of electric charge is the Coulomb (C), and the charge of a single electron is approximately -1.6×10^{-19} C.

Electric charges can be stationary or moving. When stationary, they create an electric field around them. When moving, they generate both an electric and a magnetic field. The movement of charges is what constitutes an electric current.

Electric Field

An electric field is a vector field that surrounds a charged particle or object. It represents the force that a charged particle would experience if placed in the field. The strength of the electric field (E) is measured in volts per meter (V/m) and is defined by the force per unit charge:

$$E = \frac{f}{q}$$

where F is the force experienced by the charge and q is the charge itself.

Electric fields exert forces on charged particles, and the direction of the force depends on the charge of the particle. Positive charges move in the direction of the electric field, while negative charges move in the opposite direction.

Magnetic Field

A magnetic field is a vector field that surrounds a magnetic object or a current-carrying conductor. Magnetic fields are created by moving electric charges (currents) and can exert forces on other moving charges or magnetic materials. The strength of a magnetic field is measured in Tesla (T) or Gauss (G), with 1 Tesla = 10,000 Gauss.

The force experienced by a moving charge in a magnetic field is known as the Lorentz force, given by: $F = q(v \times B)$ where q is the charge, v is the velocity of the charge, and B is the magnetic field. This force is always perpendicular to both the velocity of the particle and the magnetic field, causing the particle to move in a circular or spiral path.

Electromagnetic Induction

One of the key principles connecting electricity and magnetism is electromagnetic induction, discovered by Michael Faraday. It states that a changing magnetic field can induce an electric current in a conductor. This is the fundamental principle behind transformers, electric generators, and motors.

Faraday's Law of Induction is expressed as:

$$\mathcal{E} = -\frac{d\Phi_B}{dt}$$

where E is the induced electromotive force (emf), and Φ_B is the magnetic flux through a loop. The negative sign indicates that the induced emf opposes the change in magnetic flux (Lenz's Law).

Applications of Electricity and Magnetism

Electricity and magnetism have widespread applications in modern technology. Electric motors convert electrical energy into mechanical energy using magnetic fields and current. Transformers transfer electrical energy between circuits using electromagnetic induction, while generators convert mechanical energy into electrical energy.

Circuits, Voltage, and Current

An electric circuit is a closed loop that allows electric current to flow from a power source, through conductive components, and back to the source. Circuits are used in virtually all electronic devices, from simple household appliances to complex computer systems. Understanding the key concepts of voltage, current, and resistance is critical for analyzing how circuits work.

Electric Current

Electric current is the flow of electric charge through a conductor, typically carried by electrons in a metal wire. The unit of current is the ampere (A), and 1 ampere represents a flow of 1 Coulomb of charge per second:

$$I = \frac{Q}{t}$$

where I is the current, Q is the charge, and t is the time. In most circuits, current flows from the positive terminal of a power source to the negative terminal, although the electrons move in the opposite direction (conventional current).

There are two main types of current: direct current (DC) and alternating current (AC). In DC circuits, the current flows in one direction, while in AC circuits, the current alternates its direction periodically.

Voltage

Voltage, also known as electric potential difference, is the amount of energy per unit charge available to move charges through a circuit. The unit of voltage is the volt (V), and 1 volt represents 1 joule of energy per coulomb of charge:

$$V = \frac{W}{Q}$$

where V is the voltage, W is the energy in joules, and Q is the charge. Voltage is often described as the "pressure" that pushes current through a circuit. Higher voltage means more energy is available to move charges, resulting in a stronger current.

Voltage can be supplied by various sources, such as batteries or power supplies. In a battery, chemical energy is converted into electrical energy, creating a potential difference between the two terminals.

Resistance

Resistance is a measure of how much a material opposes the flow of electric current. The unit of resistance is the ohm (Ω), and Ohm's Law relates resistance (R), current (I), and voltage (V) in a circuit: V=IR This equation indicates that the current in a circuit is directly proportional to the voltage and inversely proportional to the resistance. Materials with low resistance, such as copper, allow current to flow easily, while materials with high resistance, such as rubber, prevent current flow.

Series and Parallel Circuits

In a series circuit, components are connected end-to-end, and the current flows through each component one after the other. The total resistance in a series circuit is the sum of the individual resistances: $R_{total} = R_1 + R_2 + R_3 + ...$ The voltage is divided across the components, but the current remains the same throughout the circuit.

In a parallel circuit, components are connected across the same voltage source. The total resistance in a parallel circuit is given by:

$$\frac{1}{R_{total}} = \frac{1}{R_1} + \frac{1}{R_2} + \frac{1}{R_3} + ...$$

In this case, the voltage across each branch is the same, but the current is divided among the different paths.

Power in Electrical Circuits

The power consumed or supplied by an electrical device is the rate at which electrical energy is converted into another form of energy, such as heat, light, or mechanical work. Power is measured in watts (W), and it is calculated using the formula: P=VI where P is the power, V is the voltage, and I is the current. Another useful formula is: $P=I^2R$ which is used to calculate the power dissipated as heat in a resistor.

Applications of Circuits

Circuits are the building blocks of all electronic devices. Understanding how to design, analyze, and troubleshoot circuits is essential for working in fields such as electrical engineering, computer science, and robotics. Circuits are found in everything from smartphones and computers to household appliances and industrial machinery.

Chapter 5: Optics

Optics is the branch of physics that deals with the behavior and properties of light, including its interactions with matter and the construction of instruments that use or detect light. In the context of the MCAT, optics primarily focuses on the fundamental principles governing light, its reflection, refraction, diffraction, and wave-particle duality. Understanding these principles is essential for interpreting how light behaves in different media, how optical instruments function, and how vision works in biological systems.

Light is an electromagnetic wave, meaning it consists of oscillating electric and magnetic fields that propagate through space. The speed of light in a vacuum is approximately 3.00×10^8 m/s, and it slows down when it travels through other media like water or glass. The relationship between the speed of light in a vacuum (c) and the speed of light in a medium (v) is given by the refractive index (n) of the medium, where: $n = \frac{c}{v}$.

The refractive index describes how much light slows down when it enters a medium. A higher refractive index means light travels more slowly through that medium. The refractive index of a vacuum is 1, and for other materials, it is greater than 1.

When studying optics, one must grasp the nature of light as both a particle and a wave. The wave aspect explains phenomena such as interference, diffraction, and polarization, while the particle aspect explains photoelectric effects, where light ejects electrons from a material.

Geometric Optics

Geometric optics is a simplified model of optics that treats light as rays that travel in straight lines, allowing us to predict how light behaves when it strikes surfaces like mirrors and lenses. There are two primary phenomena in geometric optics: reflection and refraction.

Geometric optics is useful for understanding how light interacts with mirrors, lenses, prisms, and other optical devices. These tools are used extensively in everyday applications such as eyeglasses, cameras, microscopes, and telescopes.

Reflection

Reflection occurs when light bounces off a surface and returns to the medium from which it originated. The law of reflection states that the angle of incidence (the angle between the incoming light ray and the normal to the surface) is equal to the angle of reflection (the angle between the reflected ray and the normal). Mathematically, this is represented as: $\theta_i = \theta_r$

Where:
- θ_i is the angle of incidence.
- θ_r is the angle of reflection.

Reflection can be classified into two types: specular reflection and diffuse reflection.
- Specular Reflection: This occurs on smooth, shiny surfaces, such as mirrors or polished metals, where light reflects in a uniform direction. In specular reflection, parallel incident rays remain parallel after reflection, creating a clear image. This principle is used in mirrors and other reflective devices, allowing us to see our own reflection.

- Diffuse Reflection: This occurs on rough, uneven surfaces, where light reflects in multiple directions. In diffuse reflection, the reflected light rays scatter, making it impossible to see a clear image. This scattering effect is what enables us to see most objects in our environment, as light bounces off surfaces irregularly and enters our eyes from various angles.

Plane Mirrors

Plane mirrors are flat reflective surfaces that form virtual images behind the mirror. The size of the image formed by a plane mirror is equal to the size of the object, and the image appears to be the same distance behind the mirror as the object is in front of it. This is why when you stand 1 meter in front of a plane mirror, your reflection seems to be 1 meter behind it.

The image formed in a plane mirror is upright, laterally inverted (left and right are swapped), and virtual, meaning it cannot be projected onto a screen. These properties of plane mirrors are frequently tested on the MCAT.

Curved Mirrors

Curved mirrors can be concave or convex, and they follow the same law of reflection, but their curved surfaces cause light rays to converge or diverge.

- Concave Mirrors: These mirrors curve inward, like the inside of a spoon, and are also known as converging mirrors. Parallel light rays incident on a concave mirror converge at a focal point after reflection. Concave mirrors can produce real, inverted images if the object is beyond the focal point, or virtual, upright images if the object is closer to the mirror than the focal point.
- Convex Mirrors: These mirrors curve outward, like the back of a spoon, and are also known as diverging mirrors. Parallel light rays reflect outward, as if they are diverging from a focal point behind the mirror. Convex mirrors always produce virtual, upright, and diminished images, regardless of the object's position. Convex mirrors are often used in security and vehicle side mirrors because they provide a wider field of view.

Refraction

Refraction is the bending of light as it passes from one medium to another with a different refractive index. This change in speed causes the light ray to change direction at the boundary between the two media. The angle of refraction (the angle between the refracted ray and the normal) depends on the refractive indices of the two media and the angle of incidence. This relationship is governed by Snell's law, expressed as:

$$n_1 \sin \theta_1 = n_2 \sin \theta_2$$

Where n_1 is the refractive index of the first medium.
n_2 is the refractive index of the second medium.
θ_1 is the angle of incidence.
θ_2 is the angle of refraction.

When light enters a medium with a higher refractive index (e.g., from air to water), it slows down and bends toward the normal. Conversely, when light enters a medium with a lower refractive index (e.g., from water to air), it speeds up and bends away from the normal.

Lenses and Refraction

Lenses rely on refraction to focus or disperse light. A lens is a transparent object, typically made of glass or plastic, that refracts light to form an image. Lenses are classified as either converging (convex) or diverging (concave), depending on their shape.

- Convex Lenses (Converging Lenses): These lenses are thicker in the middle than at the edges. They bend light rays toward each other, causing them to converge at a focal point. Convex lenses can form real, inverted images when the object is beyond the focal point or virtual, upright images when the object is within the focal length.
- Concave Lenses (Diverging Lenses): These lenses are thinner in the middle and thicker at the edges. They cause light rays to diverge as if they originated from a focal point behind the lens. Concave lenses always produce virtual, upright, and diminished images.

The behavior of light as it passes through lenses is essential for understanding optical instruments like microscopes and corrective lenses. The ability of lenses to focus light is described by the lens-maker's equation:

$$\frac{1}{f} = (n - 1)\left(\frac{1}{R_1} - \frac{1}{R_2}\right)$$

Where: f is the focal length of the lens.
n is the refractive index of the lens material.
R_1 and R_2 are the radii of curvature of the two surfaces of the lens.

Chapter 6: Thermodynamics

Thermodynamics is the branch of physics that deals with the relationships between heat, work, temperature, and energy. It provides a framework for understanding the behavior of systems, particularly those involving energy exchanges, and is governed by a set of fundamental principles known as the laws of thermodynamics.

At its core, thermodynamics explores how energy is transferred from one form to another and how it affects matter. This subject is essential in a wide range of fields, including engineering, chemistry, biology, and even cosmology. For students of the MCAT, having a solid grasp of thermodynamics is vital as it underpins much of the biochemical processes in the body, such as cellular respiration and energy metabolism.

Key Concepts in Thermodynamics

1. System and Surroundings:
   - A system refers to the part of the universe that is being studied, while the surroundings are everything outside the system. Systems can be open (exchange of matter and energy), closed (exchange of energy but not matter), or isolated (no exchange of matter or energy).
2. Types of Processes:
   - Isothermal: Temperature remains constant.
   - Adiabatic: No heat exchange occurs.
   - Isobaric: Pressure remains constant.
   - Isochoric: Volume remains constant.
3. State Functions:
   - A state function depends only on the state of the system and not on how it reached that state. Examples include internal energy, pressure, volume, temperature, and entropy.
4. Internal Energy (U):
   - The total energy contained within a system, consisting of kinetic and potential energies of the molecules. Changes in internal energy can be caused by heat (q) and work (W), according to the first law of thermodynamics.
5. Enthalpy (H):
   - A measure of the total heat content of a system at constant pressure. It is defined as $H=U+PV$, where P is pressure and V is volume.
6. Entropy (S): A measure of the disorder or randomness in a system. A higher entropy indicates a greater level of disorder. Entropy tends to increase in spontaneous processes, reflecting the second law of thermodynamics.
7. Gibbs Free Energy (G): Gibbs free energy is used to determine the spontaneity of a process. The change in Gibbs free energy (ΔG) is given by the equation:

$$\Delta G = \Delta H - T\Delta S$$

where ΔH is the change in enthalpy,
T is the temperature in Kelvin, and
ΔS is the change in entropy. A negative
ΔG indicates a spontaneous process, while a positive value indicates a non-spontaneous process.

Heat Transfer and Laws of Thermodynamics

Heat Transfer

Heat transfer refers to the movement of thermal energy from one object or system to another, typically from regions of higher temperature to regions of lower temperature. There are three main mechanisms of heat transfer:

1. Conduction:
   - Conduction is the transfer of heat through a material or between materials that are in direct contact. In conduction, energy is passed along by collisions between molecules or atoms. This process is most efficient in solids, particularly metals, which have free electrons that facilitate the energy transfer.
   - Example: When you touch a metal spoon that has been sitting in a pot of hot water, the heat from the water is transferred to the spoon by conduction.
2. Convection:
   - Convection involves the transfer of heat by the movement of fluids (liquids or gases). It can be either natural (caused by buoyancy forces due to temperature differences) or forced (caused by external forces, such as a fan or pump).
   - Example: Boiling water on a stove exhibits convection as the heated water at the bottom rises and cooler water sinks, creating a circulation pattern.
3. Radiation:
   - Radiation is the transfer of heat in the form of electromagnetic waves, such as infrared radiation. It does not require a medium, meaning heat can be transferred through the vacuum of space.
   - Example: The heat we feel from the sun is a result of radiation, as energy is transmitted through space and absorbed by our skin.

Laws of Thermodynamics

The laws of thermodynamics are the fundamental principles that describe how energy is transferred and transformed. There are four laws, typically numbered from zero to three.

1. Zeroth Law of Thermodynamics:
   - The zeroth law establishes the concept of temperature and thermal equilibrium. It states that if two systems are each in thermal equilibrium with a third system, they are in thermal equilibrium with each other. This law allows for the definition of temperature as a fundamental property.
2. First Law of Thermodynamics (Law of Energy Conservation):
   - The first law is essentially the principle of the conservation of energy. It states that energy cannot be created or destroyed, only transferred or converted from one form to another. In mathematical form:

$$\Delta U = Q - W$$

where ΔU is the change in internal energy of the system,

Q is the heat added to the system, and

W is the work done by the system.

- Example: When a gas is heated in a closed container, the added heat increases the internal energy of the gas, which may result in an increase in temperature or cause the gas to do work by expanding.
3. Second Law of Thermodynamics:
    - The second law states that the total entropy of an isolated system can never decrease over time, and it can only remain constant in a reversible process. In other words, natural processes tend to move towards a state of greater disorder or randomness. This law also implies that heat naturally flows from hot objects to cold ones.
    - Example: Ice melting in a warm room is a natural process where the system moves from a state of lower entropy (ice) to higher entropy (liquid water).
4. Third Law of Thermodynamics:
    - The third law states that as a system approaches absolute zero (0 Kelvin), the entropy of the system approaches a minimum value. For a perfectly crystalline substance, this entropy approaches zero at absolute zero.
    - Example: It is impossible to reach absolute zero, as doing so would require removing all energy from the system, which violates the third law.

Chapter 7: Fluid Dynamics

Fluid dynamics is the branch of physics that deals with the study of fluids (liquids and gases) in motion. It focuses on understanding how fluids behave under various conditions and how they interact with their environment. In the context of MCAT physics, fluid dynamics is crucial because it helps explain several natural phenomena, from blood flow in arteries to the principles governing airplane flight.

Basic Concepts of Fluid Dynamics

1. Density (ρ): Density is defined as mass per unit volume of a fluid. Mathematically, it is represented as: $\rho = \frac{m}{v}$. Where m is mass and V is volume. In SI units, density is expressed in kilograms per cubic meter (kg/m³). Fluids can vary in density, which influences their behavior under different conditions. For example, water is denser than air, which affects how they flow and exert pressure.
2. Pressure (P): Pressure is the force exerted by a fluid per unit area. It is a scalar quantity and is represented as: $p = \frac{F}{A}$. Where F is the force and A is the area. The SI unit of pressure is the Pascal (Pa). In fluid dynamics, pressure is a key factor in determining how fluids move and how they exert forces on objects.
3. Flow Rate (Q): The flow rate of a fluid is the volume of fluid passing through a cross-sectional area per unit of time. It is given by: Q=A·V. Where A is the cross-sectional area and v is the fluid velocity. Flow rate is often measured in cubic meters per second (m³/s). Understanding flow rate is essential for calculating how fluids move through different channels, such as pipes or blood vessels.
4. Viscosity (η): Viscosity refers to the internal friction within a fluid that resists flow. Fluids with higher viscosity, such as honey, flow more slowly than low-viscosity fluids, like water. Viscosity is critical when dealing with real-life fluid systems because it affects the speed and pattern of fluid flow.
5. Laminar vs. Turbulent Flow: In laminar flow, fluid moves in parallel layers with minimal mixing between layers. This type of flow is smooth and orderly. Conversely, turbulent flow is characterized by chaotic, irregular fluid motion. The Reynolds number (Re) determines whether a flow is laminar or turbulent, with values below 2,000 typically indicating laminar flow, and values above 4,000 indicating turbulence.

Continuity Equation

The continuity equation is a fundamental principle of fluid dynamics that expresses the conservation of mass in fluid flow. It states that the flow rate of an incompressible fluid remains constant along a streamline, which implies:

$$A_1 \cdot v_1 = A_2 \cdot v_2$$

Where A1 and $v1$ are the cross-sectional area and velocity at one point, and A2 and $v2$ are the area and velocity at another point. This equation means that when the cross-sectional area decreases, the fluid velocity must increase to maintain the same flow rate, and vice versa.

Bernoulli's Equation and Applications

Bernoulli's equation is derived from the principle of conservation of energy for fluid flow. It relates the pressure, velocity, and height at different points in a moving fluid and is especially useful for describing fluid behavior under ideal conditions (inviscid, incompressible fluids). Bernoulli's equation is stated as:

$$P + \frac{1}{2}\rho v^2 + \rho g h = \text{constant}$$

Where: P is the fluid pressure, ρ is the fluid density, v is the fluid velocity, g is the acceleration due to gravity, h is the height above a reference point.

Explanation of the Terms

1. Pressure Energy (P): This term accounts for the energy due to fluid pressure. In regions where the fluid pressure is high, there is more pressure energy available for the fluid's motion or other uses.
2. Kinetic Energy ($\frac{1}{2}\rho v$) This term represents the kinetic energy of the fluid, which is associated with its velocity. Fluids moving at higher velocities have more kinetic energy.
3. Potential Energy (ρgh): This term accounts for the gravitational potential energy of the fluid. Fluids at higher elevations have more potential energy due to their position relative to a reference point.

Applications of Bernoulli's Equation

Bernoulli's equation has widespread applications in both natural and engineered systems. Its utility lies in its ability to describe how fluid speed, pressure, and height are interrelated under steady flow conditions.

1. Airplane Wings (Lift):

One of the most well-known applications of Bernoulli's principle is the generation of lift in airplane wings. Air moving over the curved top surface of a wing travels faster than air moving beneath the flatter bottom surface. According to Bernoulli's equation, the higher velocity on top leads to a lower pressure, creating a pressure difference that generates lift, enabling the airplane to stay in the air.

2. Venturi Effect:

The Venturi effect describes the reduction in pressure that occurs when a fluid flows through a constricted section of pipe. This is a direct consequence of Bernoulli's equation: as the cross-sectional area of the pipe decreases, the velocity of the fluid increases, leading to a corresponding drop in pressure. This principle is used in devices such as Venturi meters, which measure flow rates, and in carburetors, where it helps mix air and fuel.

3. Blood Flow in Arteries:

Bernoulli's principle also applies to the human circulatory system. In areas where blood vessels narrow, such as in stenosed arteries, the velocity of blood increases, leading to a drop in pressure. This explains some of the hemodynamic changes that occur in diseases involving blood vessels.

4. Pitot Tubes:

Pitot tubes are devices used to measure fluid velocity, particularly in airspeed measurements for aircraft. A pitot tube works by comparing the fluid pressure in a flowing stream to the pressure in a static stream. The difference between these pressures, when applied to Bernoulli's equation, can be used to calculate the velocity of the fluid.

5. Chimneys and Drafts:

Chimneys exploit Bernoulli's principle to enhance the draft (the upward movement of air or gases). Air flows faster at the top of the chimney due to lower external pressure compared to the pressure inside the chimney. This pressure difference causes smoke or gases to rise, helping vent them out of the chimney.

6. Sprayers and Atomizers:

Bernoulli's principle is also utilized in devices like sprayers and atomizers. When air flows quickly over a liquid, the pressure above the liquid decreases, causing the liquid to rise and form a spray. This application is used in everything from perfume bottles to industrial applications.

Limitations of Bernoulli's Equation

Bernoulli's equation assumes that the fluid is incompressible and inviscid (having no internal friction). However, in real-world applications, most fluids exhibit some degree of viscosity and compressibility, which can cause deviations from ideal behavior. For example, in very narrow or highly viscous flows, energy losses due to friction (viscous drag) become significant, and Bernoulli's equation must be modified to account for these factors.

Practical Question For Section 5:

1. Which of the following is a scalar quantity?
A) Velocity
B) Force
C) Speed
D) Displacement

2. What is the unit of force in the SI system?
A) Newton
B) Joule
C) Kilogram
D) Meter

3. According to Newton's First Law of Motion, an object will remain at rest unless:
A) It loses energy
B) A net external force acts on it
C) It is in a vacuum
D) Its inertia changes

4. What does Newton's Second Law state about force and acceleration?
A) Force is inversely proportional to acceleration
B) Force is directly proportional to acceleration
C) Force is inversely proportional to mass
D) Acceleration is independent of force

5. If an object is moving with constant velocity, the net force acting on it is:
A) Positive
B) Negative
C) Zero
D) Equal to its mass

6. Which of the following is an example of non-contact force?
A) Friction
B) Tension
C) Normal force
D) Gravitational force

7. The tendency of an object to resist changes in its state of motion is called:
A) Inertia
B) Acceleration
C) Friction
D) Velocity

8. A car accelerates uniformly from rest to a speed of 20 m/s in 10 seconds. What is the acceleration of the car?
A) 2 m/s^2
B) 10 m/s^2

C) 5 m/s²
D) 20 m/s²

9. **Which of the following is true about objects in uniform motion?**
A) They experience a constant net force
B) Their velocity changes
C) Their acceleration is zero
D) Their displacement is zero

10. **In which direction does friction act on a moving object?**
A) Opposite to the direction of motion
B) In the same direction as motion
C) Perpendicular to the surface
D) Randomly

11. **If the net force acting on an object is zero, the object will:**
A) Come to rest
B) Accelerate uniformly
C) Continue at constant velocity
D) Increase in mass

12. **The force that acts perpendicular to the surface of contact between two objects is called:**
A) Frictional force
B) Normal force
C) Tension
D) Applied force

13. **Which law states that the force acting between two objects is equal in magnitude and opposite in direction?**
A) Newton's First Law
B) Newton's Second Law
C) Newton's Third Law
D) Law of Universal Gravitation

14. **The acceleration due to gravity on Earth is approximately:**
A) 1 m/s²
B) 9.8 m/s²
C) 3.5 m/s²
D) 5 m/s²

15. **Which of the following does not affect the magnitude of the frictional force?**
A) The mass of the object
B) The nature of the surfaces in contact
C) The velocity of the object
D) The normal force acting on the object

16. **What is the relationship between mass and inertia?**
A) Inertia increases with velocity

B) Inertia is independent of mass
C) Inertia decreases as mass increases
D) Inertia increases as mass increases

17. What is the net force on an object moving at constant speed in a straight line?
A) Equal to its mass
B) Equal to the force of gravity
C) Zero
D) Equal to its weight

18. If a constant force is applied to an object, the object will:
A) Stop immediately
B) Move with constant velocity
C) Accelerate in the direction of the force
D) Move in the opposite direction of the force

19. An object is in free fall. What force is acting on it?
A) Tension
B) Normal force
C) Gravitational force
D) Air resistance

20. An object thrown vertically upward will have zero velocity at the highest point of its path because:
A) The force acting on it is zero
B) The net force is upward
C) Gravity is pulling it downwards
D) Air resistance acts upward

21. What is the SI unit of work?
a) Newton
b) Joule
c) Watt
d) Pascal

22. If a force is applied but no displacement occurs, how much work is done?
a) Positive work
b) Negative work
c) Zero work
d) Infinite work

23. Which of the following formulas correctly represents the work done by a constant force?
a) $W = Fd\sin(\theta)$
b) $W = Fd\cos(\theta)$
c) $W = \dfrac{fd}{\cos(\theta)}$

d) $W = \dfrac{fd}{\sin(\theta)}$

24. Kinetic energy depends on which two factors?
a) Mass and acceleration
b) Mass and velocity
c) Velocity and displacement
d) Force and velocity

25. What is the kinetic energy of an object with a mass of 5 kg moving at a velocity of 10 m/s?
a) 50 J
b) 100 J
c) 250 J
d) 500 J

26. **Which of the following is true about potential energy?**
a) It depends on the object's velocity
b) It depends on the object's mass and height
c) It is maximum when the object is in motion
d) It is zero at the highest point of an object's motion

27. **Gravitational potential energy is given by which formula?**
a) $PE = \dfrac{1}{2}mv^2$
b) $PE = mgh$
c) $PE = \dfrac{1}{2}kx^2$
d) $PE = ma$

28. If an object is lifted to double its original height, what happens to its gravitational potential energy?
a) It is halved
b) It doubles
c) It stays the same
d) It quadruples

29. Which quantity represents the rate at which work is done?
a) Force
b) Power
c) Kinetic energy
d) Potential energy

30. **Which of the following is a scalar quantity?**
a) Work
b) Force
c) Displacement
d) Momentum

31. According to the work-energy theorem, the net work done on an object is equal to:
a) The change in its potential energy
b) The change in its kinetic energy
c) The sum of its kinetic and potential energy
d) Its power

32. A car's kinetic energy increases by a factor of four. What happens to its velocity?
a) It doubles
b) It triples
c) It quadruples
d) It halves

33. If the speed of an object is doubled, by what factor does its kinetic energy change?
a) It doubles
b) It triples
c) It quadruples
d) It halves

34. In a frictionless system, which principle states that total mechanical energy remains constant?
a) Newton's First Law
b) Law of Conservation of Energy
c) Work-Energy Theorem
d) Pascal's Principle

35. Which of the following scenarios is an example of negative work?
a) Pushing a car uphill
b) Lifting a box from the floor
c) Friction slowing down a moving object
d) Throwing a ball upward

36. What happens to the total mechanical energy of a system when only conservative forces act on it?
a) It increases
b) It decreases
c) It remains constant
d) It oscillates

37. Which of the following factors does not affect the potential energy of an object?
a) Mass
b) Height
c) Velocity
d) Gravity

38. What is the work done by gravity when an object moves horizontally on a frictionless surface?
a) Positive work

b) Negative work
c) Zero work
d) Infinite work

39. In which of the following situations is work NOT being done on the object?
a) A person pushing a box up a hill
b) A person holding a book still above their head
c) A car accelerating on a highway
d) A falling rock

40. What is the power output if 400 J of work is done in 20 seconds?
a) 10 W
b) 20 W
c) 15 W
d) 5 W

41. Which of the following best defines the term "frequency" in the context of sound waves?
A) The speed at which sound waves travel
B) The number of oscillations per second
C) The distance between two consecutive compressions
D) The maximum displacement of particles in the medium

42. What unit is frequency measured in?
A) Decibels
B) Pascals
C) Hertz
D) Watts

43. In sound waves, amplitude is most closely related to which of the following?
A) Pitch
B) Loudness
C) Wavelength
D) Speed of sound

44. Resonance occurs when:
A) A system is driven at a frequency higher than its natural frequency
B) A system is driven at a frequency equal to its natural frequency
C) The speed of the wave is constant
D) The amplitude of a wave decreases over time

45. Which of the following represents the formula for calculating frequency?
A) $F = \lambda / v$
B) $F = v / \lambda$
C) $f = \lambda v$
D) $F = 1 / v\lambda$

46. What happens to the wavelength if the frequency of a sound wave is doubled?
A) It is halved
B) It is doubled
C) It remains constant
D) It becomes zero

47. The decibel scale is used to measure:
A) The frequency of a sound wave
B) The loudness of a sound
C) The wavelength of a sound wave
D) The speed of sound

48. Which of the following is an example of resonance in everyday life?
A) A radio picking up a signal
B) A vibrating guitar string
C) A car horn blaring
D) A person speaking

49. The loudness of a sound is directly proportional to:
A) Frequency
B) Wavelength
C) Amplitude
D) Resonance frequency

50. In which medium does sound travel the fastest?
A) Air
B) Water
C) Vacuum
D) Steel

51. When sound waves travel from air into water, what happens to their speed?
A) It increases
B) It decreases
C) It remains the same
D) It becomes zero

52. Which characteristic of sound changes when you adjust the volume on a speaker?
A) Frequency
B) Amplitude
C) Wavelength
D) Resonance

53. What is the primary factor that determines the pitch of a sound?
A) Amplitude
B) Frequency
C) Wavelength
D) Speed of sound

54. If the frequency of a sound wave is 500 Hz and the speed of sound is 340 m/s, what is the wavelength of the wave?
A) 0.68 m
B) 170 m
C) 1.47 m
D) 0.34 m

55. What is the natural frequency of an object?
A) The highest frequency at which it can vibrate
B) The frequency at which it vibrates when disturbed without external force
C) The frequency of the loudest sound it can produce
D) The average of all possible vibrational frequencies

56. The amplitude of a wave is:
A) The distance between two successive compressions
B) The height of the wave from its equilibrium position
C) The number of vibrations per second
D) The time taken for one complete cycle

57. Which of the following will increase if the amplitude of a sound wave is increased?
A) Pitch
B) Frequency
C) Loudness
D) Wavelength

58. Which of the following conditions is necessary for resonance to occur?
A) The medium must be air
B) The driving frequency must match the natural frequency
C) The wave must have a low amplitude
D) The wave must have a high frequency

59. A wave has a frequency of 1000 Hz and travels at a speed of 340 m/s. What is its wavelength?
A) 0.34 m
B) 3.4 m
C) 0.034 m
D) 34 m

60. Which term describes the point where a sound wave's pressure is at its maximum?
A) Rarefaction
B) Compression
C) Crest
D) Trough

61. Which of the following best defines electric current?
A) The flow of electric charge
B) The amount of energy used by a device

C) The resistance to electric flow
D) The potential difference between two points

62. The unit of electric current is:
A) Volt
B) Ampere
C) Ohm
D) Joule

63. Ohm's Law is represented by which of the following equations?
A) V=IR
B) P=IV
C) F=q(v×B)
D) E= F/Q

64. In a series circuit, the total resistance is:
A) The product of individual resistances
B) The sum of individual resistances
C) The inverse of the sum of individual resistances
D) The difference between the highest and lowest resistance

65. Which of the following is a characteristic of a parallel circuit?
A) The same current flows through each component
B) The total resistance is higher than any individual resistance
C) The voltage across each component is the same
D) The total voltage is the sum of the individual voltages

66. The unit of electrical resistance is:
A) Ampere
B) Coulomb
C) Ohm
D) Volt

67. What happens to the current if the voltage is increased while the resistance remains constant?
A) The current increases
B) The current decreases
C) The current remains the same
D) The current becomes zero

68. Which of the following components stores electrical energy in a circuit?
A) Resistor
B) Capacitor
C) Diode
D) Inductor

69. Which law relates the magnetic field around a conductor to the current passing through it?
A) Coulomb's Law
B) Faraday's Law
C) Ampere's Law
D) Kirchhoff's Law

70. Electromagnetic induction occurs when:
A) A conductor is placed in a stationary magnetic field
B) A magnetic field is applied to a stationary conductor
C) The magnetic field around a conductor changes
D) A conductor is heated

71. What is the SI unit of magnetic flux?
A) Weber
B) Tesla
C) Gauss
D) Henry

72. What force acts on a moving charge in a magnetic field?
A) Gravitational force
B) Electric force
C) Lorentz force
D) Nuclear force

73. The relationship between voltage, current, and resistance in a circuit is governed by:
A) Lenz's Law
B) Kirchhoff's Current Law
C) Ohm's Law
D) Faraday's Law

74. Which quantity remains constant in a series circuit?
A) Voltage
B) Current
C) Resistance
D) Power

75. The direction of induced current in a conductor due to a changing magnetic field is given by:
A) Ohm's Law
B) Lenz's Law
C) Coulomb's Law
D) Ampere's Law

76. The electric potential difference between two points in a circuit is known as:
A) Current
B) Voltage

C) Power
D) Capacitance

77. What happens to the total resistance if more resistors are added in parallel to a circuit?
A) It increases
B) It decreases
C) It remains the same
D) It becomes infinite

78. Which of the following devices is used to measure current in a circuit?
A) Voltmeter
B) Ohmmeter
C) Ammeter
D) Galvanometer

79. In which of the following circuits is the power dissipated the highest?
A) A circuit with high voltage and low current
B) A circuit with low voltage and high current
C) A circuit with high voltage and high resistance
D) A circuit with low voltage and high resistance

80. Which of the following is true about alternating current (AC)?
A) It flows in only one direction
B) It has a constant voltage
C) It changes direction periodically
D) It is used only in batteries

81. Which of the following correctly represents the law of reflection?
A) $\theta i + \theta r = 90°$
B) $\theta i = \theta r$
C) $\theta i = 2\theta r$
D) $\theta r = \sin^{-1}(\theta i)$

82. When light passes from air into water, it:
A) Speeds up and bends toward the normal
B) Slows down and bends toward the normal
C) Slows down and bends away from the normal
D) Speeds up and bends away from the normal

83. In a concave mirror, what kind of image is formed when the object is placed beyond the focal point?
A) Virtual and upright
B) Real and inverted
C) Virtual and diminished
D) Real and enlarged

84. A convex mirror is used in vehicles because:
A) It produces a magnified image
B) It produces a virtual, upright, and diminished image

C) It produces a real, inverted image
D) It converges light rays to a single point

85. Which formula correctly expresses Snell's law of refraction?
A. $n_1 \sin\theta_1 = n_2 \sin\theta_2$
B. $n_1 \sin\theta_1 = n_2 \cos\theta_2$
C. $n_1 \cos\theta_1 = n_2 \sin\theta_2$
D. $n_1 + n_2 = \theta_2 + \theta_2$

86. What is the refractive index of a medium if light travels through it with a speed of 2.25×10^8 m/s? (Assume the speed of light in vacuum is 3.00×10^8 m/s)
A) 1.50
B) 1.33
C) 1.67
D) 2.00

87. In which of the following situations does total internal reflection occur?
A) Light passes from air to water
B) Light passes from water to glass
C) Light passes from glass to water
D) Light passes from glass to air at an angle greater than the critical angle

88. The focal length of a concave mirror is:
A) Always positive
B) Always negative
C) Positive when the object is far away
D) Dependent on the size of the object

89. A light ray is incident at an angle of 30° on a glass-air interface. If the refractive index of glass is 1.5, what is the angle of refraction in the air?
A) 19.47°
B) 41.81°
C) 48.59°
D) 60.00°

90. Which of the following lenses is used to correct myopia (nearsightedness)?
A) Convex lens
B) Concave lens
C) Cylindrical lens
D) Bifocal lens

91. The image formed by a plane mirror is:
A) Real, inverted, and the same size as the object
B) Virtual, upright, and smaller than the object
C) Virtual, upright, and the same size as the object
D) Real, inverted, and larger than the object

92. What happens to the speed of light as it passes from glass into air?
A) It decreases

B) It remains the same
C) It increases
D) It becomes zero

93. When a ray of light travels parallel to the principal axis and hits a concave mirror, it:
A) Passes through the center of curvature
B) Reflects back parallel to the principal axis
C) Passes through the focal point
D) Reflects through the vertex of the mirror

94. Which of the following best describes the critical angle in optics?
A) The angle of incidence at which total reflection occurs
B) The angle of incidence at which the angle of refraction is 90°
C) The angle of incidence at which no reflection occurs
D) The angle of incidence at which light travels at the speed of sound

95. For a concave lens, which of the following is true about the image formed?
A) Real, inverted, and enlarged
B) Virtual, upright, and diminished
C) Virtual, inverted, and enlarged
D) Real, upright, and diminished

96. The refractive index of diamond is 2.42. What is the speed of light inside diamond?
A) 1.24×10^8 m/s
B) 1.86×10^8 m/s
C) 2.42×10^8 m/s
D) 3.00×10^8 m/s

97. A ray of light passes from air to glass. Which statement about its behavior is true?
A) Its speed increases and it bends toward the normal
B) Its speed decreases and it bends away from the normal
C) Its speed decreases and it bends toward the normal
D) Its speed remains the same and it bends away from the normal

98. The power of a convex lens is measured in:
A) Meters
B) Diopters
C) Newtons
D) Pascals

99. What is the magnification of an image produced by a concave mirror if the object is placed at the focal point?
A) Zero
B) Infinity
C) Positive
D) Negative

100. The angle between the incident ray and the reflected ray in specular reflection is:
A) Equal to the angle of incidence

B) Twice the angle of incidence
C) Always 90°
D) Equal to the angle of refraction

101. Which of the following is a state function in thermodynamics?
A) Work
B) Heat
C) Enthalpy
D) Path

102. In an adiabatic process, which of the following occurs?
A) No work is done
B) No heat is exchanged
C) Pressure remains constant
D) Volume remains constant

103. What does the first law of thermodynamics state?
A) Energy can be created but not destroyed
B) Energy cannot be created or destroyed, only transferred
C) Entropy of a system always decreases
D) All processes are reversible

104. Heat transfer through a solid is primarily due to:
A) Radiation
B) Convection
C) Conduction
D) Evaporation

105. Which law of thermodynamics states that absolute zero cannot be reached?
A) Zeroth law
B) First law
C) Second law
D) Third law

106. Which of the following is an example of a reversible process?
A) Free expansion of a gas
B) Melting of ice at 0°C
C) Combustion of fuel
D) Mixing of two gases

107. In which process does heat flow from a hotter object to a cooler one without any physical medium?
A) Conduction
B) Convection
C) Radiation
D) Sublimation

108. What happens to the entropy of an isolated system during a spontaneous process?
A) It increases
B) It decreases
C) It remains the same
D) It can increase or decrease

109. The total internal energy of a system depends on:
A) The temperature of the surroundings
B) The amount of work done by the system
C) The state of the system
D) The volume of the system only

110. Which equation represents the change in internal energy in a thermodynamic system?
A) Q=W−UQ
B) ΔU=Q−W
C) Q=U+PV
D) ΔG=ΔH−TΔS

111. Which of the following processes does not involve heat transfer?
A) Isothermal
B) Adiabatic
C) Isochoric
D) Isobaric

112. Which quantity always increases in a spontaneous process?
A) Gibbs free energy
B) Enthalpy
C) Internal energy
D) Entropy

113. Which of the following statements is true for a cyclic process?
A) The change in internal energy is zero
B) The entropy of the system decreases
C) The total work done is zero
D) The heat added equals the work done

114. The Zeroth Law of Thermodynamics helps define which physical property?
A) Entropy
B) Temperature
C) Pressure
D) Heat

115. In a heat engine, what is the efficiency defined as?
A) The ratio of work done to heat added
B) The ratio of heat added to work done
C) The ratio of heat transferred to the surroundings
D) The amount of entropy generated

116.   Which of the following is not a mechanism of heat transfer?
A) Conduction
B) Convection
C) Radiation
D) Reflection

117.   During which process is no change in temperature observed?
A) Isothermal
B) Adiabatic
C) Isochoric
D) None of the above

118.   In which type of heat transfer do molecules of the substance move from one place to another?
A) Conduction
B) Convection
C) Radiation
D) None of the above

119.   According to the second law of thermodynamics, which of the following is true?
A) Energy can be completely converted into work
B) Entropy of an isolated system tends to decrease
C) No process is possible in which the sole result is the transfer of heat from a cooler to a hotter body
D) Work can be done without any loss of energy

120.   The Carnot engine operates between two temperature reservoirs at 500 K and 300 K. What is the maximum possible efficiency?
A) 40%
B) 60%
C) 20%
D) 50%

121.   What physical quantity is conserved in the continuity equation?
A) Energy
B) Pressure
C) Mass
D) Volume

122.   Bernoulli's equation is a statement of which of the following principles?
A) Conservation of momentum
B) Conservation of energy
C) Conservation of mass
D) Conservation of force

123.   Which of the following is an application of Bernoulli's principle?
A) Determining the viscosity of a fluid

B) Measuring the velocity of a fluid using a Pitot tube

C) Calculating the force of gravity on a fluid

D) Finding the volume of a liquid

124. What does the term $\frac{1}{2}\rho v^2$ represent in Bernoulli's equation?

A) Pressure energy

B) Kinetic energy per unit volume

C) Gravitational potential energy

D) Mass per unit volume

125. According to Bernoulli's principle, what happens to the pressure in a fluid as its velocity increases?

A) Pressure increases

B) Pressure decreases

C) Pressure remains constant

D) Pressure fluctuates

126. The Venturi effect is an application of which fluid dynamics principle?

A) Pascal's principle

B) Bernoulli's principle

C) Archimedes' principle

D) Newton's second law

127. In fluid flow, when the cross-sectional area decreases, what happens to the fluid velocity according to the continuity equation?

A) Velocity decreases

B) Velocity remains constant

C) Velocity increases

D) Velocity becomes zero

128. What is the SI unit of pressure used in fluid dynamics?

A) Newton

B) Pascal

C) Joule

D) Watt

129. What is the main factor that distinguishes turbulent flow from laminar flow?

A) Density of the fluid

B) Temperature of the fluid

C) Reynolds number

D) Continuity of flow

130. In Bernoulli's equation, the term ρgh represents which type of energy?

A) Kinetic energy

B) Pressure energy

C) Gravitational potential energy

D) Thermal energy

131. What causes lift in an airplane wing according to Bernoulli's principle?
A) Higher velocity of air below the wing
B) Higher pressure on the top surface of the wing
C) Higher velocity of air over the top of the wing
D) Higher temperature on the wing surface

132. The Reynolds number is used to determine which type of flow?
A) Ideal flow
B) Laminar vs. turbulent flow
C) Constant flow
D) Isothermal flow

133. Which of the following conditions must be met for Bernoulli's equation to apply?
A) The fluid must be compressible
B) The fluid must be viscous
C) The fluid must be incompressible and non-viscous
D) The flow must be turbulent

134. What does the continuity equation suggest about fluid speed in narrower pipes?
A) The speed decreases
B) The speed increases
C) The speed remains the same
D) The speed fluctuates

135. In which of the following systems is Bernoulli's equation least likely to apply accurately?
A) Ideal gas flowing through a wide pipe
B) Water flowing in a laminar manner
C) Oil flowing through a narrow tube with high viscosity
D) Airflow over a smooth surface

136. Which of the following quantities is not explicitly considered in Bernoulli's equation?
A) Fluid density
B) Fluid viscosity
C) Fluid velocity
D) Fluid pressure

137. In a Venturi meter, what happens to the pressure of a fluid as it passes through a constriction?
A) Pressure increases
B) Pressure decreases
C) Pressure remains constant
D) Pressure fluctuates rapidly

Answers and Explanation

1. C. Speed. – Speed is a scalar quantity because it only has magnitude, not direction. Other options like velocity and displacement are vector quantities because they involve both magnitude and direction.
2. Newton. – The SI unit of force is the Newton (N), which is equivalent to kg·m/s^2. It measures the force required to accelerate a 1 kg mass by 1 meter per second squared.
3. B. A net external force acts on it. – According to Newton's First Law (the law of inertia), an object will remain at rest or in uniform motion unless acted upon by a net external force.
4. B. Force is directly proportional to acceleration. – Newton's Second Law of Moton states that the force acting on an object is directly proportional to its acceleration, as expressed in the equation F=ma.
5. C. Zero. – If an object is moving with constant velocity, the net force acting on it is zero. According to Newton's First Law, objects in motion at a constant velocity will continue to do so unless acted on by a net external force.
6. D. Gravitational force. – Gravitational force is a non-contact force that acts over a distance without requiring physical contact between objects, unlike friction or tension.
7. A. Inertia. – Inertia is the property of an object that resists changes to its state of motion. The more mass an object has, the greater its inertia.
8. A. 2 m/s^2. – The car's acceleration is calculated by dividing the change in velocity (20 m/s) by the time taken (10 s), giving an acceleration of a=2m/s^2
9. C. Their acceleration is zero. – Objects in uniform motion have a constant velocity and thus no acceleration, meaning the net force on them is zero.
10. A. Opposite to the direction of motion. – Friction always acts in the direction opposite to the motion of an object, resisting its movement.
11. C. Continue at constant velocity. – According to Newton's First Law, if the net force on an object is zero, it will continue moving at a constant velocity or remain at rest.
12. B. Normal force. – The normal force is the force exerted by a surface perpendicular to the object in contact with it, balancing the object's weight.
13. C. Newton's Third Law. – Newton's Third Law states that for every action, there is an equal and opposite reaction. This means that forces between two interacting objects are equal in magnitude and opposite in direction.
14. B. 9.8 m/s^2. – The acceleration due to gravity on Earth is approximately 9.8m/s^2, which is the rate at which objects accelerate when falling under the influence of Earth's gravitational pull.
15. C. The velocity of the object. – The magnitude of the frictional force depends on the normal force and the nature of the surfaces in contact, but not on the velocity of the object.
16. D. Inertia increases as mass increases. – Inertia is directly related to mass; as an object's mass increases, its inertia also increases, meaning more force is required to change its state of motion.

17. C. Zero. – If an object is moving at constant speed in a straight line, the net force acting on it is zero, according to Newton's First Law.
18. C. Accelerate in the direction of the force. – According to Newton's Second Law, if a constant force is applied, the object will accelerate in the direction of the force.
19. C. Gravitational force. – When an object is in free fall, the only force acting on it is gravity, which causes it to accelerate downward.
20. C. Gravity is pulling it downwards. – At the highest point of its path, the object's velocity becomes zero for an instant before it starts descending, but gravity continues to act downward, pulling the object back to the ground.
21. B. Joule. - The joule is the SI unit of work, defined as one newton of force applied over a distance of one meter.
22. C. Zero work. - Work is only done if there is displacement. If no movement occurs, the work done is zero, even if a force is applied.
23. B. W=Fdcos(θ). - Work is calculated as the force multiplied by displacement and the cosine of the angle between the force and the direction of movement.
24. B. Mass and velocity. - Kinetic energy depends on both the mass and the velocity of the object, as given by the formula $KE = \frac{1}{2}MV^2$
25. D. 500 J. - Using the kinetic energy formula, $KE = \frac{1}{2}MV^2$ we calculate: $KE = \frac{1}{2} \times 5 \times 10^2$ =500 J
26. B. It depends on the object's mass and height. - Gravitational potential energy is proportional to both the mass of the object and its height above a reference point, PE=mgh.
27. B. PE=mgh. - Gravitational potential energy is calculated using the object's mass, the acceleration due to gravity, and its height above the reference point.
28. B. It doubles. - Gravitational potential energy is directly proportional to height. If the height is doubled, the potential energy doubles.
29. B. Power. - Power is the rate at which work is done or energy is transferred. It is measured in watts (joules per second).
30. A. Work. - Work is a scalar quantity, meaning it has magnitude but no direction. It only describes the amount of energy transferred.
31. B. The change in its kinetic energy. - According to the work-energy theorem, the net work done on an object is equal to the change in its kinetic energy.
32. A. It doubles. - The kinetic energy of an object is proportional to the square of its velocity. A fourfold increase in kinetic energy corresponds to a doubling of velocity.
33. C. It quadruples. - Kinetic energy depends on the square of velocity. If the velocity doubles, the kinetic energy increases by a factor of four.
34. B. Law of Conservation of Energy. - This principle states that in a closed system with only conservative forces, the total mechanical energy remains constant.

35. C. Friction slowing down a moving object. - Negative work occurs when the force and the displacement are in opposite directions, such as friction acting against motion.
36. C. It remains constant. - In a system where only conservative forces (like gravity) act, the total mechanical energy (sum of kinetic and potential energy) remains constant.
37. C. Velocity. - Potential energy is determined by mass, height, and gravity, not velocity, which affects kinetic energy instead.
38. C. Zero work. - Gravity only does work when there is vertical displacement. On a horizontal surface, gravity doesn't change the object's energy, so no work is done.
39. B. A person holding a book still above their head. - Work requires displacement. If there is no movement (displacement), no work is done, even if a force is applied.
40. B. 20 W. - Power is calculated as $P = W/t$. Here, $P = 400j/20s$.
41. B. The number of oscillations per second. - Frequency refers to how many complete cycles of a wave occur in one second, measured in hertz (Hz).
42. C. Hertz. - Frequency is measured in hertz (Hz), which represents the number of wave cycles per second.
43. B. Loudness. - Amplitude determines the loudness or intensity of a sound. Higher amplitude results in a louder sound.
44. B. A system is driven at a frequency equal to its natural frequency. - Resonance occurs when an external force drives a system at its natural frequency, resulting in increased amplitude.
45. B. - $F = v/\lambda$. The formula $F = v/\lambda$ represents the relationship between frequency (f), wave speed (v), and wavelength (λ).
46. A. It is halved. - If frequency is doubled, the wavelength is inversely proportional and will be halved, given the wave speed remains constant.
47. B. The loudness of a sound. - The decibel scale measures sound intensity or loudness, with a logarithmic relationship to power.
48. B. A vibrating guitar string. - Resonance occurs when a vibrating object (like a guitar string) amplifies sound at a specific frequency.
49. C. Amplitude. - Loudness is directly related to the amplitude of a sound wave. Greater amplitude means a louder sound.
50. D. Steel. - Sound travels fastest in solids like steel because particles are more closely packed, allowing efficient energy transfer.
51. A. It increases. - Sound travels faster in water than in air because water molecules are closer together, facilitating faster energy transfer.
52. B. Amplitude. - Adjusting the volume of a speaker changes the amplitude of the sound wave, increasing or decreasing its loudness.
53. B. Frequency. - The pitch of a sound is determined by its frequency. Higher frequency sounds correspond to higher-pitched tones.

54. C. 0.68 m. The wavelength λ can be calculated using $F = v/\lambda = 300/500 = 0.68$ m.
55. B. The frequency at which it vibrates when disturbed without external force. - An object's natural frequency is the frequency at which it tends to vibrate when set in motion without external force.
56. B. The height of the wave from its equilibrium position. - Amplitude is the maximum displacement from the rest position (equilibrium), which determines the wave's energy.
57. C. Loudness. - Increasing the amplitude of a sound wave increases its loudness, as loudness is proportional to the square of amplitude.
58. B. The driving frequency must match the natural frequency. - For resonance to occur, the external force must match the system's natural frequency, resulting in amplified vibrations.
59. A. 0.34 m. Using the formula $F = v/\lambda = 300/1000 = 0.34$ m, the wavelength is calculated to be 0.34 meters.
60. B. Compression. - In sound waves, compression refers to the point where particles are closest together, resulting in maximum pressure.
61. A. The flow of electric charge. – Electric current is defined as the movement of electric charge, typically measured in amperes (A), through a conductor.
62. B. Ampere. – The ampere (A) is the SI unit of electric current, representing one coulomb of charge passing through a conductor per second.
63. A. V=IR. – Ohm's Law states that voltage (V) is equal to the current (I) multiplied by the resistance (R) in a circuit.
64. B. The sum of individual resistances. – In a series circuit, the total resistance is the sum of all individual resistances because the current has only one path to follow.
65. C. The voltage across each component is the same. – In a parallel circuit, each component is connected across the same voltage source, so the voltage remains the same for all components.
66. C. Ohm. – The ohm (Ω) is the SI unit of electrical resistance, representing the opposition to the flow of electric current.
67. A. The current increases. – According to Ohm's Law, if the voltage increases while the resistance remains constant, the current will also increase.
68. B. Capacitor. – A capacitor stores electrical energy in an electric field and can release it when required in the circuit.
69. C. Ampere's Law. – Ampere's Law relates the magnetic field around a conductor to the electric current passing through it.
70. C. The magnetic field around a conductor changes. – Electromagnetic induction occurs when there is a change in the magnetic field surrounding a conductor, which induces a current.
71. A. Weber. – The SI unit of magnetic flux is the weber (Wb), which measures the total magnetic field passing through a given area.
72. C. Lorentz force. – The Lorentz force is the force experienced by a moving charge in a magnetic field, which is perpendicular to both the velocity of the charge and the magnetic field.

73. C. Ohm's Law. – Ohm's Law relates voltage (V), current (I), and resistance (R) in an electric circuit by the equation V=IR.
74. B. Current. – In a series circuit, the same current flows through all components, while the voltage is divided across them.
75. B. Lenz's Law. – Lenz's Law states that the direction of the induced current in a conductor is such that it opposes the change in magnetic flux that caused it.
76. B. Voltage. – Voltage, or electric potential difference, is the energy per unit charge between two points in a circuit, driving the current flow.
77. B. It decreases. – Adding more resistors in parallel reduces the total resistance of the circuit, as the current has more paths to flow through.
78. C. Ammeter. – An ammeter is a device used to measure the electric current in a circuit, connected in series with the circuit elements.
79. B. A circuit with low voltage and high current. – Power is proportional to the product of voltage and current (P=VI), so high current with some voltage leads to higher power dissipation.
80. C. It changes direction periodically. – Alternating current (AC) changes direction periodically, unlike direct current (DC) which flows in only one direction.
81. B. $\theta_i=\theta_r$ - The law of reflection states that the angle of incidence is equal to the angle of reflection.
82. B. Slows down and bends toward the normal - When light enters a denser medium like water, it slows down and bends toward the normal due to the change in speed.
83. B. Real and inverted - In a concave mirror, when the object is placed beyond the focal point, a real and inverted image is formed.
84. B. It produces a virtual, upright, and diminished image - Convex mirrors always form virtual, upright, and smaller images, which is useful for providing a wider field of view.
85. A. $n_1 \sin\theta_1 = n_2 \sin\theta_2$ - Snell's law relates the angle of incidence and the angle of refraction based on the refractive indices of the two media.
86. A. 1.50 - The refractive index is calculated by dividing the speed of light in a vacuum by the speed of light in the medium: $n = \frac{3.00 \times 10^8}{2.25 \times 10^8}$
87. D. Light passes from glass to air at an angle greater than the critical angle - Total internal reflection occurs when light passes from a denser to a less dense medium and the angle of incidence exceeds the critical angle.
88. B. Always negative - The focal length of a concave mirror is negative because it is a converging mirror.
89. C. 48.59° - Using Snell's law: $\sin\theta_2 = \frac{\sin 30}{1.5}$, solve to get the angle of refraction.
90. B. Concave lens - A concave (diverging) lens is used to correct myopia by diverging light rays before they enter the eye, so they focus correctly on the retina.
91. C. Virtual, upright, and the same size as the object - A plane mirror always forms virtual, upright images that are the same size as the object.

92. C. It increases - When light passes from a denser medium (glass) to a less dense medium (air), it speeds up.
93. C. Passes through the focal point - In a concave mirror, parallel rays of light converge at the focal point after reflecting off the mirror.
94. B. The angle of incidence at which the angle of refraction is 90° - The critical angle is the angle of incidence at which light is refracted at 90°, causing it to travel along the boundary between two media.
95. B. Virtual, upright, and diminished - Concave lenses always produce virtual, upright, and diminished images regardless of the object's position.
96. A. 1.24×10^8 m/s - The speed of light in diamond is calculated by dividing the speed of light in a vacuum by the refractive index of diamond: $3.00 \times 10^8 / 2.42$
97. C. Its speed decreases and it bends toward the normal - When light passes from air to glass (a denser medium), it slows down and bends toward the normal.
98. B. Diopters - The power of a lens is measured in diopters, which is the reciprocal of the focal length in meters.
99. B. Infinity - When the object is placed at the focal point of a concave mirror, the image is formed at infinity.
100. B. Twice the angle of incidence - The angle between the incident ray and the reflected ray is twice the angle of incidence since the reflected ray forms the same angle on the opposite side of the normal.
101. C. Enthalpy. - Enthalpy is a state function because it depends only on the initial and final states of the system, not the path taken.
102. B. No heat is exchanged. - In an adiabatic process, the system does not exchange heat with its surroundings.
103. B. Energy cannot be created or destroyed, only transferred. - The first law of thermodynamics is the principle of conservation of energy.
104. C. Conduction. - Conduction occurs when heat is transferred through a solid material by the direct contact of particles.
105. D. Third law. - The third law of thermodynamics states that absolute zero cannot be achieved because entropy reaches a minimum value at that temperature.
106. B. Melting of ice at 0°C. - A reversible process is one that can be reversed without leaving any trace on the surroundings, such as phase transitions at equilibrium.
107. C. Radiation. - Radiation transfers heat through electromagnetic waves, and it doesn't require a medium.
108. A. It increases. - In a spontaneous process, entropy always increases, according to the second law of thermodynamics.
109. C. The state of the system. - The internal energy of a system is a state function and depends on variables like temperature, pressure, and volume.
110. B. $\Delta U = Q - W$. - The first law of thermodynamics is expressed as the change in internal energy equals heat added minus work done by the system.

111. B. Adiabatic. - An adiabatic process involves no heat transfer between the system and its surroundings.
112. D. Entropy. - Entropy always increases in a spontaneous process, according to the second law of thermodynamics.
113. A. The change in internal energy is zero. - In a cyclic process, the system returns to its initial state, meaning the change in internal energy is zero.
114. B. Temperature. - The Zeroth Law of Thermodynamics establishes the concept of temperature by stating that thermal equilibrium implies equal temperatures.
115. A. The ratio of work done to heat added. - Efficiency in a heat engine is defined as the ratio of the work output to the heat input.
116. D. Reflection. - Reflection is not a heat transfer mechanism; it refers to the bouncing of light or heat off a surface.
117. A. Isothermal. - In an isothermal process, the temperature remains constant.
118. B. Convection. - Convection involves the movement of fluid molecules carrying heat from one place to another.
119. C. No process is possible in which the sole result is the transfer of heat from a cooler to a hotter body. - The second law of thermodynamics prohibits the spontaneous transfer of heat from cold to hot without work being done.
120. A. 40%. - The Carnot efficiency is calculated as $1 - T_{cold}/T_{hot}$, which in this case is $1 - 300/500 = 0.40$, or 40%.
121. C. Mass - The continuity equation is based on the conservation of mass, ensuring that the mass flow rate remains constant.
122. B. Conservation of energy - Bernoulli's equation is derived from the principle of conservation of mechanical energy for a flowing fluid.
123. B. Measuring the velocity of a fluid using a Pitot tube - A Pitot tube measures fluid velocity by applying Bernoulli's principle to the difference in pressure.
124. B. Kinetic energy per unit volume - The term $\frac{1}{2}\rho v^2$ represents the kinetic energy per unit volume in Bernoulli's equation.
125. B. Pressure decreases - According to Bernoulli's principle, as fluid velocity increases, pressure decreases.
126. B. Bernoulli's principle - The Venturi effect occurs when a fluid's velocity increases as it passes through a constriction, leading to a decrease in pressure, as described by Bernoulli's principle.
127. C. Velocity increases - According to the continuity equation, when the cross-sectional area decreases, the velocity of the fluid must increase to maintain the same flow rate.
128. B. Pascal - The SI unit of pressure is the Pascal (Pa), which is equivalent to one Newton per square meter.
129. C. Reynolds number - The Reynolds number helps determine whether fluid flow is laminar or turbulent. Low values indicate laminar flow, while high values suggest turbulence.

130. C. Gravitational potential energy - The term ρgh in Bernoulli's equation represents the gravitational potential energy of the fluid per unit volume.
131. C. Higher velocity of air over the top of the wing - Bernoulli's principle explains that the faster-moving air over the curved top of the wing creates lower pressure, leading to lift.
132. B. Laminar vs. turbulent flow - The Reynolds number is used to determine whether fluid flow is laminar (smooth) or turbulent (chaotic).
133. C. The fluid must be incompressible and non-viscous - Bernoulli's equation applies to incompressible, non-viscous fluids in steady, non-turbulent flow.
134. B. The speed increases - The continuity equation shows that the fluid speed must increase as it flows through narrower sections of a pipe.
135. C. Oil flowing through a narrow tube with high viscosity - Bernoulli's equation is less accurate when viscosity is significant, as it assumes an ideal, non-viscous fluid.
136. B. Fluid viscosity - Bernoulli's equation assumes that the fluid has negligible viscosity, meaning internal friction within the fluid is not considered.
137. B. Pressure decreases - According to Bernoulli's principle, as the fluid passes through a constriction, its velocity increases, causing a drop in pressure.

SECTION 6: Psychology and Sociology

Chapter 1: Cognitive Processes

Cognitive processes are the mental activities that allow individuals to acquire, store, retrieve, and use knowledge. These processes are critical in helping us interpret and interact with the world. They include a range of mental functions such as perception, attention, memory, reasoning, problem-solving, and decision-making. Understanding cognitive processes is essential in the study of psychology and neuroscience because they form the foundation of how we think, learn, and adapt to different environments.

One of the core aspects of cognitive processes is the concept of information processing. This model suggests that the human brain functions similarly to a computer, where information is input through our senses, processed by our cognitive systems, and output through behaviors or decisions. Cognitive processes are not linear; rather, they often overlap and interact with each other. For example, attention plays a critical role in how we perceive the world, and memory affects how we process new information based on prior knowledge.

Cognitive processes are central to everyday life, guiding everything from mundane tasks like driving a car to complex problem-solving in academic or professional settings. To understand cognitive processes fully, it is important to break down some of their key components, such as perception, attention, and memory.

Perception

Perception refers to the process by which individuals organize and interpret sensory information from the environment to form a meaningful understanding of the world around them. This is not a passive activity but an active process where the brain continuously interprets signals from the sensory organs (such as eyes, ears, and skin) to construct a coherent view of reality. Without perception, we would be unable to make sense of the myriad of stimuli that we encounter daily.

Perception involves multiple stages:
- Sensation: Sensory organs detect external stimuli such as light, sound, or temperature.
- Organization: The brain organizes the raw sensory data into recognizable patterns.
- Interpretation: The brain uses prior experiences, expectations, and context to interpret these patterns and give them meaning.

Perception is subjective, meaning that individuals may interpret the same stimuli in different ways. This is influenced by several factors, including prior experiences, cultural background, expectations, and even the current emotional state. For example, a person who is afraid of heights may perceive a high ledge as more dangerous than someone who is not.

Another critical aspect of perception is top-down and bottom-up processing. Bottom-up processing refers to the way our brain processes incoming data from the environment in real-time, using sensory input to build a perception. In contrast, top-down processing is driven by prior knowledge and expectations, which help the brain quickly interpret familiar stimuli. Both of these processes are integral to how we perceive the world.

Attention

Attention is the cognitive process of selectively focusing on specific stimuli while ignoring others. It acts as a filter, allowing us to concentrate on what is most relevant or important at any given moment. Without attention, it would be impossible to process the vast amounts of information we encounter every second. Instead, attention helps allocate cognitive resources to tasks that require focus.

There are different types of attention, each serving a unique function:
- Selective Attention: This type involves focusing on a particular object or task while excluding other irrelevant stimuli. For example, when studying in a noisy environment, selective attention allows you to focus on reading while tuning out background noise.
- Divided Attention: Also known as multitasking, this type allows a person to attend to more than one task simultaneously. However, divided attention often leads to a decrease in performance because the brain has limited cognitive resources to allocate to multiple tasks.
- Sustained Attention: Also referred to as concentration, sustained attention is the ability to maintain focus on a specific task or stimulus over an extended period. This is particularly important for tasks that require continuous monitoring, such as air traffic control or long periods of study.
- Shifting Attention: Also called attentional switching, this refers to the ability to shift focus from one task to another. This flexibility is important in dynamic environments, such as when driving, where attention must be rapidly shifted between different stimuli.

Attention is not an unlimited resource; it is subject to cognitive overload. When we try to attend to too many things at once, or when we are tired or stressed, our ability to focus declines. Moreover, attention can be influenced by factors such as motivation, interest, and fatigue. For instance, you are more likely to maintain focus on a task that you find enjoyable or rewarding than one that is boring or difficult.

Memory

Memory is the cognitive process involved in encoding, storing, and retrieving information. It allows individuals to retain knowledge over time and plays a key role in learning, problem-solving, and decision-making. Memory is not a singular entity but is composed of multiple systems that interact with each other. These systems are generally categorized into sensory memory, short-term memory, and long-term memory.

1. Sensory Memory: This is the initial stage of memory, where sensory information from the environment is stored for a very brief period, usually less than a second. Sensory memory acts as a buffer for incoming stimuli, allowing the brain to process relevant information. It is divided into categories such as iconic memory (visual information) and echoic memory (auditory information).
2. Short-Term Memory (STM): Short-term memory, also known as working memory, holds information temporarily for processing. STM typically lasts for about 20 to 30 seconds and has a limited capacity, often cited as "7±2" items. It is where conscious thought occurs, and it

allows for the manipulation of information, such as solving math problems or remembering a phone number long enough to dial it.
3. Long-Term Memory (LTM): Long-term memory is where information is stored more permanently, allowing it to be retrieved later. LTM has a much larger capacity than short-term memory and can store information for years or even a lifetime. There are two main types of long-term memory:
    - Declarative Memory: This is memory of facts and events, which can be consciously recalled. It includes episodic memory (events and personal experiences) and semantic memory (general knowledge and facts).
    - Procedural Memory: This type involves memory of how to perform tasks, such as riding a bike or typing on a keyboard. Procedural memories are often unconscious and are learned through repetition and practice.

Memory Retrieval is the process of recalling information stored in long-term memory. It can be influenced by cues, emotional states, and even the context in which the memory was encoded. Sometimes memory retrieval is inaccurate, leading to distortions or false memories. Factors such as stress, aging, and trauma can also affect memory performance, leading to difficulties in recalling information.

Chapter 2: Learning and Behavior

Learning is a fundamental process through which organisms acquire, retain, and utilize knowledge, skills, or behaviors. In psychology, learning refers to relatively permanent changes in behavior or mental processes resulting from experience. Behavior, in this context, encompasses any observable action made by an organism in response to stimuli. The study of learning and behavior examines how individuals or animals interact with their environments and how these interactions influence their actions and decision-making.

At the core of learning and behavior theories lies the relationship between stimuli and responses. When individuals learn, they establish associations between specific events, stimuli, or consequences and their resulting actions. The ability to adapt and change based on experience is a vital survival mechanism, allowing organisms to avoid harm, increase efficiency, and optimize responses to environmental challenges.

Types of Learning

1. Associative Learning: This type of learning occurs when an organism makes a connection between two stimuli or between a behavior and a consequence. Classical and operant conditioning are the primary forms of associative learning, both focusing on how stimuli can shape behavior.
2. Non-associative Learning: This involves learning that occurs without forming associations. Examples include habituation (decreasing response to a repeated stimulus) and sensitization (increased response to a repeated stimulus).
3. Observational Learning: Also called social learning, this type occurs when individuals learn by watching others perform a behavior and then imitating that behavior. Observational learning highlights the importance of models in shaping behavior.

Classical and Operant Conditioning

Both classical and operant conditioning are forms of associative learning. They differ in their mechanisms of forming associations and how these associations influence behavior.

Classical Conditioning

Classical conditioning was first described by Ivan Pavlov, a Russian physiologist, in the early 20th century. It involves learning through association between two stimuli. In Pavlov's famous experiment with dogs, he demonstrated how a neutral stimulus (a bell) could become associated with an unconditioned stimulus (food) to elicit a conditioned response (salivation).

1. Key Elements of Classical Conditioning:
    - Unconditioned Stimulus (US): A stimulus that naturally elicits a response. For example, food causes a dog to salivate.
    - Unconditioned Response (UR): The natural, unlearned reaction to the unconditioned stimulus. In Pavlov's experiment, the dog's salivation in response to food is the unconditioned response.
    - Conditioned Stimulus (CS): A previously neutral stimulus that, after association with the unconditioned stimulus, comes to trigger a conditioned response. The bell in Pavlov's experiment is the conditioned stimulus.

- Conditioned Response (CR): The learned response to the conditioned stimulus. In Pavlov's case, the salivation in response to the bell alone became the conditioned response.
2. Stages of Classical Conditioning:
   - Acquisition: This is the initial stage where the neutral stimulus is repeatedly paired with the unconditioned stimulus. During this phase, the organism begins to make the association between the two stimuli.
   - Extinction: If the conditioned stimulus is repeatedly presented without the unconditioned stimulus, the conditioned response will gradually weaken and disappear. This process is called extinction.
   - Spontaneous Recovery: After extinction, if the conditioned stimulus is presented again after a period of rest, the conditioned response can reappear, although typically weaker than before.
   - Generalization: Once a response has been conditioned, stimuli that are similar to the conditioned stimulus may also trigger the conditioned response. For example, a dog conditioned to salivate at the sound of a bell might also salivate at similar sounds.
   - Discrimination: This occurs when the organism learns to differentiate between the conditioned stimulus and other similar stimuli that do not predict the unconditioned stimulus.
3. Applications of Classical Conditioning:
   - Phobias: Many irrational fears develop through classical conditioning, where a neutral stimulus becomes associated with a traumatic or frightening event.
   - Taste Aversion: Individuals can develop an aversion to a food if it has been associated with illness, even if the food was not the cause of the sickness.
   - Advertising: Marketers often pair products with positive stimuli (such as attractive imagery or pleasant music) to condition positive emotional responses toward the product.

Operant Conditioning

Operant conditioning, described by B.F. Skinner, focuses on how consequences shape behavior. In contrast to classical conditioning, where an organism learns to associate two stimuli, operant conditioning involves learning the association between a behavior and its consequence. Behaviors are either strengthened or weakened depending on whether they are followed by reinforcement or punishment.

1. Key Elements of Operant Conditioning:
   - Reinforcement: Any event that strengthens or increases the likelihood of a behavior.
     - Positive Reinforcement: Involves the presentation of a rewarding stimulus after a behavior, increasing the likelihood of that behavior being repeated. For example, giving a dog a treat for sitting on command is positive reinforcement.
     - Negative Reinforcement: Involves the removal of an aversive stimulus following a behavior, which also increases the likelihood of that behavior. An example is taking painkillers to relieve a headache.

- Punishment: Any event that decreases the likelihood of a behavior.
    - Positive Punishment: Involves presenting an unpleasant stimulus after a behavior, decreasing the likelihood of that behavior. For example, scolding a child for misbehaving is positive punishment.
    - Negative Punishment: Involves the removal of a desired stimulus after a behavior, decreasing the likelihood of that behavior. For instance, taking away a child's toy for breaking a rule is negative punishment.

2. Reinforcement Schedules:
    - Continuous Reinforcement: Every instance of a desired behavior is reinforced. This is effective during the initial stages of learning but may not be practical for long-term behavior maintenance.
    - Partial Reinforcement: Behaviors are reinforced intermittently, leading to greater resistance to extinction. Partial reinforcement schedules include:
        - Fixed-Ratio Schedule: Reinforcement occurs after a specific number of responses. For example, a salesperson receiving a bonus after selling five items.
        - Variable-Ratio Schedule: Reinforcement occurs after an unpredictable number of responses. This schedule leads to high response rates and is often used in gambling.
        - Fixed-Interval Schedule: Reinforcement occurs after a fixed amount of time has passed, provided the behavior is performed. An example is a paycheck received every two weeks.
        - Variable-Interval Schedule: Reinforcement occurs at unpredictable time intervals, leading to slow and steady behavior patterns.

3. Shaping: In operant conditioning, shaping refers to gradually guiding behavior toward a desired goal through successive approximations. For example, teaching a dog to fetch a ball involves reinforcing each small step toward the final behavior, such as looking at the ball, moving toward it, picking it up, and finally bringing it back.

4. Applications of Operant Conditioning:
    - Behavior Modification: Operant conditioning is often used in behavior modification programs to reinforce positive behaviors and reduce unwanted ones. This is particularly useful in education, therapy, and training environments.
    - Token Economies: A system of behavior modification based on operant conditioning, where individuals earn tokens for performing desirable behaviors and can exchange these tokens for rewards.
    - Parenting and Discipline: Operant conditioning principles are commonly used in parenting, where reinforcement and punishment shape a child's behavior.

Both classical and operant conditioning provide valuable insights into the learning process and have numerous practical applications in fields like education, therapy, and behavior modification

Chapter 3: Sociological Theories

Sociological theories are frameworks that provide insight into how society functions, offering explanations for social phenomena, behaviors, and structures. These theories form the foundation for analyzing the dynamics of social groups, interactions, and institutions. Key sociological theories include Functionalism, Conflict Theory, and Symbolic Interactionism, each offering distinct perspectives on society.

Functionalism

Functionalism, also known as structural-functional theory, views society as a complex system with interconnected parts working together to promote stability and order. This perspective, rooted in the work of sociologists like Émile Durkheim and Talcott Parsons, emphasizes the role of social institutions in maintaining equilibrium in society. Each institution, such as the family, education system, or government, plays a specific function that contributes to the overall stability of society. In functionalism, society is seen as an organism where each part has a function. For example, the family is responsible for socializing children, while schools transmit knowledge and values, and the legal system enforces norms. When all parts of society function properly, societal stability is maintained. Functionalists believe that any disruption or dysfunction in one part of society can lead to social instability, but over time, societies adapt to restore balance. For example, if the economy experiences a downturn, families may adapt by altering consumption patterns, and governments may intervene through policies like unemployment benefits.

Criticism of functionalism includes its tendency to overlook inequalities and power dynamics, as it emphasizes harmony and consensus. It often fails to account for how social structures may benefit some groups over others, perpetuating inequality.

Conflict Theory

Conflict theory offers a contrasting perspective, focusing on the inherent power struggles and inequalities within society. Karl Marx is one of the most influential figures in the development of this theory, which centers on the idea that society is in a state of perpetual conflict due to competition for limited resources. Conflict theory suggests that social order is maintained by domination and power, rather than consensus and cooperation.

In this view, society is divided into two main classes: the bourgeoisie (capitalist class) and the proletariat (working class). The bourgeoisie controls the means of production, while the proletariat sells their labor. Conflict theorists argue that the bourgeoisie exploits the proletariat to maximize profits, which leads to class struggles. Over time, these struggles may lead to social change, as the working class seeks to overthrow the capitalist system.

While Marx's ideas focused primarily on class conflict, modern conflict theory has expanded to include other forms of inequality, such as race, gender, and ethnicity. Feminist theory, for example, highlights the ways in which gender inequality is rooted in patriarchal structures. Similarly, racial conflict theory explores how racial and ethnic minorities face systemic discrimination and exclusion.

Conflict theory has been criticized for its emphasis on division and neglect of social cohesion. Critics argue that it overlooks how individuals and groups work together for the common good, focusing too heavily on oppression and inequality.

Symbolic Interactionism

Symbolic interactionism focuses on the micro-level of social interaction, emphasizing how individuals create meaning through social interactions. This theory, associated with George Herbert Mead and Herbert Blumer, explores how people use symbols—such as language, gestures, and objects—to communicate and develop their identities.

According to symbolic interactionism, society is built on the everyday interactions between individuals. These interactions are shaped by the meaning's individuals attach to symbols. For instance, a handshake, smile, or word can convey different meanings depending on the context and the individuals involved. Social reality, in this sense, is constructed through human interpretation.

One important concept within symbolic interactionism is the "self" and the idea of the "looking-glass self," developed by Charles Cooley. This concept suggests that individuals form their self-identity based on how they believe others perceive them. Social roles and behaviors are constantly negotiated and redefined through interaction.

While symbolic interactionism provides valuable insights into individual interactions and meaning-making, it has been criticized for neglecting larger social structures and forces that influence behavior. It focuses heavily on subjective experiences, making it difficult to analyze societal-level phenomena like inequality or power dynamics.

Social Structures and Institutions

Social structures and institutions are the building blocks of society, providing an organized framework for social interactions and relationships. Social structures refer to the recurring patterns of behavior that govern individuals' actions and expectations, while institutions are the formal and informal systems that guide and regulate these behaviors. Together, they form the backbone of societal organization, shaping everything from daily interactions to large-scale social change.

Social Structures

Social structures are the organized patterns of relationships and roles that influence how people behave and interact. These structures include hierarchical systems such as class, race, gender, and age. They provide a framework for individuals' positions in society and their relationships with one another. Social structures are maintained through social norms, laws, and expectations, which help guide behavior.

For example, the class structure divides society into different economic levels, such as upper, middle, and lower classes. These divisions shape individuals' access to resources, opportunities, and power. Similarly, gender roles are social structures that define expected behaviors for men and women, influencing everything from career choices to family dynamics.

Social structures are not static; they evolve over time in response to cultural, political, and economic changes. For instance, changes in gender roles over the past few decades have seen a shift towards greater gender equality in many parts of the world. However, social structures often reinforce inequality, as certain groups may be privileged while others are marginalized.

Social Institutions

Social institutions are established systems that shape and regulate human behavior. They provide the guidelines and rules necessary for maintaining order in society. Key social institutions include the family, education, religion, government, and economy.

- Family: The family is one of the most fundamental social institutions. It is responsible for the socialization of children, providing emotional and economic support, and establishing social roles and values. Families can take many forms, including nuclear families, extended families, and single-parent families.
- Education: The education system is another critical social institution that transmits knowledge, skills, and values to individuals. Schools not only provide formal education but also play a role in socializing students, teaching them norms and expectations.
- Religion: Religion serves as a social institution that provides a moral framework for individuals and communities. It offers explanations for the meaning of life, sets moral standards, and often influences laws and customs.
- Government: The government is the institution responsible for maintaining order and enforcing laws. It holds the power to create and enforce regulations, ensuring the safety and welfare of its citizens. Governments can take many forms, from democracies to authoritarian regimes.
- Economy: The economy is the institution that organizes the production, distribution, and consumption of goods and services. It shapes individuals' access to resources and opportunities and influences their roles in society.

Social institutions are interdependent, meaning that changes in one institution often lead to changes in others. For example, economic changes can affect family dynamics, with job losses or economic growth influencing marriage rates, birth rates, and household structures.

Chapter 4: Identity and Self-Concept

Identity refers to how individuals define themselves, encompassing personal beliefs, values, and the roles they play in society. It is not a static attribute but a dynamic process influenced by various factors throughout life. Understanding identity involves recognizing both individual characteristics and external influences, such as social roles, experiences, and cultural context. In psychology, identity formation is a crucial part of development, particularly during adolescence when people begin to solidify who they are in relation to the world around them.

Self-concept refers to the collection of beliefs and perceptions a person holds about themselves. It encompasses aspects such as personality traits, skills, and personal values. Self-concept affects not only how individuals see themselves but also how they interact with others and the decisions they make. A person's self-concept can be influenced by their social interactions, personal achievements, and the feedback they receive from others.

Self-concept is typically divided into three components:

1. Self-image: This is how people see themselves in terms of physical appearance, personality, and social roles. For example, a person may perceive themselves as intelligent, compassionate, or athletic.
2. Self-esteem: This refers to how people evaluate their self-image. It reflects their emotional response to their own self-assessment, such as feeling confident or self-critical.
3. Ideal self: This is the version of themselves a person aspires to be. It represents their goals, dreams, and personal ideals. Discrepancies between a person's actual self and their ideal self can lead to feelings of dissatisfaction or motivation to improve.

Factors Influencing Identity and Self-Concept

1. Socialization: One of the most significant factors in shaping identity and self-concept is socialization, the process through which individuals learn the norms, values, and behaviors appropriate to their culture. Family, peers, education, and media all play critical roles in this process. For example, family dynamics can shape a person's understanding of their roles, while peer groups might influence aspects of personality, such as extroversion or introversion.
2. Cultural Background: Identity and self-concept are also heavily influenced by a person's cultural background. Culture affects how individuals see themselves in relation to others, the importance of independence versus interdependence, and what traits are valued in a society. For instance, in collectivist cultures, identity is often tied to family and community, while in individualist cultures, personal achievements and independence might be more highly valued.
3. Life Experiences: Identity is continuously shaped by life experiences, including education, career, relationships, and major life events. Positive or negative experiences can affect a person's self-esteem and how they view their abilities. For example, achieving a major career goal can enhance self-concept, while repeated failures can lead to self-doubt.
4. Biological Factors: Identity can also be influenced by biological factors such as genetics and brain chemistry. Traits like temperament, which are present from early childhood, can play a role in shaping personality and self-concept. Additionally, mental health conditions can impact self-esteem and how individuals perceive themselves.

5. Social Roles: People often define themselves based on the roles they play in society. These roles can include being a parent, student, friend, or professional. The way people perceive their success in these roles can significantly impact their self-concept. A person who feels they are a good parent may have higher self-esteem in that area, while struggles in professional life may negatively affect self-image.
6. Feedback from Others: The opinions and feedback individuals receive from others contribute significantly to shaping their self-concept. Positive reinforcement from peers, family, and mentors can strengthen confidence, while criticism or negative feedback can lower self-esteem.

Gender and Cultural Identity

Gender identity refers to a person's deeply felt internal experience of gender, which may or may not align with the sex they were assigned at birth. It is how individuals perceive themselves as male, female, a blend of both, or neither, and how they choose to express this identity. Gender identity is distinct from sexual orientation, which refers to a person's attraction to others.

1. Formation of Gender Identity: Gender identity typically begins to form in early childhood, influenced by a combination of biological, social, and cultural factors. Children observe gender roles and behaviors modeled by family members, teachers, peers, and media, which helps them understand societal expectations of gender. By around age 3, most children can identify themselves as male or female, and their understanding of gender norms continues to evolve throughout adolescence and adulthood.
2. Social Influences on Gender Identity: Society plays a significant role in shaping gender identity through gender norms and expectations. From a young age, individuals are often exposed to specific roles and behaviors associated with being male or female. These expectations can be seen in various areas, such as the types of toys children are encouraged to play with, the activities they participate in, and the clothing they wear. While some societies maintain rigid gender norms, others are more accepting of a diverse range of gender identities and expressions.
3. Gender Expression: Gender expression refers to how individuals present their gender identity to the world. This can include choices in clothing, hairstyle, behavior, and voice. Gender expression can conform to traditional gender roles or challenge them. It is important to note that gender expression does not always align with a person's gender identity or biological sex.
4. Challenges Faced by Gender Nonconforming Individuals: People whose gender identity does not align with societal expectations often face discrimination, stigma, and misunderstanding. These challenges can affect their mental health and well-being, contributing to issues such as anxiety, depression, and social isolation. Supportive environments that recognize and respect diverse gender identities are crucial for the mental and emotional health of gender nonconforming individuals.

Cultural identity refers to a person's sense of belonging to a particular culture or ethnic group. It involves a shared connection to cultural practices, language, traditions, and values. Cultural identity helps individuals make sense of their place in the world and provides a framework for how they interact with others.

1. Cultural Identity and Socialization: Like gender identity, cultural identity is shaped by socialization. From birth, individuals are introduced to the cultural practices and values of their family, community, and broader society. This process helps individuals develop an understanding of their cultural heritage and traditions, which can be passed down through generations. Cultural identity is often strengthened through participation in cultural rituals, religious practices, and communal celebrations.
2. Multiculturalism and Cultural Identity: In today's globalized world, many individuals grow up in multicultural environments where they are exposed to multiple cultural influences. This can lead to the development of a bicultural or multicultural identity, where individuals identify with more than one culture. While this can provide a rich and diverse perspective on life, it can also present challenges in reconciling conflicting cultural norms or expectations.
3. Cultural Identity and Self-Concept: Cultural identity is closely tied to self-concept. A strong cultural identity can provide a sense of belonging, purpose, and pride, while difficulties in reconciling one's cultural background with the dominant culture can lead to identity conflicts or feelings of alienation. In situations where individuals are part of a minority culture, they may face pressure to assimilate into the dominant culture, which can affect their self-concept and cultural pride.
4. Impact of Migration and Globalization: Migration and globalization have a profound effect on cultural identity. Immigrants often face challenges in maintaining their cultural identity while adapting to new social environments. This can create a sense of dual identity, where individuals must balance their cultural heritage with the need to integrate into a new society.

Chapter 5: Social Relationships

Social relationships are the fundamental connections between individuals that shape human interactions, influence behavior, and support emotional well-being. They range from casual acquaintances to deep emotional bonds, such as friendships, familial ties, and romantic partnerships. Social relationships are key to both personal development and social stability, providing individuals with emotional support, a sense of belonging, and community. These connections are built on mutual trust, respect, communication, and shared experiences.

Humans are inherently social beings, and establishing meaningful relationships is a critical part of life. These relationships influence not only how individuals feel about themselves but also how they interact with society. Through social bonds, people gain emotional security, companionship, and assistance during times of need. Such connections can also motivate personal growth by offering new perspectives and encouraging healthy behavior.

Social relationships function through various types of connections, including:

- Familial Relationships: Bonds between family members, which are typically the first social connections people form. These relationships provide foundational emotional and practical support.
- Friendships: Emotional bonds between non-related individuals that are usually formed based on mutual interests, trust, and companionship.
- Romantic Relationships: Deep emotional connections often based on love and attraction, which can provide both emotional support and a sense of intimacy.
- Professional Relationships: These relationships form in the workplace or professional environments, built on mutual respect, shared goals, and professional ethics.

The quality and stability of social relationships are often measured by factors such as communication, trust, reciprocity, and mutual understanding. Relationships that lack these elements may become strained or dissolve over time. Additionally, positive social relationships contribute to better mental and physical health, as they reduce feelings of loneliness, depression, and anxiety.

In contrast, toxic relationships, marked by manipulation, lack of trust, or disrespect, can have detrimental effects on an individual's well-being, leading to emotional distress, low self-esteem, and even physical health issues. Therefore, it is important to cultivate healthy social relationships and to recognize the signs of harmful ones.

Group Dynamics, Socialization, and Communication

Group Dynamics

Group dynamics refer to the patterns of interaction between members of a group, which influence how individuals behave and relate to one another. These dynamics can be influenced by factors such as group size, the roles of individual members, the group's goals, and the established norms within the group. Understanding group dynamics is crucial in understanding how people function within social structures, whether in informal settings like friendship circles or formal environments such as workplaces.

Several important aspects of group dynamics include:
- Roles: Within any group, individuals may take on specific roles, whether formally assigned or naturally developed. Some members may emerge as leaders, guiding the group's direction and decisions, while others may play supportive roles, offering assistance or maintaining group harmony. These roles help shape how the group operates and whether it can meet its goals effectively.
- Norms: Norms are the informal rules and expectations that govern behavior within a group. They dictate what is considered acceptable or unacceptable behavior. Groups with clear and healthy norms tend to function more effectively, as members understand their boundaries and what is expected of them.
- Cohesion: Group cohesion refers to the sense of unity and camaraderie among group members. A cohesive group is more likely to collaborate effectively, resolve conflicts, and work towards shared goals. High cohesion is often associated with better group performance, but it can also lead to issues like groupthink, where the desire for harmony suppresses critical thinking.

Group dynamics are particularly important in situations where cooperation is required to achieve shared goals, such as in project teams, sports, or social movements. Positive group dynamics, where communication is open and roles are well-defined, can lead to high performance and member satisfaction. On the other hand, poor group dynamics can result in misunderstandings, conflicts, and decreased group productivity.

Socialization

Socialization is the lifelong process through which individuals learn the norms, values, behaviors, and social skills appropriate to their culture and society. It begins in childhood but continues throughout life as individuals encounter new environments and social contexts. Socialization helps people understand how to interact with others, how to behave in various social settings, and how to fulfill the roles that society expects of them.

Socialization occurs through several key agents:
- Family: The family is typically the first and most important agent of socialization, as it is where individuals first learn about norms, values, language, and acceptable behavior. Parents, siblings, and extended family play significant roles in shaping one's social identity and understanding of social roles.
- Education: Schools are critical socialization agents, where individuals not only acquire academic knowledge but also learn how to interact with peers and authority figures. Schools teach societal values such as respect for others, discipline, and the importance of following rules.
- Peers: Peer groups become especially influential during adolescence and young adulthood. Peers offer opportunities for individuals to explore their identities, form friendships, and establish independence from family. Peer groups often provide social reinforcement for behaviors that are valued within the group, both positive and negative.

- Media: In contemporary society, mass media plays a significant role in shaping individuals' perceptions of the world. From television and films to social media, the content individuals consume can influence their views on societal norms, relationships, and their role in society.

Socialization is critical for integrating individuals into their society, helping them learn how to participate in social life effectively and how to navigate different social roles. Failures in socialization can lead to difficulties in communication, misunderstandings in social contexts, and conflicts with societal norms.

Communication

Communication is the process of sharing information, thoughts, and feelings between individuals or groups. It is a fundamental part of human interaction and essential for forming and maintaining social relationships. Effective communication involves not only the words spoken but also non-verbal cues such as body language, tone of voice, and facial expressions.

There are several forms of communication:

- Verbal Communication: This involves the use of spoken or written language to convey messages. Effective verbal communication requires clarity, active listening, and an understanding of the audience's needs.
- Non-Verbal Communication: This includes body language, facial expressions, gestures, and posture. Non-verbal cues can reinforce what is being said or, in some cases, contradict it. For example, someone may say they are fine, but their body language may suggest otherwise.
- Interpersonal Communication: This occurs between individuals and is the most common form of communication. It involves exchanging messages in face-to-face settings, over the phone, or through digital means. The quality of interpersonal communication often determines the strength of social relationships.
- Group Communication: This involves exchanging messages within a group. It can be more complex than one-on-one communication because it requires managing multiple relationships and messages simultaneously. Group communication often requires the management of group dynamics, ensuring all voices are heard, and fostering collaboration.

Effective communication is key to socialization and maintaining healthy group dynamics. Miscommunication, whether through unclear messages, failure to listen, or cultural misunderstandings, can lead to conflicts, strained relationships, and reduced group cohesion. To prevent this, individuals need to develop strong communication skills, including active listening, clarity in speech, and sensitivity to non-verbal cues.

Chapter 6: Mental Health Disorders

Mental health disorders are conditions that affect mood, thinking, and behavior. These conditions range from mild to severe and impact a person's ability to function in daily life. They are a significant concern in healthcare, as mental health issues can also influence physical health, particularly in settings like rehabilitation or long-term care. Mental health disorders can be classified into various categories, such as mood disorders, anxiety disorders, personality disorders, and psychotic disorders.

Mental health is essential in maintaining overall well-being, and when it is disrupted by illness, it can lead to impairments in cognitive and emotional functioning. Early diagnosis and treatment of mental health disorders are critical to improving patient outcomes. These conditions often require a multidisciplinary approach, involving psychiatrists, psychologists, nurses, and social workers to develop a comprehensive treatment plan. Below, we explore three of the most common mental health disorders: depression, anxiety, and personality disorders.

Depression

Definition and Overview:

Depression is one of the most common mood disorders and is characterized by persistent feelings of sadness, hopelessness, and a lack of interest in activities once found enjoyable. It affects how a person thinks, feels, and handles daily activities. Depression can be triggered by various factors, including biological, genetic, environmental, and psychological influences.

Symptoms:

Symptoms of depression can vary in intensity, but some of the most common include:

- Persistent sadness or low mood
- Loss of interest in activities previously enjoyed
- Fatigue or loss of energy
- Difficulty concentrating or making decisions
- Changes in appetite or weight (either increase or decrease)
- Sleep disturbances (insomnia or excessive sleeping)
- Feelings of worthlessness or guilt
- Suicidal thoughts or behaviors

Types of Depression:

1. Major Depressive Disorder (MDD): This type of depression involves severe symptoms that interfere with the individual's ability to work, sleep, study, eat, and enjoy life. Episodes can occur once or multiple times throughout a person's life.
2. Persistent Depressive Disorder (PDD): Also known as dysthymia, this is a long-term form of depression with less severe symptoms, but they last for at least two years.
3. Seasonal Affective Disorder (SAD): SAD is a type of depression related to changes in seasons, typically occurring in the winter months due to reduced sunlight.
4. Postpartum Depression (PPD): This form of depression occurs after childbirth, affecting a mother's ability to care for her baby and herself.

Treatment Options:
1. Medication: Antidepressants like selective serotonin reuptake inhibitors (SSRIs) are commonly prescribed to balance chemicals in the brain linked to mood regulation.
2. Psychotherapy: Cognitive Behavioral Therapy (CBT) and other forms of talk therapy are used to help individuals manage their thoughts and behaviors.
3. Lifestyle Changes: Exercise, maintaining a healthy diet, and adequate sleep can help alleviate symptoms of depression.
4. Electroconvulsive Therapy (ECT): In severe cases where medication and therapy are not effective, ECT may be used to treat major depressive disorder.

Anxiety

Definition and Overview:
Anxiety disorders involve excessive fear or worry that is difficult to control and affects daily activities. While anxiety is a normal response to stress, anxiety disorders involve more intense, persistent fear or anxiety about everyday situations. These disorders are among the most common mental health conditions, impacting individuals of all ages.

Symptoms:
Anxiety disorders manifest through a variety of symptoms, including:
- Excessive worry or fear
- Restlessness or feeling "on edge"
- Fatigue
- Difficulty concentrating
- Irritability
- Muscle tension
- Sleep disturbances, such as difficulty falling asleep or staying asleep

Types of Anxiety Disorders:
1. Generalized Anxiety Disorder (GAD): This disorder involves chronic, exaggerated worry and tension, even when there is little or nothing to provoke it.
2. Panic Disorder: Characterized by sudden and repeated episodes of intense fear, known as panic attacks, these can include physical symptoms like chest pain, heart palpitations, and shortness of breath.
3. Social Anxiety Disorder (SAD): This condition involves intense anxiety or fear of being judged, negatively evaluated, or rejected in social or performance situations.
4. Phobias: Phobias are an excessive and irrational fear of specific objects or situations, such as heights, flying, or certain animals.

Treatment Options:
1. Medications: Anti-anxiety medications, such as benzodiazepines, and antidepressants, such as SSRIs, are commonly used to manage anxiety symptoms.
2. Cognitive Behavioral Therapy (CBT): This form of therapy helps individuals identify and challenge negative thinking patterns that contribute to their anxiety.

3. Exposure Therapy: This technique helps individuals gradually confront their fears in a controlled environment, reducing anxiety over time.
4. Relaxation Techniques: Methods like deep breathing, meditation, and progressive muscle relaxation can help manage acute anxiety symptoms.

Personality Disorders

Definition and Overview:

Personality disorders are a group of mental health conditions characterized by enduring patterns of behavior, cognition, and inner experience that deviate significantly from the expectations of an individual's culture. These patterns are pervasive, inflexible, and lead to distress or impairment in social, occupational, or other areas of functioning.

Types of Personality Disorders:

1. Borderline Personality Disorder (BPD): People with BPD experience intense emotions, unstable relationships, and an unclear sense of self. They may engage in impulsive behaviors and have a deep fear of abandonment.
2. Narcissistic Personality Disorder (NPD): Individuals with NPD have an inflated sense of their own importance, a deep need for admiration, and a lack of empathy for others. They often feel superior to others and are preoccupied with fantasies of success, power, or brilliance.
3. Antisocial Personality Disorder (ASPD): This disorder is characterized by a disregard for the rights of others, often leading to behaviors that are deceitful, manipulative, or harmful. Individuals with ASPD may engage in criminal behavior without feeling guilt or remorse.
4. Obsessive-Compulsive Personality Disorder (OCPD): Different from Obsessive-Compulsive Disorder (OCD), OCPD involves a preoccupation with orderliness, perfectionism, and control at the expense of flexibility and efficiency.

Symptoms:

Common symptoms across various personality disorders include:
- Rigid and unhealthy patterns of thinking and behavior
- Difficulty in relationships, both personal and professional
- An inability to adapt to changing circumstances
- Intense emotional responses to stress
- Impulsivity and risk-taking behaviors

Treatment Options:

1. Psychotherapy: Dialectical Behavior Therapy (DBT) is particularly effective for Borderline Personality Disorder. Other therapies, like psychodynamic therapy and group therapy, can also help.
2. Medications: While no medication specifically treats personality disorders, antidepressants, mood stabilizers, and antipsychotic medications may help manage certain symptoms.

Chapter 7: Demographics and Social Inequality

Demographics refer to the statistical characteristics of a population. Key factors in demographics include age, gender, race, ethnicity, income, education level, and employment status. These characteristics help to categorize and understand the makeup of a society, providing insights into trends that affect social institutions like healthcare, education, and the labor market.

Demographic studies often use tools such as population pyramids to visually represent age and sex distribution. For example, a population pyramid with a broad base and narrow top indicates a young population with high birth rates, common in developing countries. On the other hand, a more rectangular shape suggests a stable or aging population, as seen in developed countries with low birth rates.

Changes in demographics, such as aging populations in many developed nations, impact social services and healthcare systems. As the proportion of older individuals increases, there is greater demand for pensions, healthcare, and long-term care services. Governments and policymakers rely on demographic data to make informed decisions about allocating resources and planning for future needs.

In addition to age, other demographic factors like migration, fertility rates, and mortality rates contribute to the overall structure and dynamics of a population. Migration, both voluntary and involuntary, has a significant impact on the workforce, housing, and public services. For instance, an influx of young workers into a region can stimulate economic growth, while a mass exodus may lead to labor shortages and economic decline.

Social Inequality: The Uneven Distribution of Resources

Social inequality refers to the unequal distribution of resources and opportunities within a society. These resources can include wealth, education, healthcare, employment, and political power. Social inequality can exist on both individual and systemic levels, with certain groups of people experiencing advantages or disadvantages based on their demographic characteristics.

One of the primary forms of social inequality is economic inequality, which refers to disparities in income and wealth distribution. In many societies, the wealthiest individuals control a disproportionate share of resources, while lower-income individuals may struggle to access basic necessities like food, shelter, and healthcare. Economic inequality is closely linked to issues such as poverty, unemployment, and access to education, which further perpetuate social disparities.

Another critical aspect of social inequality is racial and ethnic inequality. Historically marginalized groups, including racial and ethnic minorities, often face systemic discrimination that limits their access to quality education, healthcare, and employment opportunities. In many cases, these inequalities are deeply embedded in the social and legal systems, creating barriers that are difficult to overcome. For example, racial discrimination in housing policies has led to segregated neighborhoods, contributing to disparities in access to quality education and healthcare.

Gender inequality is another pervasive form of social inequality. Women and gender minorities often face discrimination in the workplace, such as lower wages, fewer opportunities for advancement, and limited access to leadership positions. These disparities are often compounded by the unpaid labor that women disproportionately perform in domestic roles, such as childcare and caregiving. Gender inequality also extends to healthcare, where women and gender minorities may experience inadequate access to reproductive health services and face gender bias in medical treatment.

Education and Social Inequality

Education plays a crucial role in shaping social inequality. Access to quality education is a key factor that can either mitigate or exacerbate social disparities. In many societies, individuals from wealthier families have access to better educational resources, including well-funded schools, experienced teachers, and extracurricular activities that enhance learning opportunities. In contrast, individuals from low-income families often attend underfunded schools with fewer resources, leading to lower academic achievement and limited access to higher education.

The concept of the "achievement gap" refers to the disparities in academic performance between students from different socioeconomic, racial, and ethnic backgrounds. This gap is often driven by factors such as unequal access to early childhood education, differences in school funding, and varying levels of parental involvement. As a result, students from disadvantaged backgrounds may struggle to complete high school or pursue higher education, limiting their opportunities for upward social mobility.

The relationship between education and social inequality is cyclical: individuals who receive a lower quality education are less likely to secure high-paying jobs, which in turn affects their ability to provide quality education for their children. Breaking this cycle requires addressing systemic inequalities in educational funding, access to early childhood programs, and support for disadvantaged students.

Healthcare and Social Inequality

Healthcare is another area where social inequality is starkly evident. Access to quality healthcare is often determined by an individual's income, employment status, and geographic location. In countries without universal healthcare systems, individuals from low-income backgrounds may struggle to afford medical treatment, leading to poorer health outcomes and higher rates of chronic diseases. Even in countries with public healthcare systems, disparities in the quality of care can exist based on factors such as race, ethnicity, and geographic location.

For instance, in the United States, racial and ethnic minorities are more likely to be uninsured or underinsured, limiting their access to preventive care and timely medical treatment. These disparities contribute to higher rates of chronic conditions such as diabetes, hypertension, and heart disease among minority populations. Additionally, rural communities often face challenges in accessing healthcare due to a shortage of medical providers and facilities, leading to higher rates of untreated illnesses.

Social determinants of health, such as education, housing, and employment, play a significant role in shaping health outcomes. Individuals living in poverty are more likely to experience food insecurity, unstable housing, and hazardous working conditions, all of which negatively impact their health. Addressing social inequality in healthcare requires a multifaceted approach that includes expanding access to affordable healthcare, addressing systemic discrimination in medical settings, and improving social support systems.

Political Power and Social Inequality

Political power is closely tied to social inequality, as individuals and groups with greater economic resources often have more influence over political decision-making. This power imbalance can lead to policies that disproportionately benefit the wealthy, while marginalized groups struggle to have their voices heard. For example, campaign finance laws in many countries allow wealthy individuals and corporations to contribute large sums of money to political campaigns, giving them greater access to lawmakers and the ability to shape public policy in their favor.

Political inequality is also evident in voter suppression efforts that disproportionately affect racial and ethnic minorities, low-income individuals, and other marginalized groups. These efforts may include restrictive voter ID laws, gerrymandering, and limited access to polling places, all of which reduce the political representation of disadvantaged groups. As a result, policies that address social inequality, such as raising the minimum wage or expanding access to healthcare, may face significant opposition from those in power.

Efforts to reduce social inequality often focus on increasing political participation among marginalized groups, advocating for policies that promote economic and social justice, and addressing systemic discrimination in political institutions.

Practical Question For Section 6:

1. **Which of the following is NOT considered a cognitive process?**
   a) Memory
   b) Attention
   c) Digestion
   d) Perception

2. **In perception, what is the process called when the brain organizes and interprets sensory information?**
   a) Sensation
   b) Attention
   c) Perception
   d) Encoding

3. **Top-down processing in perception is influenced by:**
   a) Incoming sensory data
   b) Prior knowledge and expectations
   c) Random stimuli
   d) External stimuli only

4. **Which type of memory lasts for less than a second and involves the storage of sensory information?**
   a) Short-term memory
   b) Long-term memory
   c) Sensory memory
   d) Procedural memory

5. **Selective attention allows an individual to:**
   a) Focus on multiple tasks simultaneously
   b) Ignore irrelevant stimuli and focus on a single task
   c) Retain information for long periods
   d) Encode sensory input directly into long-term memory

6. **What is the capacity of short-term memory according to the "magic number" theory?**
   a) 5±1 items
   b) 7±2 items
   c) 10±3 items
   d) 12±4 items

7. **Which of the following is an example of bottom-up processing?**
   a) Reading a book based on prior knowledge of the subject
   b) Identifying a song you've heard before
   c) Recognizing an unfamiliar object based on its sensory features
   d) Understanding a concept based on your expectations

8. **Which of the following is a type of declarative memory?**
   a) Procedural memory

b) Semantic memory
   c) Sensory memory
   d) Iconic memory
9. **What is the role of working memory in cognitive processes?**
   a) Long-term storage of facts and events
   b) Short-term manipulation and processing of information
   c) Passive reception of sensory information
   d) Automatic retrieval of learned skills
10. **Divided attention refers to:**
    a) Focusing on one task exclusively
    b) Switching attention between tasks quickly
    c) Paying attention to multiple tasks simultaneously
    d) Concentrating for extended periods of time
11. **Which part of the memory process involves retaining information over time?**
    a) Encoding
    b) Retrieval
    c) Storage
    d) Sensation
12. **Sustained attention is most important for which of the following activities?**
    a) Checking your phone while watching TV
    b) Reading a novel for an extended period
    c) Answering multiple-choice questions on an exam
    d) Listening to a conversation while driving
13. **Which of the following statements best describes episodic memory?**
    a) Memory of facts and knowledge
    b) Memory of how to perform tasks
    c) Memory of personal experiences and events
    d) Memory of sensory experiences
14. **The "cocktail party effect" is an example of:**
    a) Selective attention
    b) Divided attention
    c) Sensory overload
    d) Bottom-up processing
15. **Which of the following influences how we perceive stimuli from the environment?**
    a) Sensory data only
    b) Prior knowledge, expectations, and context
    c) Perceptual constancies
    d) Reflexive responses
16. **In attention research, the term "attentional bottleneck" refers to:**
    a) The limited capacity of the brain to process information

b) The brain's ability to multitask
   c) A strategy to avoid distractions
   d) A technique to improve focus
17. **Iconic memory is associated with which sense?**
    a) Taste
    b) Hearing
    c) Sight
    d) Touch
18. **What type of memory involves the recall of motor skills and habits?**
    a) Procedural memory
    b) Semantic memory
    c) Working memory
    d) Sensory memory
19. **Which of the following is an example of top-down processing?**
    a) Recognizing a familiar face in a crowd
    b) Identifying a new object based on its parts
    c) Reacting to an unexpected loud sound
    d) Memorizing a new vocabulary word
20. **Which type of memory is most likely to be used when solving a math problem mentally?**
    a) Long-term memory
    b) Sensory memory
    c) Working memory
    d) Episodic memory
21. **Which of the following is a type of associative learning?**
    a) Observational learning
    b) Habituation
    c) Classical conditioning
    d) Sensitization
22. **In classical conditioning, the stimulus that naturally triggers a response is called the:**
    a) Conditioned stimulus (CS)
    b) Unconditioned response (UR)
    c) Conditioned response (CR)
    d) Unconditioned stimulus (US)
23. **What is the process by which a conditioned response fades when the conditioned stimulus is no longer paired with the unconditioned stimulus?**
    a) Generalization
    b) Extinction
    c) Spontaneous recovery
    d) Discrimination

24. **Which of the following is an example of positive reinforcement?**
    a) Removing a restriction after good behavior
    b) Giving a treat for completing homework
    c) Scolding after misbehavior
    d) Taking away privileges after breaking a rule
25. **Which of the following describes negative reinforcement?**
    a) Adding an aversive stimulus to decrease behavior
    b) Removing a pleasant stimulus to decrease behavior
    c) Adding a pleasant stimulus to increase behavior
    d) Removing an aversive stimulus to increase behavior
26. **Which schedule of reinforcement provides reinforcement after an unpredictable number of responses?**
    a) Fixed-ratio
    b) Variable-ratio
    c) Fixed-interval
    d) Variable-interval
27. **In operant conditioning, what is the process of rewarding successive approximations to a desired behavior called?**
    a) Shaping
    b) Extinction
    c) Generalization
    d) Discrimination
28. **Which of the following best describes classical conditioning?**
    a) Learning through observation
    b) Learning through association between a stimulus and a response
    c) Learning through consequences
    d) Learning through imitation
29. **What happens during spontaneous recovery in classical conditioning?**
    a) A response weakens over time
    b) A learned behavior is completely forgotten
    c) An extinguished conditioned response reappears
    d) New behaviors are learned rapidly
30. **What is it called when an organism responds to stimuli that are similar to the conditioned stimulus in classical conditioning?**
    a) Discrimination
    b) Generalization
    c) Extinction
    d) Habituation

31. In operant conditioning, which of the following is an example of negative punishment?
    a) Giving a child a time-out
    b) Removing a toy after bad behavior
    c) Praising a child for good behavior
    d) Giving extra homework for misbehavior
32. Which of the following is an example of classical conditioning in everyday life?
    a) A dog salivating when it hears a bell
    b) A student studying harder to avoid failing
    c) A child receiving a reward for doing chores
    d) A person learning how to drive by observing others
33. In operant conditioning, reinforcement that occurs after a set number of responses is known as:
    a) Variable-ratio
    b) Fixed-ratio
    c) Fixed-interval
    d) Variable-interval
34. Which of the following is an example of generalization in classical conditioning?
    a) A dog responding only to a specific bell sound
    b) A dog salivating at any sound resembling a bell
    c) A dog stopping its response after repeated exposure
    d) A dog performing different actions for different stimuli
35. What type of learning occurs when behavior is influenced by observing others?
    a) Classical conditioning
    b) Operant conditioning
    c) Observational learning
    d) Associative learning
36. Which of the following is an example of positive punishment?
    a) Adding extra chores for bad behavior
    b) Removing a toy for bad behavior
    c) Praising good behavior
    d) Taking away privileges for bad behavior
37. In operant conditioning, what type of reinforcement schedule results in the highest response rates and is most resistant to extinction?
    a) Fixed-interval
    b) Variable-ratio
    c) Fixed-ratio
    d) Variable-interval
38. Which element of classical conditioning is responsible for triggering a learned response?
    a) Unconditioned stimulus
    b) Conditioned stimulus

c) Unconditioned response
d) Conditioned response

39. **What does the term "extinction" refer to in operant conditioning?**
    a) Decreasing the frequency of a behavior by removing reinforcement
    b) Removing a conditioned stimulus
    c) Increasing a behavior by applying punishment
    d) Preventing any new learning from taking place

40. **Which of the following is an example of fixed-interval reinforcement?**
    a) Receiving a paycheck every two weeks
    b) Winning on a slot machine after a random number of pulls
    c) Receiving praise after every homework assignment
    d) Being rewarded after every third correct response

41. **Which sociological theory views society as a system of interconnected parts working together to maintain stability?**
    a) Conflict Theory
    b) Functionalism
    c) Symbolic Interactionism
    d) Feminist Theory

42. **Who is primarily associated with the development of Conflict Theory?**
    a) Émile Durkheim
    b) Max Weber
    c) Karl Marx
    d) George Herbert Mead

43. **Which concept refers to the belief that society is held together by power and coercion, according to Conflict Theory?**
    a) Social consensus
    b) Social cooperation
    c) Social inequality
    d) Social equilibrium

44. **According to Functionalism, what happens when one part of society is not functioning properly?**
    a) Society collapses
    b) Social institutions cease to exist
    c) Society adapts to restore balance
    d) Social conflict emerges

45. **Symbolic Interactionism primarily focuses on:**
    a) Macro-level social structures
    b) Social interactions at the individual level
    c) Economic inequalities
    d) Class struggles

46. What concept is central to Symbolic Interactionism and refers to the symbols individuals use to communicate and form relationships?
    a) Social roles
    b) Cultural norms
    c) Social symbols
    d) Social institutions
47. The "looking-glass self" is a concept developed by:
    a) Karl Marx
    b) Charles Cooley
    c) Émile Durkheim
    d) Herbert Spencer
48. Which theory argues that social inequality is a key driving force in societal change?
    a) Functionalism
    b) Conflict Theory
    c) Symbolic Interactionism
    d) Social Exchange Theory
49. Feminist theory, which highlights gender inequality, is most closely associated with which broader sociological perspective?
    a) Functionalism
    b) Conflict Theory
    c) Symbolic Interactionism
    d) Structuralism
50. Which sociological theory would be most likely to explore the role of language in shaping individual identity?
    a) Functionalism
    b) Conflict Theory
    c) Symbolic Interactionism
    d) Postmodernism
51. Social structures are primarily concerned with:
    a) The material wealth of individuals
    b) The recurring patterns of social behavior
    c) Individual psychology
    d) Legal regulations
52. Which of the following is an example of a social institution?
    a) A personal hobby
    b) A law enforcement agency
    c) A random group of friends
    d) A sports team
53. Which of the following is considered the most fundamental social institution?
    a) Economy

b) Government
c) Family
d) Education

54. In modern societies, the institution responsible for transmitting knowledge and values to individuals is:
   a) Family
   b) Religion
   c) Education
   d) Media

55. What is a key function of the government as a social institution?
   a) Socialization of children
   b) Maintaining order and enforcing laws
   c) Production and distribution of goods
   d) Offering religious guidance

56. Social structures like class, race, and gender are examples of:
   a) Social institutions
   b) Social norms
   c) Social roles
   d) Social hierarchies

57. Which of the following best defines social inequality?
   a) Equal access to resources
   b) Unequal distribution of wealth, power, and opportunities
   c) Social cooperation between groups
   d) Social harmony among classes

58. Social institutions tend to work together because they are:
   a) Completely independent
   b) Based on individual choices
   c) Interdependent and interconnected
   d) Unchanging and static

59. What is the primary role of religion as a social institution?
   a) Enforcing government laws
   b) Providing economic services
   c) Offering a moral framework and shared values
   d) Transmitting scientific knowledge

60. The economic system, as a social institution, primarily deals with:
   a) Socialization and cultural transmission
   b) Distribution of goods and services
   c) Regulation of moral behavior
   d) Enforcement of legal norms

61. **What is self-concept primarily composed of?**
    a) Beliefs about society
    b) Personal skills and experiences
    c) Public opinions
    d) Personality traits, skills, and values
62. **Which of the following best defines self-esteem?**
    a) The ability to achieve personal goals
    b) A person's perception of how others view them
    c) The emotional evaluation of one's own self-image
    d) The confidence one has in their social roles
63. **Which component of self-concept refers to how people see themselves physically and socially?**
    a) Self-esteem
    b) Self-image
    c) Ideal self
    d) Ego
64. **Discrepancies between a person's actual self and their ideal self often result in:**
    a) Increased motivation
    b) Social isolation
    c) A sense of satisfaction
    d) Feelings of dissatisfaction
65. **Which factor primarily influences the development of identity and self-concept during adolescence?**
    a) Social media presence
    b) Peer interaction and social roles
    c) Parental expectations
    d) Biological changes
66. **Self-concept is often shaped by feedback from:**
    a) Internal beliefs alone
    b) Personal reflection
    c) Family, peers, and social interactions
    d) Academic performance
67. **What is the role of socialization in identity formation?**
    a) It is the biological process of development
    b) It teaches individuals societal norms, values, and behaviors
    c) It focuses on independent achievements
    d) It emphasizes natural personality traits
68. **In which cultural context is personal achievement most likely to be a significant factor in identity formation?**
    a) Collectivist cultures

b) Nomadic cultures
   c) Rural cultures
   d) Individualist cultures
69. **Which of the following best describes a collectivist approach to identity?**
   a) Focus on personal achievement
   b) Strong emphasis on individuality
   c) Identity connected to family and community roles
   d) Minimal regard for social roles
70. **How does life experience influence self-concept?**
   a) Life experiences are unrelated to self-concept development
   b) Positive experiences typically decrease self-esteem
   c) Negative experiences can lead to self-doubt and lower self-esteem
   d) Self-concept remains static despite life experiences
71. **Gender identity refers to:**
   a) A person's biological sex
   b) The roles assigned by society based on sex
   c) A person's internal experience and perception of gender
   d) The level of influence gender has on social roles
72. **At what age do most children begin to recognize and identify their gender?**
   a) 1 year old
   b) 3 years old
   c) 5 years old
   d) 8 years old
73. **Which term best describes the outward expression of one's gender identity?**
   a) Gender role
   b) Gender expression
   c) Gender fluidity
   d) Sexual orientation
74. **In which situation is gender expression most evident?**
   a) Internal belief systems
   b) External appearance and behavior
   c) Private thoughts and feelings
   d) Family expectations
75. **What is a common challenge faced by gender nonconforming individuals?**
   a) Increased societal acceptance
   b) Lack of opportunities for social mobility
   c) Discrimination and misunderstanding
   d) Enhanced mental health outcomes
76. **Cultural identity is primarily formed through:**
   a) Biological traits

b) Personal achievements
   c) Socialization and cultural exposure
   d) Economic status
77. **Cultural identity provides a sense of:**
   a) Economic power
   b) Personal isolation
   c) Belonging and shared connection
   d) Political influence
78. **A multicultural identity typically develops when:**
   a) A person adheres strictly to one culture
   b) An individual is exposed to multiple cultural influences
   c) Social roles do not influence identity
   d) Personal identity is determined by economic factors
79. **What is one of the main effects of globalization on cultural identity?**
   a) Cultural identities remain unchanged
   b) Individuals are more likely to reject their own cultural heritage
   c) People are more exposed to multiple cultures, leading to a dual or multicultural identity
   d) It makes traditional cultural practices obsolete
80. **Which of the following best describes the concept of bicultural identity?**
   a) Strong adherence to a single cultural tradition
   b) Identifying with two or more cultures simultaneously
   c) Rejecting all cultural influences
   d) Avoiding participation in cultural traditions
81. **Which of the following best defines social relationships?**
   a) Emotional connections with oneself
   b) Bonds between individuals that shape interactions
   c) Financial interactions between people
   d) Relationships formed exclusively in the workplace
82. **What is the primary agent of socialization in early childhood?**
   a) Media
   b) Schools
   c) Family
   d) Peer groups
83. **Which of the following is NOT a key element of group dynamics?**
   a) Group cohesion
   b) Individual isolation
   c) Norms
   d) Roles

84. **What term describes the informal rules and expectations that govern behavior within a group?**
    a) Roles
    b) Cohesion
    c) Norms
    d) Hierarchies
85. **Which type of relationship typically provides the most foundational emotional support?**
    a) Professional relationships
    b) Romantic relationships
    c) Familial relationships
    d) Acquaintances
86. **What is the process by which individuals learn the norms and values of their society?**
    a) Communication
    b) Socialization
    c) Cohesion
    d) Group dynamics
87. **Which of the following is most likely to lead to groupthink?**
    a) Open communication
    b) Low group cohesion
    c) High group cohesion
    d) Clear role differentiation
88. **In the context of social relationships, what is a toxic relationship?**
    a) A relationship based on manipulation and disrespect
    b) A professional relationship between colleagues
    c) A relationship based on mutual support and respect
    d) A casual friendship
89. **Which agent of socialization becomes more influential during adolescence?**
    a) Family
    b) Peers
    c) Media
    d) Schools
90. **What term refers to the sense of unity and camaraderie within a group?**
    a) Group dynamics
    b) Group cohesion
    c) Socialization
    d) Communication
91. **Which form of communication involves exchanging messages without spoken words?**
    a) Verbal communication
    b) Non-verbal communication
    c) Interpersonal communication

d) Group communication

92. Which is NOT an example of non-verbal communication?
    a) Facial expressions
    b) Hand gestures
    c) Body language
    d) Written words

93. What is the primary role of peer groups in socialization?
    a) Teaching professional skills
    b) Providing independence from family
    c) Offering financial support
    d) Introducing family values

94. Which type of communication is most complex due to managing multiple relationships and messages?
    a) Interpersonal communication
    b) Group communication
    c) Non-verbal communication
    d) Verbal communication

95. Which agent of socialization plays a significant role in shaping individuals' perceptions through content consumption?
    a) Family
    b) Schools
    c) Media
    d) Peers

96. Which of the following is an example of verbal communication?
    a) Email
    b) Eye contact
    c) Handshake
    d) Posture

97. What term is used to describe the roles and patterns of behavior expected within a group?
    a) Norms
    b) Group cohesion
    c) Hierarchies
    d) Social structures

98. Which of the following can negatively impact group performance by suppressing critical thinking?
    a) Group cohesion
    b) Groupthink
    c) Role differentiation
    d) Clear communication

99. **What is the key element that defines a healthy social relationship?**
    a) Manipulation
    b) Lack of trust
    c) Mutual respect
    d) Dependency
100. **Which of the following best describes socialization through mass media?**

    a) Learning directly from family members
    b) Interactions with teachers and peers
    c) Shaping beliefs through content on TV, internet, and social media
    d) Acquiring language skills from parents
101. **Which of the following is a hallmark symptom of major depressive disorder (MDD)?**
    a) Increased energy levels
    b) Persistent sadness or low mood
    c) Heightened irritability only during the night
    d) Excessive fear of specific objects or situations
102. **Which of the following neurotransmitters is most commonly associated with mood regulation in depression?**
    a) Acetylcholine
    b) Dopamine
    c) Serotonin
    d) Glutamate
103. **In anxiety disorders, what is the most common symptom experienced by individuals?**
    a) Increased concentration
    b) Elevated sense of confidence
    c) Excessive worry
    d) Reduced heart rate
104. **Which of the following best defines Generalized Anxiety Disorder (GAD)?**
    a) Sudden, intense episodes of fear accompanied by physical symptoms
    b) A persistent and exaggerated worry over everyday things
    c) Fear of social judgment in public situations
    d) Fear triggered by a specific object or situation
105. **Which type of therapy is most commonly used to treat individuals with Borderline Personality Disorder (BPD)?**
    a) Cognitive Behavioral Therapy (CBT)
    b) Dialectical Behavior Therapy (DBT)
    c) Exposure Therapy
    d) Acceptance and Commitment Therapy
106. **Which symptom is NOT typically associated with depression?**
    a) Loss of interest in activities

b) Sudden bursts of energy and activity
c) Changes in sleep patterns
d) Difficulty concentrating

107. **Which of the following personality disorders is characterized by an inflated sense of self-importance?**
a) Antisocial Personality Disorder
b) Borderline Personality Disorder
c) Obsessive-Compulsive Personality Disorder
d) Narcissistic Personality Disorder

108. **Panic disorder is often accompanied by which physical symptom?**
a) Shortness of breath
b) Heightened memory recall
c) Lack of sleep
d) Loss of appetite

109. **Which of the following is a common symptom of Antisocial Personality Disorder (ASPD)?**
a) Excessive guilt
b) Deceitful and manipulative behavior
c) Fear of judgment by others
d) Recurrent panic attacks

110. **In Major Depressive Disorder, which of the following changes are typically observed in sleep patterns?**
a) Increased sleep duration without any disturbances
b) Sleep disturbances such as insomnia or excessive sleeping
c) Sudden onset of vivid dreams
d) No changes in sleep patterns

111. **Social Anxiety Disorder is primarily marked by which of the following fears?**
a) Fear of heights
b) Fear of being judged or rejected in social situations
c) Fear of closed spaces
d) Fear of the dark

112. **Which of the following disorders is most commonly linked to a lack of empathy and manipulative behaviors?**
a) Borderline Personality Disorder
b) Narcissistic Personality Disorder
c) Antisocial Personality Disorder
d) Obsessive-Compulsive Personality Disorder

113. **Which of the following neurotransmitters plays a significant role in the development of anxiety disorders?**
a) Dopamine

b) Serotonin
c) Acetylcholine
d) Norepinephrine

114. **Which type of personality disorder is characterized by a preoccupation with perfectionism and control?**
    a) Narcissistic Personality Disorder
    b) Borderline Personality Disorder
    c) Obsessive-Compulsive Personality Disorder
    d) Schizotypal Personality Disorder

115. **Which of the following types of depression is typically triggered by reduced sunlight exposure in winter months?**
    a) Postpartum Depression
    b) Seasonal Affective Disorder (SAD)
    c) Major Depressive Disorder
    d) Dysthymia

116. **A person with Generalized Anxiety Disorder (GAD) will likely experience which of the following?**
    a) Intense fear of judgment in social settings
    b) Persistent and excessive worry about multiple areas of life
    c) A fear of specific animals, objects, or situations
    d) Panic attacks lasting for more than an hour

117. **Which of the following is NOT considered a mood disorder?**
    a) Major Depressive Disorder
    b) Bipolar Disorder
    c) Anxiety Disorder
    d) Dysthymia

118. **Which of the following treatment methods is most commonly used for anxiety disorders?**
    A) Antipsychotic medications
    B) Exposure therapy
    C) Stimulant medications
    D) Dialectical Behavior Therapy

119. **Which of the following is true about Borderline Personality Disorder?**
    a) Individuals are primarily concerned with perfectionism
    b) Individuals exhibit a consistent fear of abandonment
    c) The disorder is characterized by frequent panic attacks
    d) People with BPD often exhibit empathy and sympathy toward others

120. **In depression, which brain region is most commonly associated with the regulation of mood and emotions?**
    a) Hippocampus

b) Amygdala
c) Thalamus
d) Prefrontal cortex

121. **Which of the following is NOT considered a key demographic characteristic?**
    a) Age
    b) Gender
    c) Height
    d) Income

122. **A population pyramid with a broad base and narrow top typically represents what kind of population?**
a) Aging population
    a) b) Declining population
    b) Young population with high birth rates
    c) Population with equal birth and death rates

123. **Economic inequality refers to disparities in the distribution of which of the following?**
    a) Healthcare services
    b) Wealth and income
    c) Educational opportunities
    d) Voting rights

124. **Which factor is most directly associated with racial inequality?**
    a) Birth rates
    b) Education level
    c) Systemic discrimination
    d) Geographic location

125. **Social inequality can be defined as the unequal distribution of what?**
    a) Natural resources
    b) Opportunities and resources
    c) Population density
    d) Birth and death rates

126. **Which form of inequality is characterized by disparities in wages and access to leadership positions based on gender?**
    a) Racial inequality
    b) Economic inequality
    c) Gender inequality
    d) Social inequality

127. **The "achievement gap" in education typically refers to disparities between students based on which factors?**
    a) School size and funding
    b) Academic performance and resources
    c) Racial and socioeconomic background

d) Parental involvement and teacher experience

128. **Which of the following is a social determinant of health that contributes to social inequality?**
   a) Employment status
   b) Technological advancement
   c) Climate change
   d) National security policies

129. **In countries without universal healthcare systems, access to healthcare is most directly influenced by which factor?**
   a) Religious affiliation
   b) Geographic location
   c) Income and employment status
   d) Nationality

130. **What is the relationship between social inequality and voter suppression?**
   a) Voter suppression disproportionately affects wealthy individuals
   b) Voter suppression policies are implemented to reduce voter turnout
   c) Voter suppression disproportionately affects marginalized groups
   d) Voter suppression has no direct connection to social inequality

131. **In demographic studies, migration has which of the following impacts on a society?**
   a) Reduces population size permanently
   b) Increases the birth rate
   c) Affects workforce size and economic growth
   d) Creates more natural resources

132. **Gender inequality in healthcare can be exemplified by which of the following?**
   a) Equal access to reproductive health services
   b) Gender bias in medical treatment
   c) Universal healthcare coverage for all genders
   d) Men receiving fewer medical diagnoses

133. **Which of the following demographic factors most directly affects the demand for pensions and healthcare services?**
   a) High birth rates
   b) Increasing aging population
   c) Rural-to-urban migration
   d) Population density

134. **In terms of political power, which of the following can contribute to maintaining social inequality?**
   a) Equal representation in government
   b) Campaign finance laws favoring large donations
   c) Laws that increase the minimum wage
   d) Affordable housing policies

135. Which of the following is a key characteristic of systemic social inequality?
    a) It affects only individuals based on personal choices
    b) It can be easily eliminated by individual action
    c) It is embedded in social and legal systems
    d) It arises spontaneously without any historical context
136. Which demographic trend is common in developed countries?
    a) High fertility rates
    b) High mortality rates
    c) Aging population
    d) Increasing youth population
137. Social mobility refers to an individual's ability to:
    a) Move from one country to another
    b) Access higher-quality healthcare
    c) Improve their social and economic status
    d) Maintain their current socioeconomic level
138. Racial segregation in housing policies has historically contributed to social inequality in which of the following areas?
    a) Availability of natural resources
    b) Access to quality education and healthcare
    c) Birth rates and death rates
    d) Technological innovation
139. Which of the following is an example of economic inequality?
    a) Equal access to public transportation
    b) Unequal income distribution among different social classes
    c) Disparities in climate change awareness
    d) Equal representation in political office
140. Which factor is often cited as a key barrier to reducing social inequality in healthcare?
    a) Overpopulation in rural areas
    b) Discriminatory practices in medical settings
    c) Universal access to healthcare
    d) Surplus of healthcare workers

Answers and Explanation

1. c) Digestion. – Digestion is a biological process, not a cognitive process. Cognitive processes involve mental activities like memory and perception.
2. c) Perception. – Perception is the process by which the brain organizes and interprets sensory information to create a meaningful experience of the world.
3. b) Prior knowledge and expectations. – Top-down processing is influenced by what we already know and expect, helping us interpret sensory information more efficiently.
4. c) Sensory memory. – Sensory memory stores incoming sensory information for a very brief period, typically less than a second, before it's processed or forgotten.
5. b) Ignore irrelevant stimuli and focus on a single task. – Selective attention enables individuals to focus on specific stimuli while filtering out irrelevant distractions.
6. b) 7±2 items. – Short-term memory is limited in capacity, typically holding between 5 to 9 items (often cited as 7±2).
7. c) Recognizing an unfamiliar object based on its sensory features. – Bottom-up processing starts with incoming sensory data, building a perception from the raw information.
8. b) Semantic memory. – Semantic memory is a type of declarative memory that involves knowledge of facts and concepts.
9. b) Short-term manipulation and processing of information. – Working memory is used for temporarily holding and manipulating information, such as solving math problems or following a recipe.
10. c) Paying attention to multiple tasks simultaneously. – Divided attention refers to the ability to focus on more than one task at the same time, often at the cost of reduced efficiency.
11. c) Storage. – Storage is the process of maintaining information over time so that it can be retrieved later when needed.
12. b) Reading a novel for an extended period. – Sustained attention is the ability to focus on a task continuously without becoming distracted over a long period.
13. c) Memory of personal experiences and events. – Episodic memory refers to memories of specific events or experiences from one's personal life.
14. a) Selective attention. – The cocktail party effect is the phenomenon where you can focus on a single conversation in a noisy environment, highlighting selective attention.
15. b) Prior knowledge, expectations, and context. – Perception is influenced by what we already know, our expectations, and the context in which stimuli are presented.
16. a) The limited capacity of the brain to process information. – The attentional bottleneck refers to the brain's limited capacity to process multiple pieces of information at once.
17. c) Sight. – Iconic memory is a type of sensory memory related to visual information.
18. a) Procedural memory. – Procedural memory involves the storage of motor skills and habits, such as riding a bike or tying shoes.
19. a) Recognizing a familiar face in a crowd. – Top-down processing uses prior knowledge, such as recognizing a familiar face, to make sense of stimuli.

20. c) Working memory. – Working memory is responsible for holding and manipulating information temporarily, like mentally solving a math problem.
21. C. Classical conditioning. - Classical conditioning is a type of associative learning where an organism learns to associate two stimuli together. It differs from non-associative learning forms like habituation and sensitization.
22. D. Unconditioned stimulus (US). - The unconditioned stimulus (US) is a stimulus that naturally triggers an unlearned, automatic response, such as food triggering salivation in Pavlov's experiment.
23. B. Extinction. - Extinction occurs when the conditioned response gradually diminishes because the conditioned stimulus is no longer paired with the unconditioned stimulus.
24. B. Giving a treat for completing homework. - Positive reinforcement involves adding a reward following a behavior to increase the likelihood of that behavior being repeated.
25. D. Removing an aversive stimulus to increase behavior. - Negative reinforcement occurs when an aversive stimulus is removed after a behavior, which increases the likelihood of the behavior occurring again.
26. B. Variable-ratio. - A variable-ratio schedule provides reinforcement after an unpredictable number of responses, which is commonly seen in gambling scenarios like slot machines.
27. A. Shaping. - Shaping is the process in operant conditioning where behaviors are gradually guided toward a desired goal through successive approximations.
28. B. Learning through association between a stimulus and a response. - In classical conditioning, learning occurs by associating a neutral stimulus with an unconditioned stimulus, leading to a conditioned response.
29. C. An extinguished conditioned response reappears. - Spontaneous recovery is the sudden reappearance of a previously extinguished conditioned response after a rest period without further conditioning.
30. B. Generalization. - Generalization occurs when an organism responds to stimuli that are similar to the original conditioned stimulus, which shows that the association can spread to related stimuli.
31. B. Removing a toy after bad behavior. - Negative punishment involves taking away a desirable stimulus, like a toy, to decrease the likelihood of a behavior being repeated.
32. A. A dog salivating when it hears a bell. - This is a classic example of classical conditioning, where the dog learns to associate the sound of the bell (conditioned stimulus) with food (unconditioned stimulus).
33. B. Fixed-ratio. - In a fixed-ratio schedule, reinforcement is provided after a set number of responses. For example, a reward is given for every 5th correct response.
34. B. A dog salivating at any sound resembling a bell. - Generalization in classical conditioning refers to the tendency of the conditioned response to be triggered by stimuli similar to the conditioned stimulus.
35. C. Observational learning. - Observational learning occurs when behavior is learned by watching others and imitating their actions, rather than through direct reinforcement.

36. A. Adding extra chores for bad behavior. - Positive punishment involves presenting an aversive stimulus, like extra chores, after an undesirable behavior to reduce its occurrence.
37. B. Variable-ratio. - A variable-ratio schedule provides reinforcement after an unpredictable number of responses, which leads to the highest response rates and is most resistant to extinction.
38. B. Conditioned stimulus. - In classical conditioning, the conditioned stimulus (CS) is the previously neutral stimulus that, after being paired with the unconditioned stimulus, triggers the conditioned response.
39. A. Decreasing the frequency of a behavior by removing reinforcement. - In operant conditioning, extinction occurs when reinforcement is removed, leading to a decrease in the behavior over time.
40. A. Receiving a paycheck every two weeks. - A fixed-interval schedule provides reinforcement after a set amount of time has passed, as seen with regular paychecks.
41. B. Functionalism - Functionalism views society as a system of interconnected parts, where each institution serves a function to maintain social stability and equilibrium.
42. C. Karl Marx - Karl Marx is the key figure behind Conflict Theory, which emphasizes the struggles between social classes, particularly the capitalist (bourgeoisie) and working class (proletariat).
43. C. Social inequality - Conflict Theory argues that society is held together by the power dynamics and social inequality, where dominant groups maintain control over resources and institutions.
44. C. Society adapts to restore balance - According to Functionalism, if a part of society is dysfunctional, adjustments are made to restore stability and balance within the system.
45. B. Social interactions at the individual level - Symbolic Interactionism focuses on small-scale social interactions, analyzing how individuals create and interpret meanings through their interactions with others.
46. D. Social institutions - In Symbolic Interactionism, symbols like language, gestures, and objects are crucial in shaping interactions and relationships. These symbols are the foundation of social reality.
47. B. Charles Cooley - The "looking-glass self" is a concept developed by Charles Cooley, suggesting that individuals form their self-concept based on how they think others perceive them.
48. B. Conflict Theory - Conflict Theory posits that social change is driven by struggles over resources, inequality, and power. Inequality is seen as the key factor in societal change.
49. B. Conflict Theory - Feminist theory, which addresses gender inequality, is rooted in Conflict Theory. It focuses on the power imbalances and systemic inequalities that disadvantage women.
50. C. Symbolic Interactionism - Symbolic Interactionism would focus on language and symbols as they shape individual identity and social interactions, emphasizing micro-level processes.

51. B. The recurring patterns of social behavior - Social structures refer to the organized patterns of social relationships, norms, and roles that shape behavior and expectations in society.
52. B. A law enforcement agency - Social institutions are formal and organized systems that regulate behavior. A law enforcement agency is part of the institution of government, maintaining law and order.
53. C. Family - The family is the most fundamental social institution, responsible for primary socialization, nurturing, and instilling values in individuals from an early age.
54. C. Education - Education is the social institution responsible for transmitting knowledge, values, and skills to individuals, preparing them for societal roles and participation.
55. B. Maintaining order and enforcing laws - The government is responsible for maintaining order, enforcing laws, and regulating societal behavior to ensure the welfare of the population.
56. D. Social hierarchies - Social structures like class, race, and gender create hierarchical divisions in society, organizing individuals into ranked categories that affect their access to resources and opportunities.
57. B. Unequal distribution of wealth, power, and opportunities - Social inequality refers to the unequal access to resources, opportunities, and power between different groups in society.
58. C. Interdependent and interconnected - Social institutions like family, education, religion, government, and economy are interdependent, meaning they influence and rely on one another to maintain social order.
59. C. Offering a moral framework and shared values - Religion provides individuals and communities with a set of moral guidelines, shared values, and beliefs that influence behavior and social cohesion.
60. B. Distribution of goods and services - The economy is the institution responsible for organizing the production, distribution, and consumption of goods and services, shaping individuals' access to material resources.
61. B. Personal skills and experiences. – Self-concept refers to the collection of beliefs about one's own skills, personality, and abilities, which shape how individuals see themselves.
62. C. The emotional evaluation of one's own self-image. – Self-esteem is the evaluative aspect of self-concept, reflecting how positively or negatively individuals feel about their own perceived qualities.
63. B. Self-image. – Self-image is how individuals perceive themselves, including their physical appearance and social roles, which forms an essential part of self-concept.
64. D. Feelings of dissatisfaction. – When there is a significant difference between a person's actual self and their ideal self, it often leads to feelings of dissatisfaction and a desire for change.
65. B. Peer interaction and social roles. – During adolescence, peers play a critical role in identity formation as individuals experiment with different social roles and relationships.
66. C. Family, peers, and social interactions. – Self-concept is shaped by the feedback individuals receive from others, including family, friends, and broader social interactions.

67. B. It teaches individuals societal norms, values, and behaviors. – Socialization is the process through which individuals learn the norms and values of their society, which influences their identity and self-concept.
68. D. Individualist cultures. – In individualist cultures, personal achievement and independence are highly valued, and identity is often shaped by personal success and self-reliance.
69. C. Identity connected to family and community roles. – In collectivist cultures, identity is often defined by the roles individuals play within their family and community, emphasizing interdependence.
70. C. Negative experiences can lead to self-doubt and lower self-esteem. – Life experiences, especially failures or negative feedback, can diminish self-esteem and cause individuals to question their abilities.
71. C. A person's internal experience and perception of gender. – Gender identity refers to how an individual perceives and experiences their gender, which may differ from societal expectations or biological sex.
72. B. 3 years old. – By age 3, most children can identify themselves as male or female and begin to understand the associated societal roles and expectations.
73. B. Gender expression. – Gender expression is the outward display of one's gender identity, including choices in clothing, hairstyle, and behavior, which may or may not align with societal expectations.
74. B. External appearance and behavior. – Gender expression is most evident through how individuals present themselves to others, such as through appearance and actions.
75. C. Discrimination and misunderstanding. – Gender nonconforming individuals often face challenges such as societal discrimination and a lack of understanding, which can negatively affect their mental health.
76. C. Socialization and cultural exposure. – Cultural identity is developed through exposure to the cultural norms, traditions, and values of one's community or heritage, typically learned during early socialization.
77. C. Belonging and shared connection. – Cultural identity provides individuals with a sense of belonging and connection to others who share similar cultural values and practices.
78. B. An individual is exposed to multiple cultural influences. – Multicultural identity develops when individuals grow up in or are exposed to multiple cultural environments, integrating elements from each into their self-concept.
79. C. People are more exposed to multiple cultures, leading to a dual or multicultural identity. – Globalization exposes individuals to different cultural practices, which can result in the development of a bicultural or multicultural identity.
80. B. Identifying with two or more cultures simultaneously. – Bicultural identity occurs when individuals identify with two or more cultural groups and integrate aspects of both into their self-concept.

81. B. Bonds between individuals that shape interactions. - Social relationships refer to the emotional and practical connections between people that influence their interactions and behaviors.
82. C. Family. - The family is typically the first agent of socialization, where individuals learn basic norms, values, and social roles during childhood.
83. B. Individual isolation. - Group dynamics are about interactions within the group, and individual isolation is not a component of these interactions.
84. C. Norms. - Norms are the informal rules and expectations that regulate behavior in groups, ensuring predictability in interactions.
85. C. Familial relationships. - Familial relationships provide foundational emotional support from family members, which is often critical during early development.
86. B. Socialization. - Socialization is the process by which individuals learn and internalize the norms, values, and roles required to function in society.
87. C. High group cohesion. - High group cohesion can lead to groupthink, where the desire for harmony prevents critical evaluation of ideas.
88. A. A relationship based on manipulation and disrespect. - Toxic relationships involve negative patterns like manipulation, which can harm mental and emotional health.
89. B. Peers. - During adolescence, peer groups become a more dominant influence on social behavior and identity formation.
90. B. Group cohesion. - Group cohesion refers to the unity and solidarity among group members, which fosters teamwork and collaboration.
91. B. Non-verbal communication. - Non-verbal communication involves body language, facial expressions, and gestures to convey messages without spoken words.
92. D. Written words. - Written words are a form of verbal communication, while the other options are examples of non-verbal communication.
93. B. Providing independence from family. - Peer groups help individuals establish independence by offering social support outside of family influence.
94. B. Group communication. - Group communication is complex due to managing multiple relationships and ensuring all members participate in discussions.
95. C. Media. - Media plays a crucial role in shaping individuals' views on society and culture by providing constant exposure to information and ideas.
96. A. Email. - Email is a form of written verbal communication, while the other options are forms of non-verbal communication.
97. A. Norms. - Norms refer to the established rules of behavior expected within a group, helping to maintain order and cooperation.
98. B. Groupthink. - Groupthink occurs when a group prioritizes consensus over critical thinking, which can stifle diverse opinions and hinder decision-making.
99. C. Mutual respect. - A healthy social relationship is characterized by mutual respect, trust, and equality between the individuals involved.

100. C. Shaping beliefs through content on TV, internet, and social media. - Media influences socialization by exposing individuals to societal norms and values through content they consume.
101. B. Persistent sadness or low mood. - Major depressive disorder is characterized by a continuous feeling of sadness or a loss of interest in life, which significantly affects daily functioning.
102. C. Serotonin. - Serotonin is a key neurotransmitter that plays a significant role in mood regulation. Low levels of serotonin are commonly associated with depression.
103. C. Excessive worry. - Anxiety disorders are characterized by chronic worry that is difficult to control and often disproportionate to the actual situation.
104. B. A persistent and exaggerated worry over everyday things. - Generalized Anxiety Disorder (GAD) involves ongoing worry about everyday life events without a clear reason or trigger.
105. B. Dialectical Behavior Therapy (DBT). - DBT is a type of psychotherapy particularly effective for Borderline Personality Disorder (BPD), focusing on managing emotions and improving interpersonal relationships.
106. B. Sudden bursts of energy and activity. - Depression is typically marked by a lack of energy and interest in activities, not sudden bursts of energy, which is more associated with mania or hypomania.
107. D. Narcissistic Personality Disorder. - Individuals with Narcissistic Personality Disorder have an inflated sense of their own importance and a deep need for admiration, often at the expense of others' feelings.
108. A. Shortness of breath. - Panic attacks, which are common in panic disorder, often include physical symptoms such as shortness of breath, chest pain, and a rapid heartbeat.
109. B. Deceitful and manipulative behavior. - Individuals with Antisocial Personality Disorder (ASPD) tend to engage in deceitful, manipulative, and often harmful behaviors toward others without remorse.
110. B. Sleep disturbances such as insomnia or excessive sleeping. - Depression often causes disruptions in sleep patterns, including difficulty falling asleep or excessive sleep.
111. B. Fear of being judged or rejected in social situations. - Social Anxiety Disorder involves intense anxiety in social or performance situations where the individual fears being negatively evaluated.
112. C. Antisocial Personality Disorder. - People with Antisocial Personality Disorder often lack empathy and engage in manipulative and sometimes harmful behaviors toward others.
113. D. Norepinephrine. - Norepinephrine is a neurotransmitter involved in the body's fight-or-flight response, and its dysregulation is linked to anxiety disorders.
114. C. Obsessive-Compulsive Personality Disorder. - This personality disorder is characterized by a preoccupation with orderliness, perfectionism, and control, often leading to rigidity in thoughts and behaviors.

115. B. Seasonal Affective Disorder (SAD). - SAD is a type of depression that occurs at a specific time of year, typically in the winter, when exposure to sunlight decreases.
116. B. Persistent and excessive worry about multiple areas of life. - Generalized Anxiety Disorder involves chronic worry about various aspects of daily life, including work, health, and social interactions.
117. C. Anxiety Disorder. - Anxiety disorders are not classified as mood disorders. Mood disorders primarily involve disturbances in mood, such as depression or bipolar disorder.
118. B. Exposure therapy. - Exposure therapy is often used in the treatment of anxiety disorders to help individuals face and overcome their fears in a controlled environment.
119. B. Individuals exhibit a consistent fear of abandonment. - Borderline Personality Disorder is characterized by intense fear of abandonment, leading to unstable relationships and emotional instability.
120. D. Prefrontal cortex. - The prefrontal cortex plays a crucial role in regulating emotions and decision-making, and its dysfunction is linked to mood disorders such as depression.
121. C. Height. - Height is not a key demographic characteristic; demographics typically focus on factors like age, gender, and income that influence population trends and resource allocation.
122. C. Young population with high birth rates. - A broad-based population pyramid indicates a young population with high birth and fertility rates, common in developing countries.
123. B. Wealth and income. - Economic inequality specifically refers to the uneven distribution of wealth and income across individuals or groups in a society.
124. C. Systemic discrimination. - Racial inequality is often perpetuated by systemic discrimination, which affects access to resources such as education, employment, and healthcare.
125. B. Opportunities and resources. - Social inequality refers to the unequal distribution of resources and opportunities, such as wealth, education, and healthcare, within a society.
126. C. Gender inequality. - Gender inequality is characterized by disparities in wages, job opportunities, and access to leadership positions based on gender.
127. C. Racial and socioeconomic background. - The "achievement gap" refers to differences in academic performance between students of different racial and socioeconomic backgrounds, often due to unequal access to educational resources.
128. A. Employment status. - Employment status is a key social determinant of health that can affect access to healthcare, housing, and education, thereby contributing to social inequality.
129. C. Income and employment status. - In countries without universal healthcare, access to medical services is often determined by income and employment status, with low-income individuals facing greater barriers to care.
130. C. Voter suppression disproportionately affects marginalized groups. - Voter suppression efforts, such as restrictive voter ID laws, tend to disproportionately impact racial and ethnic minorities, low-income individuals, and other marginalized groups, reducing their political influence.

131. C. Affects workforce size and economic growth. - Migration can significantly impact a society's workforce, potentially boosting economic growth by providing labor or straining resources when large numbers of people leave or enter a region.
132. B. Gender bias in medical treatment. - Gender inequality in healthcare can be seen in the bias that women and gender minorities face in medical treatment, often leading to misdiagnosis or inadequate care.
133. B. Increasing aging population. - As populations age, the demand for pensions, healthcare, and other social services increases, which can strain public resources in countries with aging populations.
134. B. Campaign finance laws favoring large donations. - Campaign finance laws that allow large donations from wealthy individuals or corporations can perpetuate political inequality by giving those with more financial resources greater influence over policymakers.
135. C. It is embedded in social and legal systems. - Systemic social inequality is entrenched in societal structures, including laws, policies, and institutions, making it difficult to dismantle without significant changes to those systems.
136. C. Aging population. - Developed countries often experience aging populations due to lower birth rates and longer life expectancies, increasing the demand for healthcare and social services.
137. C. Improve their social and economic status. - Social mobility refers to the ability of individuals or groups to move up (or down) the social and economic ladder, often through education, employment, or other means.
138. B. Access to quality education and healthcare. - Racial segregation in housing policies has historically led to unequal access to quality education and healthcare, which continues to affect racial minorities today.
139. B. Unequal income distribution among different social classes. - Economic inequality is exemplified by the uneven distribution of income and wealth, where some individuals or groups hold a disproportionate amount of resources.
140. B. Discriminatory practices in medical settings. - Discriminatory practices, such as racial or gender bias, in medical settings can prevent marginalized groups from receiving adequate healthcare, thus perpetuating social inequality.

SECTION 7: Critical Analysis and Reasoning Skills (CARS)

Chapter 1: Approaching CARS Passages

Critical Analysis and Reasoning Skills (CARS) is one of the most challenging sections of the MCAT because it requires strong analytical and critical thinking skills without relying on content knowledge from other sections. The key to mastering CARS is to develop a strategic approach to passages, understanding what the test is asking for and how to efficiently manage your time.

Understanding the Structure of CARS Passages

CARS passages are generally about 500-600 words long and cover a wide range of topics, including social sciences, humanities, ethics, and philosophy. The passages often present complex arguments, sometimes requiring you to recognize subtle distinctions, underlying assumptions, or the author's intent.

The first step to mastering CARS is to familiarize yourself with the format. Passages are dense and may include unfamiliar topics. However, your task is not to memorize the content, but rather to understand the structure of the arguments and the connections between ideas. Focus on identifying the author's main point, supporting evidence, and any counterarguments presented.

Effective Reading Strategies

Many students struggle with time management on the CARS section, so adopting a consistent reading strategy is crucial. Here are some practical tips:

- Read Actively: This involves paying attention to the structure and flow of the argument, not just the content. While reading, ask yourself what the author is trying to prove, what evidence they provide, and whether they present opposing views.
- Identify the Main Idea: Every CARS passage has a central thesis or main idea. Your job is to identify this as quickly as possible. The main idea is often located in the introduction or conclusion of the passage, but it can also be found in repeated themes throughout.
- Focus on Relationships Between Ideas: Rather than getting bogged down in every detail, look for the relationships between the different points presented in the passage. For example, how does one piece of evidence support or challenge the argument? Recognizing these connections will help you answer questions that ask about the passage's structure or logical flow.
- Don't Memorize Facts: CARS questions rarely require you to recall specific facts. Instead, focus on understanding the general flow of the argument. If a question asks about a specific detail, you can always refer back to the passage.
- Stay Neutral: Avoid letting your personal opinions influence how you interpret a passage. The MCAT is testing your ability to critically evaluate arguments, not whether you agree with them. Always focus on what the author is saying, not what you think they should say.

Timing and Pacing

You have 90 minutes to complete 9 passages with 5-7 questions each. This means you should spend no more than 10 minutes per passage, including the time to answer the questions. It's important to develop a pacing strategy that works for you. If you find yourself spending too much time on a particular passage, it's better to move on and return to it later if you have time.

Some students prefer reading the questions before reading the passage, while others read the entire passage first. There is no universal best approach, so try both methods during practice and see which works better for you.

Practice is Key

The more you practice CARS passages, the better you'll get at identifying patterns in how the passages are written and how the questions are structured. Regular practice helps you to recognize common traps, such as misleading answer choices or questions that seem to ask about details but are really testing your understanding of the overall argument.

Types of Passages and Questions

Types of Passages

CARS passages are drawn from a wide variety of disciplines, but they can generally be classified into two broad categories: Humanities and Social Sciences. Each of these has unique features that affect how you approach them.

1. Humanities Passages: Humanities passages tend to focus on topics related to art, literature, history, ethics, or philosophy. These passages often involve abstract ideas and moral debates. The writing style in humanities passages may be more figurative or metaphorical, requiring careful interpretation of the author's tone and underlying message. The key challenge here is understanding the nuanced views presented, as the questions may test your ability to evaluate interpretations or alternative viewpoints.

2. Social Sciences Passages: Social sciences passages, on the other hand, often draw from fields such as psychology, sociology, political science, or economics. These passages tend to focus on empirical studies, theories, or historical events. The tone is usually more straightforward than humanities passages, but the questions can be more detailed, asking you to evaluate evidence, analyze data, or recognize the implications of certain theories. In these passages, it's important to understand the framework or theory the author is discussing and how the evidence supports or contradicts it.

Types of Questions

The types of questions you'll encounter in CARS can be broadly grouped into three categories:

1. Main Idea Questions: These questions ask you to identify the central argument or thesis of the passage. The main idea is usually a broad statement that summarizes the passage as a whole. To answer these questions, focus on the introduction and conclusion, and look for repeated themes throughout the passage.

    Example: "Which of the following best captures the author's main point in the passage?"

2. Detail Questions: Detail questions require you to locate and recall specific information from the passage. These questions often refer to a particular line or paragraph. When answering detail questions, go back to the passage and find the specific section mentioned to confirm your answer.

    Example: "According to the author, which of the following best describes the role of government in regulating the economy?"

3. Inference Questions: Inference questions test your ability to draw conclusions that are not explicitly stated in the passage but are implied by the author's argument. These are often the most challenging types of questions, as they require you to understand the broader implications of the argument and apply that understanding to new information.
   Example: "Based on the information in the passage, which of the following is most likely true about the author's perspective on international trade?"
4. Function or Purpose Questions: These questions ask you to analyze why the author included a specific statement or paragraph in the passage. These questions are testing your understanding of the role that different parts of the passage play in the overall argument.
   Example: "What is the primary purpose of the second paragraph in the context of the passage as a whole?"
5. Author's Tone and Attitude Questions: Questions in this category ask you to determine the author's tone or attitude toward the subject matter. This requires careful reading of the language used in the passage, as tone can be subtle and may change throughout the passage.
   Example: "Which of the following best describes the author's attitude toward technological advancements?"

Chapter 2; Analyzing Arguments

The ability to analyze arguments effectively is crucial for success on the MCAT's Critical Analysis and Reasoning Skills (CARS) section. In this section, you'll encounter complex texts that present various arguments, positions, and reasoning patterns. To excel, you must be able to break down the structure of these arguments, identify key components, and assess their validity.

1. Identifying Claims and Conclusions

Every argument is built around a central claim or conclusion. This is the main point the author is trying to convey. Your first task when analyzing an argument is to identify this conclusion. It is usually located at the end of a paragraph or in a summary sentence, but it can sometimes be implied rather than explicitly stated. The conclusion represents the "what" of the argument—the core assertion the author wants to persuade you to accept.

For example, an argument might conclude that "universal healthcare leads to a healthier society." This is the primary assertion the author will support with reasons or evidence.

2. Distinguishing Premises from Conclusions

Once you identify the conclusion, your next step is to recognize the premises. Premises are the supporting statements that provide reasons or evidence for the conclusion. They answer the "why" question—why should the reader accept the conclusion?

A premise might state, "Countries with universal healthcare systems have lower infant mortality rates." This is a piece of evidence the author uses to support the conclusion about the benefits of universal healthcare.

It's essential to differentiate between premises and conclusions, as they play distinct roles in an argument. Premises bolster the conclusion and provide logical foundations for it. They are not the author's main point but rather the stepping stones leading to it.

3. Identifying Assumptions

Most arguments rely on assumptions—unstated ideas or beliefs that link the premises to the conclusion. These assumptions can often be weak points in an argument because they are not supported by explicit evidence. To analyze an argument effectively, you need to identify and evaluate these assumptions.

For example, if an argument concludes that "a healthier society results from universal healthcare," it may assume that access to healthcare is the primary determinant of health outcomes. This assumption might be flawed if other factors, like education or income, also play significant roles in determining health.

Once you recognize an assumption, ask whether it is reasonable. Does the author provide sufficient evidence to justify this belief? If not, the argument may be weak.

4. Recognizing Argumentative Strategies

Authors use a variety of strategies to persuade their audience. One common strategy is appealing to authority, where the author references experts or authoritative sources to support their claims. For example, citing a study from a renowned medical journal lends credibility to an argument about healthcare policy.

Another strategy is appealing to emotions, where the author tries to evoke a response from the reader. While emotional appeals can be persuasive, they are not always based on sound reasoning. It's important to recognize when an argument relies more on emotion than on logical premises.

5. Identifying Counterarguments

In well-rounded arguments, authors often address counterarguments—opposing viewpoints or objections to their claims. Recognizing these counterarguments is crucial for thorough analysis, as they provide insight into the author's reasoning and understanding of alternative perspectives.

For example, in an argument supporting universal healthcare, the author might acknowledge that critics claim it leads to longer wait times for medical services. The author can then rebut this counterargument by presenting evidence that shows healthcare quality is not diminished by these wait times.

6. Evaluating the Strength of Evidence

Strong arguments are built on solid evidence. When analyzing an argument, always assess the quality and relevance of the evidence the author presents. Evidence can take many forms, including statistics, expert testimony, research studies, or historical examples.

For instance, if an author argues that universal healthcare improves societal health, the evidence might include comparative data on life expectancy between countries with and without universal healthcare. Consider whether the evidence is current, reliable, and directly related to the conclusion. Weak or irrelevant evidence can undermine an otherwise persuasive argument.

Main Idea, Tone, and Author's Purpose

Understanding the main idea, tone, and author's purpose in a passage is essential for mastering the CARS section. These elements reveal the core message the author is conveying, the attitude they take toward the subject, and their motivation for writing. Recognizing them will allow you to grasp the passage's overall meaning and approach questions with greater accuracy.

1. Identifying the Main Idea

The main idea of a passage is its central message or thesis. It is what the author wants to communicate above all else. In many cases, the main idea can be found in the introduction or conclusion of a passage, where the author summarizes or restates their point. However, it can also be scattered throughout the text, with clues in each paragraph building toward the overall message. For example, in a passage about environmental conservation, the main idea might be that "sustainable development is essential for the future of the planet." This statement captures the author's primary concern and the essence of the passage.

To identify the main idea, ask yourself: "What is the author primarily trying to convey or argue?" Look for repeated themes or statements that seem to carry particular weight within the passage.

2. Understanding the Author's Tone

Tone refers to the author's attitude toward the subject they are writing about. It can be neutral, enthusiastic, critical, sarcastic, or any number of other attitudes. Tone is conveyed through word choice, sentence structure, and the overall style of writing.

For example, an author discussing climate change might adopt a serious, urgent tone to stress the gravity of the issue. Alternatively, an author writing about a historical figure's contributions might use a tone of admiration and respect.

Recognizing tone is important because it can affect how you interpret the passage. A sarcastic tone, for instance, may indicate that the author doesn't fully agree with the statements being made, even if they appear to be presenting facts.

Common tones you might encounter in CARS passages include:
- Critical: The author is skeptical or challenging the subject.
- Optimistic: The author is hopeful about the outcome.
- Cautious: The author is careful in drawing conclusions.

3. Determining the Author's Purpose

The author's purpose refers to their reason for writing the passage. This is closely related to the main idea but focuses more on the "why" of the text. Understanding the purpose will help you comprehend the author's objectives and how they aim to influence the reader.

Common author purposes include:
- To inform: The author presents facts or explanations without necessarily persuading the reader.
- To persuade: The author wants to convince the reader of a particular viewpoint or action.
- To entertain: The author may write in a narrative style to engage the reader's imagination or emotions.
- To explain: The author clarifies a concept or process for better understanding.

For example, an author who writes a passage about the dangers of plastic pollution may aim to persuade the reader to adopt more environmentally friendly practices. By identifying the purpose, you can better understand the author's perspective and approach the passage's questions more effectively.

4. Main Idea, Tone, and Purpose in Context

The main idea, tone, and author's purpose are often interrelated. Together, they form the framework of the passage and influence how it should be interpreted. When analyzing a passage, consider how the author's tone supports their purpose and how the main idea ties everything together. If a passage has a critical tone and the main idea is that current healthcare policies are inadequate, the author's purpose might be to persuade readers to consider alternative healthcare models. Each of these elements works together to shape the message the author is sending.

Chapter 3: Strategies for Answering Questions

When approaching questions on the Critical Analysis and Reasoning Skills (CARS) section of the MCAT, a systematic strategy is key to success. The CARS section is designed to test your ability to read, understand, and apply information, but it also measures your critical thinking skills. Here are essential strategies to enhance your ability to answer these questions effectively:

1. **Read the Passage Carefully**: The first step in answering CARS questions is understanding the passage. Read through it thoroughly without rushing. This ensures that you fully grasp the main ideas, arguments, and supporting details presented. Pay attention to how the author structures the passage, including transitions and any shifts in tone or argument.

2. **Identify the Main Idea:** After reading, identify the passage's central argument or purpose. Most passages have one primary point that the author is trying to convey, and many questions will ask about this. Look for clues in the introduction and conclusion as they often encapsulate the main idea. If you're unsure, think about why the author wrote the passage and what they are trying to communicate.

3. **Understand the Author's Tone and Perspective:** Tone and perspective are critical in understanding the author's stance on the subject. Is the author neutral, persuasive, or critical? Recognizing the tone will help you predict the types of questions you may face and how to interpret the answers. Questions often ask about how the author feels regarding the subject matter, so being able to identify tone is essential.

4. **Anticipate the Types of Questions:** The CARS section typically contains several types of questions:
    - Main idea: These questions ask for the central theme of the passage.
    - Detail: These questions require you to recall specific information.
    - Inference: These ask you to go beyond the text and draw logical conclusions.
    - Author's tone: These test your ability to identify the author's attitude toward the subject.
    - Structure and function: These focus on the organization of the passage and the role different parts play in it.

    Understanding these question types will help you predict what you're being asked before you look at the answer choices.

5. **Prephrase an Answer Before Looking at the Choices:** Once you read a question, think of the answer in your mind before looking at the provided options. This helps prevent confusion caused by tricky wording in the answer choices. When you already have an idea of the correct answer, you can quickly identify it among the options.

6. **Use Process of Elimination:** For questions that seem difficult or tricky, eliminating wrong answers is an effective strategy. Rule out answers that don't directly address the question or contradict information in the passage. Narrowing down your options increases your chances of selecting the right answer.

7. **Beware of Extreme Language:** In most CARS questions, answers containing extreme language such as "always," "never," or "only" are usually incorrect because they imply an inflexibility that is rarely true in reasoning-based questions. The correct answers tend to be moderate and measured.
8. **Look for Direct Evidence in the Passage:** Many questions can be answered by finding a specific part of the passage that directly addresses the question. Don't rely on your outside knowledge. Everything you need to answer the question is contained in the passage itself. Go back to the text and locate the relevant portion if necessary.
9. **Manage Your Time Effectively:** Time management is essential in the CARS section. Avoid spending too much time on a single passage or question. If you're stuck, make an educated guess, mark the question if possible, and move on. You can return to it later if time permits.
10. **Practice, Practice, Practice:** The more CARS passages you practice, the better you'll become at recognizing patterns in both questions and passages. This repetition builds your ability to answer efficiently and confidently under timed conditions.

Inference, Deduction, and Application

In the CARS section, many questions focus on your ability to infer, deduce, and apply the information presented in the passage. These types of questions require you to go beyond what is explicitly stated and use logical reasoning to arrive at the correct answer. Let's break these concepts down and discuss strategies for each.

1. **Inference**

Inference questions require you to derive conclusions that aren't directly stated but are implied by the text. These questions assess your ability to read between the lines. The key to answering inference questions is identifying underlying assumptions and implied meanings within the passage.

How to approach inference questions:
- Read carefully: Ensure you fully understand what is explicitly stated in the passage before trying to infer anything.
- Identify supporting evidence: Inferences must be supported by evidence in the text. Look for subtle clues, such as the author's word choice or the way they structure an argument.
- Avoid overreaching: Don't infer too much. The correct inference will always have a strong basis in the passage. Stay within the boundaries of what's plausible based on the information provided.

Example of an inference question: "Based on the passage, the author would most likely agree with which of the following statements?" In this case, you need to infer the author's stance from the tone and evidence in the text.

2. **Deduction**

Deduction involves applying general principles presented in the passage to specific situations. These questions test your ability to logically deduce specific outcomes or statements based on the overall argument.

How to approach deduction questions:
- Understand the general rule or principle: Identify the overarching idea or rule that the author presents.
- Apply it to a specific case: Once you've identified the general principle, apply it to the situation described in the question.
- Be precise: Deductive reasoning should lead to a specific conclusion that aligns with the logic of the passage.

Example of a deduction question: "If the author's reasoning in the passage is applied to a new scenario, which of the following conclusions would be the most consistent?" This type of question requires you to apply the passage's general ideas to a new situation.

3. Application

Application questions ask you to use the concepts or arguments presented in the passage in a broader context. These questions often present a new scenario and ask you to apply the logic or principles discussed to this situation.

How to approach application questions:
- Identify the core concept: Understand the primary argument or principle presented in the passage.
- Generalize the concept: Think about how this idea could be applied in other contexts.
- Apply it carefully: Ensure that the new situation aligns with the passage's principles without deviating too far from the original context.

Example of an application question: "The author's argument about social reform would most likely apply to which of the following situations?" In this case, you need to take the author's argument and apply it to a different context while ensuring consistency with the original logic.

Chapter 4: Practice Passages

When preparing for the MCAT Critical Analysis and Reasoning Skills (CARS) section, practice passages play an essential role in honing your ability to analyze and respond to complex readings. Each passage in this section is designed to test not only your comprehension of the content but also your ability to critically evaluate and synthesize the information presented.

Structure of Practice Passages

Each CARS passage is typically around 500-600 words and is drawn from humanities, social sciences, and other non-science topics. The primary goal of practice passages is to mimic real exam conditions and give you an opportunity to apply various reading and reasoning skills. Topics may include history, literature, philosophy, or ethics, and while prior knowledge of the material is not required, your ability to reason through the arguments and information is critical.

A practice passage will include anywhere from 5 to 7 questions, and these questions can be divided into several categories:

1. Main Idea Questions: These questions ask you to determine the primary message or argument of the passage. They often require you to understand not just the explicit content but the overarching point the author is trying to convey.
2. Detail-Oriented Questions: These questions focus on specific information within the passage. They often ask about a fact or claim made by the author, and while seemingly straightforward, they require precise attention to the text.
3. Inference Questions: Inference questions ask you to draw conclusions based on the information provided, even if that conclusion is not directly stated. You need to identify implications or understand the context of statements.
4. Author's Tone and Purpose Questions: These questions focus on why the author wrote the passage. Was the purpose to inform, persuade, or criticize? Understanding the tone and intent behind the author's words is crucial in these questions.
5. Application Questions: These require you to apply the ideas presented in the passage to new scenarios. They may ask you to predict what the author might say in a different situation or how a specific argument could be used in another context.

Strategies for Approaching Practice Passages

To succeed with practice passages, a systematic approach to reading and answering questions is important:

1. Active Reading: As you read through each passage, engage with the text. Focus on understanding the structure of the passage, identifying the main argument or point, and noting any shifts in tone or perspective. Keep track of the author's key points without getting lost in minor details.
2. Annotate Key Points: While reading, jot down the main idea of each paragraph. This helps in breaking down complex passages and provides a quick reference when answering questions. Note transitional words (such as "however" or "therefore") that signal shifts in the argument.

3. Identify the Question Type: Once you begin answering questions, quickly identify what type of question it is—whether it's asking for the main idea, details, or inferences. This will guide your approach to finding the answer in the passage.
4. Refer Back to the Passage: Never rely solely on memory. Always go back to the passage to confirm details or check specific lines that might be referenced in the questions.

Importance of Consistent Practice
Regular practice with CARS passages builds familiarity with the types of reading material you'll encounter and improves both speed and accuracy. Developing a habit of practicing passages under timed conditions simulates the actual MCAT exam, allowing you to become more comfortable with the pressure and pacing required to perform well. In addition, practicing various types of passages helps you recognize different writing styles and argument structures, better preparing you for the wide range of topics the MCAT covers.

Timed CARS Questions and Explanations

The CARS section of the MCAT is a test of both your reading comprehension and your ability to answer questions under time constraints. The challenge lies in balancing the need to carefully analyze dense and sometimes unfamiliar material with the pressure to move through the section quickly. Mastering timed CARS questions requires not only critical thinking but also strategic time management.

The Importance of Timed Practice
Each CARS passage on the MCAT must be read and understood in a short period. With around 53 questions spread across 9 passages, you'll need to answer roughly one question per minute while still allocating enough time to read and analyze the passage itself. Timed practice is crucial because it helps simulate the exact conditions of the exam and forces you to make decisions efficiently.

How to Structure Timed Practice Sessions
Timed practice should involve reading passages under test-like conditions and attempting to answer all associated questions within a limited time frame. A typical breakdown for timing can be:
- Reading the Passage: Spend no more than 5 minutes reading and annotating the passage. This forces you to focus on the main points and avoid getting bogged down by unnecessary details.
- Answering Questions: Allocate about 1 minute per question, making sure to carefully consider each answer while also moving quickly.

Timed practice allows you to get used to the pace of the real exam, but it's important to strike a balance between speed and accuracy. Rushing through questions without a clear understanding of the passage will hurt your performance, while being too slow might prevent you from finishing the section.

Effective Time Management Strategies
1. Skimming for the Main Idea: During timed practice, your goal isn't to memorize every word but to extract the main points. Skim the first and last sentences of paragraphs to get an overview of the author's argument and use that as a foundation to answer questions.
2. Skip and Return to Difficult Questions: If you encounter a particularly challenging question, don't get stuck on it. Mark it, move on to the next one, and return to it if time allows. This prevents you from wasting too much time on a single question while ensuring you can answer easier questions first.
3. Eliminate Wrong Answers: In cases where you're unsure of the correct answer, use the process of elimination. Narrow down the answer choices by removing those that are clearly wrong, and then make an educated guess based on the remaining options. This technique helps save time and increases your chances of selecting the correct answer.

Reviewing Your Timed Practice Sessions

After completing a set of timed CARS questions, review both correct and incorrect answers to identify patterns in your reasoning. Pay particular attention to:

- Misunderstood Passages: If you frequently get questions wrong on certain types of passages, such as those focused on abstract philosophical topics, focus additional practice on similar material to improve.
- Answer Explanations: Carefully read through the explanations for each question, especially those you got wrong. Understand why the correct answer is right and what clues in the passage led to that conclusion.
- Timing Patterns: If you find that you consistently run out of time, adjust your reading or answering strategies. Alternatively, if you finish too quickly and make mistakes, slow down your process slightly to ensure greater accuracy.

Simulating Test Day Conditions

Timed practice is only effective if it mirrors the conditions of the actual exam. For best results, replicate test-day conditions as closely as possible. This includes:

- Setting aside uninterrupted time for practice.
- Using a quiet environment similar to a test center.
- Sticking strictly to the timing limits for each passage and set of questions.

By consistently engaging in timed practice sessions and reviewing your performance, you'll become more adept at managing your time effectively while maintaining accuracy—skills that are key to excelling on the CARS section of the MCAT.

Conclusion

The MCAT is a rigorous exam requiring strong content knowledge, critical thinking skills, and strategic test-taking approaches. As you close this review, remember that consistent practice and targeted review are key to mastering each section. Every subject you've worked through—Biology, Biochemistry, Chemistry, Physics, Psychology, Sociology, and Critical Analysis and Reasoning—contributes to a deeper understanding and a stronger ability to apply knowledge under pressure.

Focus on the following points as you wrap up your preparation:

1. Content Retention and Application: Ensure that core concepts are not only memorized but understood in a way that enables you to answer complex, multi-layered questions. This involves active recall and spaced repetition of key principles, especially in the sciences. Utilize the questions and answers in each section to regularly test your comprehension.
2. Time Management: The MCAT requires effective time management across multiple sections. Practice pacing yourself by working through timed practice exams. Break down each section and set realistic goals for time spent per passage or question.
3. Critical Analysis Skills: CARS and critical reasoning aren't just tested in one section; these skills will assist you throughout the exam. Continue refining these skills by practicing comprehension and logical reasoning exercises. Review your answers carefully to learn from each mistake.
4. Review Strategy: Focus on analyzing incorrect answers. Review each explanation thoroughly to understand where errors were made. This will improve your performance by targeting areas where you tend to struggle. Keep a log of topics and question types that need further review.
5. Balanced Preparation: While content mastery is essential, balanced preparation includes mental resilience, physical endurance, and test-day strategy. Get into the habit of full-length practice under realistic conditions. Address any test-related anxiety through relaxation techniques and by building familiarity with test structure and timing.
6. Consistency and Persistence: Success on the MCAT is built through sustained effort. Maintain a study schedule, adjust as needed based on your progress, and don't neglect areas of weakness. Revisit this book as needed and take advantage of all provided resources, including practice tests and explanations.

By following these principles and maximizing the tools provided, you're well-equipped to approach the MCAT with confidence and a solid foundation. Keep your focus on consistent improvement, and approach test day with a clear mind and readiness to apply everything you've worked to master.

SCAN THE QR CODE BELOW TO ACCESS YOUR ONLINE TEST PREP

Made in the USA
Columbia, SC
13 April 2025

56557727R00187